PACIFIC RIM CITIES IN THE WORLD ECONOMY

D1607446

Comparative Urban and Community Research

Series Editor, Michael Peter Smith

PACIFIC RIM CITIES IN THE WORLD ECONOMY

Comparative Urban and Community Research
Volume 2

Edited by

Michael Peter Smith

Transaction Publishers
New Brunswick (U.S.A.) and London (U.K.)

Second printing 2004

Copyright © 1989 by Transaction Publishers, New Brunswick, New Jersey.

This book is printed on acid-free paper that meets the American National Standard for Permanence of Paper for Printed Library Materials.

ISSN: 0892-5569
ISBN: 0-88738-735-7
Printed in the United States of America

Volume 2 comprises volume 13 of *Comparative Urban Research*

Contents

Comparative Urban and Community Research is a refereed series devoted to theoretical, empirical and applied research on the processes of urbanization and community change throughout the world. The format of *Comparative Urban and Community Research* enables the publication of manuscripts that are longer and more richly textured than the articles a quarterly journal can feature.

Editorial correspondence and manuscript submissions should be addressed to *Comparative Urban and Community Research*, Department of Human and Community Development, University of California, Davis, CA 95616-8523. Submission requirements: (1) papers should be double-spaced; (2) author's name, affiliation, address and telephone number should appear on a separate sheet; (3) papers should be submitted in hard copy as well as in a diskette in Word format.

Michael Peter Smith, Editor
University of California, Davis

Rene Francisco Poitevin and Shannon Seed Hardwicke
Editorial Assistants

INTRODUCTION

Michael Peter Smith
University of California, Davis

A score of megacities along the pacific Rim have grown in significance during the past two decades as new, economically dynamic locations where international trade, finance, communications, and corporate decision-making are carried out. Numerous other Pacific Rim cities have experienced rapid growth as industrial sites. Based on levels of economic interaction the nation-states of the "Pacific Rim" include the countries of East and Southeast Asia, North America, Australia, and New Zealand. There is now an abundant literature on the global dimension of the Pacific Rim urbanization process. This literature documents the globalization of economic activity that has taken place since the 1960s and underlines the transnationalization of capital investment processes and the development of a single world labor market for industrial labor as two key driving forces of Pacific Rim urbanization.

The latter development, often referred to as the "New International Division of Labor," has been an especially prominent framework used to explain the linked processes of urban decline in Europe and North America and the rapid industrialization of the Newly Industrialized Countries (NICs) of the Pacific Rim, such as Korea, Hong Kong, Taiwan, and Singapore, whose economies have expanded rapidly as a result of direct foreign investment and joint ventures with U.S.- and Japanese-based multinational corporations. The hyper-profits derived from the relocation of industrial production sites have in turn given rise to a third global process -- the globalization of real estate speculation -- as exemplified in Japanese corporate investment in the built environment of major U.S. cities such as Los Angeles and Seattle. A fourth global process, international labor migration, was a key feature of 19th century Asian urbanization. It is now an important dimension of population growth of post-industrial cities both within and outside the Pacific Rim, with the exception of Japan whose doors have remained closed to international migration.

Despite the acknowledged importance of international processes and relations for urban development within the Pacific Rim region, discussed extensively through this volume, the contributions to Volume 2 of *Comparative Urban and Community Research* also clearly show that the urbanization of Pacific Rim cities remains embedded in historical, national, and local development contexts which shape urban development, the types of urban issues perceived as problems, and the range of possible responses to them.

Several themes stand out in these contributions. They focus on the mediating role of state structures, national socio-cultural processes, and locally-situated social actors in the dynamic of economic growth and urban change in Pacific Rim cities.

The integration of these themes produces a powerful critique of mono-causal determinism, be it the macro-economic assumptions of structural Marxism or the micro-economic market theories of urban growth so trenchantly criticized in the review essay by Swanstrom and Kerstein. Assumptions concerning the primacy of "capital accumulation" in shaping cities and social formations underpins the New International Division of Labor (NIDL) thesis, which holds that the transformation of cities on a global scale is inexorably driven by the quest for cheap labor in the productive sphere. Even the contributors to this volume such as Henderson, who place the most stress on economic forces, pose a challenge to the reductionism of the NIDL thesis. As Henderson's case study demonstrates, in Hong Kong it was the quality of labor power, not merely its cost, which attracted transnational industrial investment there. More specifically, the *cultural habituation* of the Hong Kong work force to the requirements of a manufacturing labor process occurred prior to the rise of major foreign investment. The development of textile manufacturing ten years before the rise of its now dominant electronics sector provided foreign investors with a work force, in Henderson's words, "well on the way to being culturally proletarianized and...socially adjusted to the regimes and rigors of factory labor." In the Hong Kong case the ideological/cultural control over labor power has been a more important element in urbanization and industrial development than have strict cost considerations.

In focusing exclusively on cost factors in production, the NIDL thesis also pays insufficient attention to the important role which state policies play in mediating economic relations. In Japan, for instance, the national government regulates immigration, provides tax incentives and subsidies, and uses land use and regional planning to develop high-tech regions to offset possible job displacement caused by the "hollowing out" of its domestic economy because of its shift of heavy industrial production to other Pacific Rim locations, and for political reasons to the U.S. Although free-market ideologues such as Milton Friedman cite Hong Kong as a sterling example of market-driven development, the role of the state in that city's development also looms large. The city-state of Hong Kong has been able to underwrite its capital market by low personal and corporate taxation while simultaneously maintaining a high level of legitimation and social control through high social spending. Hong Kong has overcome the fiscal constraints which this pattern of state involvement in society entails by enforcing a system of property rights in which the state currently owns 95 percent of the land. The government periodically sells leases of its land to finance police, education, and welfare services, as well as to support a public housing system which now houses 45 percent of Hong Kong's people. Likewise, as Thorns shows, New Zealand's urban development has been powerfully shaped by a succession of shifting state policy initiatives from the Great Depression to the present, ranging from protectionism and import substitution in the 1930s, through domestic energy development policies in the 1970s, to the neo-liberal state policies of recent years which have accelerated New Zealand's integration into the international political economy.

The studies in this volume also illustrate the central role which *intra-national* socio-cultural and political practices play in mediating global economic logic in urban development. For example, as Broadbent's article shows, culturally-specific social networks connect particular Japanese politicians and business elites; the culturally defined reciprocal obligations among them is a form of agency which accounts for patterns of regional investment that contradict the strict logic of capital accumulation in both corporate decision-making and regional development policy-making. In Hong Kong the particular historical experiences shaping the development of trade unionism there have reduced the role of trade unions in shaping the class consciousness of workers; to the extent that conflict is present in the productive sphere it takes the form of a very high turnover rate among the largely female electronics production workforce, who choose "exit" as a mode of resistance to patriarchal social relations and exploitative working conditions. As the case studies of Japanese urban industrial development demonstrate, during the 1970s the international oil crisis (itself largely politically produced), *combined with* domestic pressure from the Japanese environmental movement on basic materials producing corporations, *as mediated by* facilitative state policies of financial assistance, prompted many Japanese manufacturing corporations in the heavy industrial sector to establish processing facilities in low population density Southeast Asian raw materials-producing countries.

an additional difficulty with the NIDL thesis is that by focusing on the growing fluidity and multi-lateral character of transnational economic relationships in the current epoch, it thereby downplays important forms of international economic and political interdependence which are essentially *bilateral* in character. The continuing significance of bilateral political-economic relationships is well exemplified in the studies in this volume. Most important, the bilateral relationship between the superpowers of the U.S. and Japan is a key generator of economic interpenetration of the economies of cities along the Pacific Rim. The two countries continue to be the dominant foreign investors in Pacific Rim urbanization and industrial development. In the 1960s and early 1970s the bilateral competition between these nations in electronics manufacturing was a key driving force of U.S. deindustrialization of large electronics factories by a combination of offshore relocation of assembly plants to Pacific Rim locations, automation, and subcontracting to domestic sweatshops often employing Asian immigrant female workers. By the 1980s the domestic political reaction to this in the U.S. prompted many Japanese parts manufacturing firms to move from Japan to various Pacific Rim countries, not primarily to take advantage of cheap labor but to bypass U.S. trade restrictions as well as to offset the rise of the yen on international currency markets. These political-economic pressures, along with domestic political demands in the U.S. for "local" content in Japanese products sold on the U.S. market ushered in a greater than threefold expansion of Japanese-owned auto supply firms in the U.S. between 1984 and 1987 and a level of Japanese investment in automobile assembly plants which Fujita and Hill currently estimate at S5 billion. These political-economic considerations -- avoidance of bilateral political constraints, the current state of currency exchange rates, and proximity to the U.S. domestic market have recently prompted the Japanese textile sector to invest in a S500 million textile mill in Fresno, California.

To carry this argument to another level, in the case of Hong Kong the interplay between foreign capital investment processes and the role of the city-state in subsidizing wages through an extensive social wage is further mediated by the bilateral relationship between Hong Kong and the government of the People's Republic of China (PRC). For its own political and economic reasons the state apparatus of the PRC assists in subsidizing wage labor in Hong Kong by selling Chinese produced food and clothing there at below market administered prices. According to Henderson the state policies of Hong Kong and China currently subsidize one half of the total household expenditures of Hong Kong workers.

All of the above factors are well synthesized in Rimmer's conclusion that the international forces and processes shaping Pacific Rim urban development are best viewed as in dynamic interaction with internal factors within the various Pacific Rim nations such as domestic class and political interests, relations in production, socio-cultural practices, and political culture. Moreover, it is internal processes which inevitably ground and mediate international economic and geo-political forces. This is nicely illustrated in Rimmer's analysis of the interplay between Japanese construction contractors and state policy makers which shifted economic activities away from urban areas of Japan during World War II and since the early 1970s have shifted the focus of real estate investment under three national political regimes depending on the mutual interests of both sets of actors in the context of changing international political-economic conditions and demands.

The studies in this volume thus recognize a plurality of forces interacting to produce urban change in the Pacific Rim. This recognition represents a shift of the center of gravity in urban analysis to a post-structuralist mode of thinking in which any master discourse which attributes too much mastery over social process to a single cause is viewed as reductionist. Thus, for example, the papers in this volume, in different ways, address the question of the role of "locality" or "place" in urban change by rejecting the framing of the question as forcing a choice between global or local driving forces. "And/also" is preferred to "either/or." In framing the question of the relationship between structure and agency and the global and local levels of analysis the current trend in urban studies is to ask not "Which is determinative?" but rather, "How are they connected? What is their dynamic interplay? What zone of freedom is there for human agency and local affectivity within structural constraints? What are the place-specific features of change? How do local social structures, history, and culture mediate extra-local change? How are global, national, and local political-economic and socio-cultural processes interrelated in the making, unmaking, and remaking of cities?"

Several of the contributors to "Pacific Rim Cities in the World Economy," particularly the opening overview article by Douglass, move beyond the question of causality to focus on the observed and foreseeable consequences of Pacific Rim urban development. Four central contradictions of urban development in the Pacific Rim emerge from this analysis. First, although access to and the past strength of the U.S. domestic market have been key elements in the developing urban and regional economies within the Pacific Rim, the impact of the investment shifts and attendant deindustrialization, and growing income polarization within the U.S. has been to weaken the middle income base of the vast U.S. market for consumer durables produced in Pacific Rim cities.

Second, the hyper-urbanization of a handful of mega-cities such as Tokyo, Mexico City, Jakarta, Manila, Seoul, Singapore and Los Angeles is now already outstripping the resource and ecological constraints which must be self-consciously mediated by urban political and planning processes, if even the current population living in these growing areas is to be sustained. The over-urbanization of these cities has produced a widening gap between population growth and the provision of housing, basic infrastructure, and schools. In Tokyo, as Broadbent shows, the high land prices and astronomical housing costs for home ownership have adversely affected the quality of life of the average citizen of that booming world city. In many of the mega-cities on the Pacific Rim the public health problem of waste disposal has reached crisis proportions. The slums of Manila and Jakarta and the barrios of Mexico City constitute even more obtrusive indicators of the gap between economic and social development within the new world cities.

Third, the growth of Pacific Rim cities has been geographically uneven within each society as well as internationally. Within Pacific Rim nations the growth of mega-cities has been accompanied by stagnation or decline in other urban regions. This has produced new forms of inter-local conflict and competition, a general neglect of rural development, and intensified socio-spatial inequalities.

Fourth, the neo-liberal trend toward reduced public social spending and increased tax incentives to stimulate economic investment in Pacific Rim cities has left unanswered the question of how basic levels of urban infrastructure and public services needed to sustain the population base of the growing cities are to be financed in the future and who will pay for them.

This reduced level of public spending for social and infrastructural services has been justified by the deployment of the ideology of the free market. The pitfalls of this neo-liberal ideology are implicit in the empirical studies in this volume and explicitly elucidated in the closing review essay. The ideology of market liberalism legitimates dein-dustrialization as driven by a quest for rational investment of scarce resources, thereby ignoring institutional biases in actual resource allocation processes including the role of social and political power relations in struc-turing market exchanges. Moreover, it masks the fact that employment and housing investment and disinvestment are not antithetical, but linked and mutually reinforcing processes and lead to the denigration of political demo-cracy as a mechanism for allocating social resources. Finally, on the onto-logical level, it sanctions hyper-mobility and expendability in social relations.

The studies in this volume constitute a welcome challenge to market logic. They challenge mono-causal thinking and recognize the com-plexity of the actual forces in change in Pacific Rim urbanization. By moving us beyond economistic reasoning they provide us with a more tex-tured and nuanced historical account of the dynamics of urban development within the Pacific Rim. Such an account is an essential first step toward redressing the imbalance between the economic and social development of Pacific Rim cities.

THE FUTURE OF CITIES ON THE PACIFIC RIM

Mike Douglass
University of Hawaii

The confluence of rapid urbanization and economic restructuring on the Pacific Rim has raised issues about the future of the urban habitat that are increasingly shared on an international plane. Environmental degradation and loss of arable land on a global scale are everywhere calling for innovative efforts to sustain the material and ecological bases for the expansion of human agglomerations which no longer produce food and are consuming energy and producing wastes at exponential rates. At the same time, competition to sustain the urban economy has moved across national boundaries, producing strategies to "win" transnational investment which are either unresponsive or inimical to efforts to counter widening social disparities and maintain the integrity of built and natural environments. The trend toward the concentration of urban populations in mega-cities has magnified the issues and dilemmas being confronted at the dawn of the Pacific Age and the world's first urban century.

At the beginning of the 19th century no more than an estimated three percent of the world's people lived in cities (Hay, 1977). Over the next 100 years the movement of people to cities increased rapidly, but the proportion of the world's population residing in urban places still reached a level of only 15 percent by 1900. Even by 1950 the proportion had climbed to just above 20 percent, of which three-quarters were in Europe and North America (UN, 1969; Hauser and Gardiner, 1982).[1] Since 1950, though, urbanization has accelerated around the world at a pace such that the year 2000, when for the first time half of the population of the globe will be urban, will be a watershed in world history.

By 2000 the urban transition will have been substantially completed in Europe, North America, Japan and other post-industrial nations. At least four-fifths of their citizens will reside in cities, natural population growth rates will be low, and population mobility will be marked by inter-urban rather than rural-urban migration. National development efforts in these countries will concentrate on obtaining food and energy, disposing of the waste, and providing jobs, housing and services for cities and the people who live in them. Other Newly Industrializing Countries (NICs) will also have high percentages of their population living in cities and will be faced with similar concerns.

But for the great majority of world's countries and people the year 2000 will reveal an apparent paradox in the global distribution of the urban population: in absolute numbers, almost two-thirds of the world's three billion urban inhabitants will be living in low-income countries that will still have a majority of their own population residing in villages and rural regions.[2] At the same time, relatively high natural population growth rates will combine with equally high rates of rural-urban migration to make the "hyper-urbanization" of metropolitan regions in these countries a major national concern.[3] Much of the success in managing urban development in these agrarian economies will depend on the ability to accelerate rural development as a means of decentralizing the urbanization process away from large cities and toward rural regions. But even a successful rural development effort will serve to complement, not replace, efforts to close the already large gap between the demands for housing, sewage and drainage systems, transportation and basic services in these countries' rapidly growing cities, some of which will have in excess of 15 million and as many as 30 million inhabitants.[4]

The concern of this paper is the future of cities, and the people who will inhabit them, in a dynamically expanding region of the world referred to as the Pacific Rim.[5] Three major themes serve to guide the discussion. The first is that historical and national development contexts continue to differentiate both the processes of urbanization and the specific nature of urban issues that will be confronted in the future. Existing patterns of urbanization and national development provide localized parameters on the dimensions of urban issues and the range of possible responses.

The second theme is that as the countries of the Pacific Rim become more tightly integrated through trade, investment, political arrangements, and cultural interpenetration, the future of all cities will be highly contingent not only on local and national events but increasingly on global ones. It is already clear, for example, that the economies of cities in the NICs of East Asia are highly contingent upon access to and the strength of the U.S. domestic market. What is perhaps less obvious is the trend toward the absorption of international trade within large-scale transnational corporations that source, process, manufacture, assemble, distribute and market commodities through their own world-wide networks transcending national boundaries. The economies of many cities are already highly sensitive to the locational decisionmaking of transnational corporations which select the sites for all levels of management, production and distribution on an international rather than national basis.

The third theme follows from the first two and develops the position that if cities are going to be able to provide the type of habitat that will be conducive to meeting the basic requirements of living and working into the 21st century, efforts to gain a shared, longer-term perspective on the future of cities is required.   This requirement reflects, in part, the increasing interdependencies between cities at an international level, which point to the need for longer lead times for resolving issues of concern that transcend national boundaries.   If urban issues can no longer be wholly treated as purely domestic matters, the further implication is that international fora for discussion, negotiation and mediation will also be of mutual interest to the governments and citizens of all cities of the Pacific Rim.

The discussion below is divided into three sections.   The first section gives an overview of patterns and trends in urbanization around the Pacific Rim; the second section places the future of cities on the Pacific Rim into an international context; and the third section addresses the major issues confronting the future of cities related first to resource and ecological constraints on sustaining increasing numbers and proportions of people living in cities.   Key areas of concern are food, energy, water and waste.   A second set of issues concerns the internal functioning of the cities, namely, their capacity to provide employment for their labor force and to maintain basic levels of infrastructure, housing, and welfare for their citizens. Financing the urban future in an era of diminishing central government support and increased inter-city competition for industry is also discussed.

Urbanization and Structural Change on the Pacific Rim

Over the past three decades the dominance of the North Atlantic as the core of the world economy has been challenged by the emergence of a new world region composed of countries located on the Pacific Rim.   The dynamic rates of economic growth and structural change in this region have led a number of enthusiasts to proclaim that a "Pacific Age" in world history has begun.

Urbanization, the increasing proportion of people living and working in cities, has been a central feature in the formation of this new world region.   Major cities have served as key points in a rapidly integrating network of Pacific Rim trade, communications, finance and corporate decisionmaking that serve to link the economies of this region to each other and with the rest of the world.   Within this network, the rapid growth of such cities as Los Angeles, Tokyo, Hong Kong and Singapore has itself been offered as a testament to a Pacific shift in the world economy.   Other Pacific Rim cities have in less than two decades become global centers of manufacturing and trade.

For these and related reasons, the pace and magnitude of urbanization on the Pacific Rim has reached historically unprecedented levels.

For the Pacific Rim as a whole, the urban population is expected to increase from slightly more than 700 million in 1986 to almost one billion, or 45 percent of the total Pacific Rim population, by the year 2000.[6]

In annual terms, the 1986-2000 period will see the urban population of the Pacific Rim increase by enough people to populate the greater New York metropolitan area of 17 million people every year to the end of the century -- and well beyond.

Although the rapid rate of urbanization has been very recent, the patterns of urban growth around the Pacific Rim, particularly in Asia, have been developing over long periods of time. In Japan, for example, the contemporary pattern of urbanization can be traced to the *jokamachi*, or castle towns, built in the 17th century. Other great Asian cities, such as Jakarta, Manila, Rangoon, Singapore, Hong Kong and Saigon, were created between the 17th and 19th centuries by the Dutch, Spanish, British and French in locations where only very small settlements had previously existed. In most cases these cities have become the present-day capitals of independent nation-states as well as cores of national economic development and industrial growth. Since 1950 these core urban regions have been growing at rates which double their populations in less than 20 years. What were once small or intermediate-size cities at the time of independence are now well on the way to becoming the "megacities" of the 21st century.

The location of many of these cities, established in earlier times, is a major cause of concern today. Mexico City's location was selected by the appearance of an eagle sitting on a cactus with a snake in its talons; the city expands on a site never intended for its present proportions. Los Angeles, located in what even the American Indians called the "Valley of Smoke," expands in a pollution-retaining, waterless environment that has required solutions that stretch the imagination and incur very high costs to sustain. Almost all of the large cities of the Pacific Rim, established in lowland delta regions, continue to expand into the most fertile agricultural lands of their nations, reducing their potential to feed their growing populations from domestic food production.

In addition to establishing national patterns of urbanization, historically layered experiences continue to serve as the context for emerging patterns of development within cities as well. Tokyo, currently the largest city on the Pacific Rim, struggles to adapt the realities of narrow lanes and dense land-use patterns of the seventeenth century to the imperatives of the automobile city of the late twentieth century. Bangkok, once the Venice of the Orient, is literally sinking as large-scale industries unrelentingly draw the ground water from beneath it, and is annually flooded as highways have paved over its many canals.

Bangkok, Jakarta, Los Angeles, Mexico City, Tokyo, and many other Pacific Rim cities have reached and even passed their ecological limits, and are struggling to cope with changing needs in historically defined urban structures and land-use patterns. As experience has shown in such countries as Brazil, the United Kingdom, and Tanzania, though, the capacity to relocate the functions of large cities into new towns and new capital cities, thereby achieving a new national pattern of urbanization, has met with only marginal success at best. The dynamics of structural change and economic growth giving increasing prominence to megacities of the Pacific Rim suggest that these struggles will become more pronounced in the future.

Economic restructuring has effected significant changes in patterns of urbanization on the Pacific Rim in recent years, yet inherited urban systems continue to act as the general spatial framework for economic, social and political change in most countries. When viewed from a historical perspective, any assessment of the future of cities on the Pacific Rim must also account for variations in the social, political and economic factors and conditions among cities and their national and local settings. While some governments turn to nuclear energy for their cities, others have yet to provide even first-round electricity supplies to their urban populations. While post-industrial service employment expands in cities in North America, cities in Southeast Asia have just begun to experience high rates of growth in the manufacturing sector. And while the city-state of Singapore has neither a rural hinterland population nor significant levels of international migration to absorb into its labor force or to place unrelenting pressures on its urban services, large cities in Indonesia will have rural-urban migration as a major factor with which to contend, and Los Angeles will continue to absorb great numbers of people from Mexico, Central America and Asia.

Urbanization on the Pacific Rim will undoubtedly continue to display variations which, in a more positive sense, are themselves the life of the city giving each its ambience, identity and occasion for celebration. They also suggest that although many urban issues may be of shared concern around the Pacific Rim, uniform solutions are not likely to be found.

Urbanization Trends

At even the simplest level of comparison, namely the proportion of the national population residing in urban areas, countries of the Pacific Rim display perhaps the highest variation of any region in the world. Using 1983 estimates, the proportions range from a low of 21 percent in China, the most populous country in the world, to a high of 100 percent in the small city-state of Singapore (Table 1). Rather than indicating a clear dichotomy between the "advanced" and the "less-advanced" countries, the levels suggest a number of situations. At the highest level of urbanization are the island cities of Hong Kong and Singapore which essentially have no rural hinterlands within their territorial domain and which have very small national populations of seven and three million, respectively. The nation/ colony status of these two cities, which includes powers to limit rural-urban migration from neighboring countries, has been of overriding importance in managing urban growth and providing urban services, including public housing, for the residential population.

At a slightly lower level of urbanization is the cluster of "post-industrial" countries having 75 percent or more of the national populations residing in cities. Australia, Canada, Japan, New Zealand, and the U.S. are included in this group. With less than 10 percent of the labor force working in agriculture in these countries, the demographic transition to an urban society is close to being complete, and urban employment is rapidly shifting away from manufacturing toward service sector occupations.

The NICs of Korea, Mexico and Taiwan, and including Hong Kong and Singapore, with about two-thirds of their populations residing in urban areas, form the next cluster of countries. Most of these countries are expected to reach very high levels of urbanization by the end of the century, but, unlike the high-income countries, may continue to urbanize around the growth of manufacturing industries.

A fourth group of countries includes the agrarian economies of East and Southeast Asia: China, Indonesia, Malaysia, the Philippines, and Thailand. With one-fifth to two-fifths of their national populations currently residing in cities, the commonalty of these countries is the continuing rural basis of their economies and cities. Although Malaysia, the Philippines, and Thailand, have been termed "near-NICs" by some (Ranis, 1983), levels of industrialization remain low. The mainstays of their economies continues to be natural resource extraction and cash and food crop production. Unlike the post-industrial countries and the NICs, rural-urban migration continues to be the overriding focus of urban policies in these countries. In many of these countries migrants from rural areas continue to account for as much as half of the annual increases in population in core cities. The responses have been varied. China, in officially denying migrants the right to reside in cities, represents one extreme. The result has been the very rapid increase in the "floating population" of workers who either migrate from city to city in search of construction work or who unofficially reside in the city without legal access to urban services and food rations.[7]

In other countries, slum clearance drives and removal of "informal sector" activities have been used to try to control the expansion of what is

Table 1. Pacific Rim National and Urban Population, 1980-2000*

Country	National Population millions 1986	millions 2000	Gr. Rate/Yr 1973-1983	1980-2000	Density persons/km² 1986	2000	Urban Population millions 1986	millions 2000[1]	% Urban 1983	2000	Rate/Yr 1973-1983	1980-2000	% Pacific Rim Urban Population 1986	2000
Australia	15.8	18.2	1.3	1.0	2	2	14	16	86	88	1.5	1.2	2	2
Canada	25.6	29.0	1.2	0.9	3	3	19	22	75	75	1.2	0.9	3	2
China	1,050.0	1,240.8	1.5	1.2	110	130	221	325	21	26	3.5	2.8	31	34
Hong Kong[2]	5.7	6.6	1.0	1.0	5,529	6,355	6	7	100	100	1.0	1.0	1	1
Indonesia	168.4	219.2	2.3	1.9	88	114	40	70	24	32	4.8	4.0	6	7
Japan	121.5	130.3	0.9	0.5	327	350	92	106	76	81	1.8	1.0	13	11
Malaysia	15.8	20.8	2.4	2.0	48	63	5	7	31	35	3.5	2.9	1	1
Mexico	81.7	112.3	2.9	2.3	41	57	56	88	69	79	4.1	3.3	8	8
New Zealand	3.3	3.6	0.6	0.7	12	14	3	3	83	86	0.8	0.9	0	0
Philippines	58.1	77.7	2.7	2.1	194	259	23	33	39	44	3.8	3.0	3	4
S. Korea	43.3	52.6	1.6	1.4	442	537	27	48	62	91	4.8	4.2	4	5
Singapore	2.6	3.0	1.3	1.0	4,221	4,852	3	3	100	100	1.3	1.0	0	0
Taiwan	19.6	22.8	1.5	1.1	545	635	13	18	67	78	3.0	2.2	2	2
Thailand[3]	52.8	66.9	2.3	1.7	103	130	13	19	25	29	3.6	2.7	2	2
U.S.	241.0	265.7	1.0	0.7	26	28	181	203	75	76	1.2	0.8	25	21
Pacific Rim	1,905.2	2,232.6	1.6	1.1	45	53	715	968	38	42	2.8	2.0	100	100

Sources: 1986 Population: *The 1987 Information Please Almanac*; population growth rates and % urban: World Bank, *World Development Report 1985*; U.S. Bureau of Census, *World Population 1985*.
1. based on 1973-83 urban growth rates weighed by change in total population growth rates (rate for 1973-1983 / rate for 1980-2000.
2. Hong Kong: entire colony treated as a single urban region.
3. Data on urbanization adjusted by G. Jones, *Structural Change and Prospects for Urbanization in Asian Countries*. Honolulu: East-West Center, 1983.

mistakenly viewed as an unproductive urban population.

Interestingly, international migration, which was a major force in urbanization in the 19th century in Asia but is now an insignificant feature of urban growth in that part of the world, has become of prominent feature in all but of few post-industrial cities.   On the Pacific Rim, Japan is the only post-industrial country which has maintained a strong closed-door policy to international migration. The high contrast between its urban social issues and those of the U.S., which has a de facto policy of recruiting cheap labor from other countries on a massive scale, is largely a result of the difference in migration policies.

In Japan, where the only significant minority consists of Japan's own colonial legacy of approximately 400,000 Koreans, urbanization has almost exclusively been a domestic process of rural-urban migration which reached its highest rates in the 1960s. With few exceptions, cities in Japan are marked neither by huge ethnic enclaves nor large poverty-level neighborhoods.[8]   In contrast, the U.S., which has been highly open to international migration, adds more than 500,000 legal migrants and an equal or higher number of illegal ones to its population each year. Many, especially illegal, migrants have become the underclass of American cities; they are the "domestic" source of below-minimum wage labor that allows some portions of U.S. industry to compete with East and Southeast Asia; they are the new residents of swelling ethnic barrios and slum areas in what has been called the movement of the Third World to the First World (Sassen-Koob, 1981; Soja, et al., 1983).

Another key demographic variable in the urbanization experiences on the Pacific Rim is population density. Histories of high rural densities in Asia have, in many cases, been translated into high urban densities that are in turn being manifested in problems of human congestion and land-use conflict of greater intensity than that being experienced in the low density countries of the Pacific Rim such as Australia, Canada and the U.S.   And as the NICs begin to cope with these densities more narrowly in urban terms, the very real concern of the densely-settled agrarian countries of Asia is that urbanization in the ensuing decades will continue to reflect a search for economic survival rather than upward social mobility for a vast majority of migrants from rural areas.

When population densities and levels and rates of urbanization are combined with differences in the distribution of the urban population among cities, the matrix of variations in urban experiences broadens considerably. Several extreme, if not unique, urban patterns are found among the countries of the Pacific Rim. One is Thailand, a country cited in almost every human geography textbook as having perhaps the highest concentration of urban population of any country in the world. Bangkok, the nation's capital, only major port and the center of most of Thailand's industry, is more than 60 times the size of the second largest city, Chiengmai. In contrast, the largest countries of the Pacific Rim have an equally large number of metropolises which together account for a substantial proportion of the national urban population. In China, for example, there are 70 cities with populations greater than 500,000 which together have 45 percent of the nation's urban population. Indonesia's nine large cities hold half of the urban population.

Only one major commonalty appears to cut across all of the differences noted above. Regardless of the level of urbanization or the number of very large cities, the share of population in the largest urban core regions continues to increase. In fact, one of the most marked urbanization trends on the Pacific Rim is the accelerating growth of a limited number of "megacities" with five million or more inhabitants. In many countries -- China, Indonesia, Japan, Mexico, the Philippines, South Korea and Thailand -- more than 30 percent the total urban population now resides in such urban concentrations. In Korea, the metropolitan core region of Seoul, which includes its surrounding Kyonggi Province, has almost 12 million people, or 51 percent of the total urban population. This region alone absorbed the equivalent of 84 percent of the nation's total population increase between 1980 and 1985 (Lee, 1988).[9]

Population numbers alone severely understate the command which core metropolitan regions have over their national economies. The greater Manila metropolitan area, for example, has 40 percent of the urban population, but accounts for 73 percent of the nation's manufacturing firms. Bangkok accounts for two-thirds or more of Thailand's energy consumption, industrial jobs and gross value, private investment in construction, and bank headquarters. Seoul Metropolis receives two-thirds of Korea's commercial bank investments and has more than half of the nation's automobiles (Bronger, 1985).

The trend toward the concentration of urban populations into large megacities is expected to continue well into the next century. Figure 1 shows the expected distribution of Pacific Rim megacities in the year 2000. Thinking about planning for such gargantuan agglomerations of human activity helps to crystallize many of the key questions about the future of cities. How will resources be gathered to sustain them? How will the waste they produce be disposed? How will cities house, educate, provide employment, and guarantee at least a minimum level of welfare to their citizenry? Who are the main actors in the planning process, and what are the major dynamics that need to be understood?

These concerns are accentuated by, but not confined to, the hyper-

Figure 1   Megacities of the Pacific Rim in the Year 2000

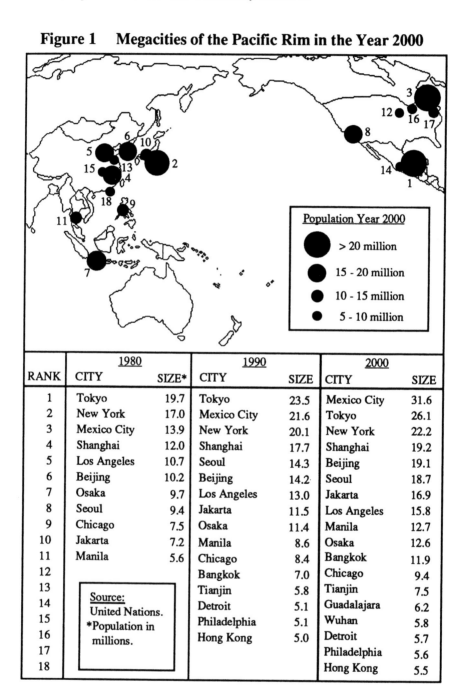

RANK	1980 CITY	SIZE*	1990 CITY	SIZE	2000 CITY	SIZE
1	Tokyo	19.7	Tokyo	23.5	Mexico City	31.6
2	New York	17.0	Mexico City	21.6	Tokyo	26.1
3	Mexico City	13.9	New York	20.1	New York	22.2
4	Shanghai	12.0	Shanghai	17.7	Shanghai	19.2
5	Los Angeles	10.7	Seoul	14.3	Beijing	19.1
6	Beijing	10.2	Beijing	14.2	Seoul	18.7
7	Osaka	9.7	Los Angeles	13.0	Jakarta	16.9
8	Seoul	9.4	Jakarta	11.5	Los Angeles	15.8
9	Chicago	7.5	Osaka	11.4	Manila	12.7
10	Jakarta	7.2	Manila	8.6	Osaka	12.6
11	Manila	5.6	Chicago	8.4	Bangkok	11.9
12			Bangkok	7.0	Chicago	9.4
13			Tianjin	5.8	Tianjin	7.5
14	Source:		Detroit	5.1	Guadalajara	6.2
15	United Nations.		Philadelphia	5.1	Wuhan	5.8
16	*Population in		Hong Kong	5.0	Detroit	5.7
17	millions.				Philadelphia	5.6
18					Hong Kong	5.5

expanding megacities. In many countries the mirror reflection of concentration in a limited number of megacities is the rapid deceleration of economic growth and industrial decline in other urban regions. In these cities, maintaining pre-existing levels of employment and public services has become the issue of the day. In either case, the rapid structural changes at local levels being brought about by economic integration on the Pacific Rim has marked the coming years as ones in which highly turbulent rather than smooth linear trajectories will be the courses charted.

Urbanization and Structural Change: Four Generalized Situations

Differences in observed patterns and processes of urbanization are associated with variations in economic structures and changes taking place in each of the Pacific Rim countries. At a very general level of discussion, these differences can be contrasted by summarizing major structural changes of the economies of each of the countries. The purpose is not to rigorously evaluate the specifics of the economic change or to suggest a uni-directional single-development-path-for-all-nations model of economic development and urbanization. Rather, it is to suggest a general typology of situations as a framework for discussion in subsequent sections. Four types of situations are identified by three factors: the overall level of non-agricultural employment in the economy; the direction of change in the manufacturing sector; and the relationship between trends in the manufacturing sector and trends in service activities (Table 2). The first situation has been popularized as that of the "post-industrial" economy and includes Australia, Canada, Japan, New Zealand and the U.S. The two defining characteristics of these countries are very low levels of agriculture-related employment, and the secular decline in manufacturing employment coupled with the rise of service activities as the main sector of employment. As mentioned above, many cities in these post-industrial countries have lost or are just now beginning to lose the industrial base that sustained their growth throughout most of this century. Even Japan has, since 1985, witnessed a declining share of employment in the manufacturing sector as the rapid rise in the value of the yen has accelerated the offshore movement of labor-intensive production processes to East and Southeast Asia.

Another defining feature of these countries is their very high levels of per capita gross domestic product (GDP). Table 2 indicates that the levels of the highest-income countries, the U.S., Canada, Australia and Japan, are ten times or more than the levels of the lowest-income countries. Care should be taken in interpreting these levels and differences. They should not be used to imply that income and welfare within these countries is either more evenly distributed or directly related to the level itself.

China, for example, has been able to substantially reduce the incidence of basic needs poverty in a situation of very low per capita income while several countries with high per capita income levels still have significant proportions of their population subsisting below basic needs poverty lines.

What the GDP/capita figures do suggest is a vast difference in the cities of the countries of the Pacific Rim. The built environment of cities in the high income countries is very complex and expresses an intensive use of a vast array of infrastructural investments, ranging from water and sewage connections for most dwellings to rapid transit systems carrying millions of people each day. In the low income countries, especially outside of the capital cities, public investments remain extremely limited, and towns expand largely through the expansion of urban villages that manage their own infrastructural needs using simple technologies and materials.

Although new industrial centers are appearing in low-wage, non-unionized regions of some of the post-industrial countries, the more substantial shifts in population and economic growth are directed toward the megacities and their hinterlands which have become the centers of corporate management functions, producer services and high technology research and development. Reflecting the spatial impact of rapid structural change, a major growth strategy of city governments in declining industrial regions in these countries has been to try to attract these new "sunrise" high technology and service industries to replace their "sunset" smokestack factories. Many have found, however, that the new jobs coming with the sunrise industries do not provide significant opportunities for the minority groups with low labor skills that moved into their inner city areas during an era of assembly-line production growth. In addition, a majority of the new service sector jobs pay wages that are substantially lower than those of the manufacturing jobs of the past and, in many cases, yield below poverty level incomes. The second situation is that of the NIC which have experienced high rates of growth in export-oriented manufacturing. Their manufacturing sector includes an entire panoply of scales and working situations, from self-employed and small-scale producers to emerging transnational corporations. Although real wage increases have lifted incomes in these countries significantly above those of the agrarian economies, they still remain substantially below those of the post-industrial countries. The further consequence of this will be that, particularly in the case of Singapore which has closed itself off to the migration of cheap labor supplies from Malaysia or Indonesia, labor shortages are becoming acute and, as wages begin to rise, future (urban) growth will greatly depend on the ability to move away from international competition for low-wage activities and toward the types of solutions being sought in the post-industrial situation.

Table 2. Selected Economic and Social Indicators of Pacific Rim Countries

Type / Country	GDP/Capita $U.S. 1986	%/yr. '65-86	% GDP Agriculture 1965	% GDP Agriculture 1986	Labor Agriculture 1965	Labor Agriculture 1981	Labor Industry 1965	Labor Industry 1981	Labor Services 1965	Labor Services 1981	Poverty %Poor 1984	Poverty top 20%/low 20%
Post-Industrial												
Australia	11,920	1.7	9	5	10	6	38	33	52	61	<5	9
Canada	14,120	2.6	6	3	11	5	33	29	56	66	<5	8
Japan	12,840	4.3	9	3	26	12	32	39	42	49	<5	4
New Zealand	7,486	1.5	—	11	13	10	36	35	51	55	<5	9
U.S.	17,480	1.6	3	2	5	2	36	32	59	66	<5	8
NICs												
Hong Kong	6,910	6.2	2	0	6	3	54	57	40	40	—	9
Singapore	7,410	7.6	3	1	6	2	26	39	68	59	—	—
Mexico	1,860	2.6	14	9	50	36	21	26	29	38	5-24	20
Taiwan[2]	3,142	5.4	18	6	—	—	13	—	—	—	—	—
Rep. Korea	2,370	6.7	38	12	58	34	13	29	29	37	5-24	8
Agrarian												
China	300	5.1	39	31	79	74	10	13	11	13	—	—
Indonesia	490	4.7	56	26	71	58	9	12	20	30	45-64	8
Malaysia	1,830	4.3	28	20	6	50	13	16	27	34	5-25	16
Thailand	810	4.0	35	24	8.2	76	5	9	13	16	25-44	9
Philippines	56	1.9	26	26	57	46	16	17	27	37	25-44	10
Pacific Rim	5,967	4.0	20	12	61	54	16	19	23	28	—	—
World[3]	2,845	2.8	26	16	—	—	—	—	—	—	—	—

Source: World Bank, *World Development Report* 1985 and 1988.
1. Percent poor defined as the proportion of households with incomes below the level needed to purchase minimum package of basic food, shelter and other daily requirements. Relative poverty defined as the ratio of the income of the top 20% of households to the lowest 20 percent. Source: GAIA, *An Atlas of Planet Management* (Anchor, 1984), p. 220.
2. Source: Asia Development Bank, *Key Indicators, 1986*
3. Excludes USSR and Eastern Europe

In all the NICs the pace of incorporation of labor into the production of standardized products for international markets has brought intensive pressure to house, transport from home to work and provide basic urban services for densely-settled urban populations. In the case of Korea, housing shortages in Seoul have become chronic despite substantial construction of high-rise public apartment buildings. It is now common for two families to live in apartments meant for one nuclear family. But variations exist even among the NICs. Unlike Korea, for example, Singapore and, for the moment, Hong Kong have been able to use their positions as city-states to stem migration and thereby slow the growth of their (urban) populations in a manner which has allowed public investments, such as in housing, to be much more effective in meeting social needs.

The third situation characterizes most of the countries of Southeast Asia which are industrializing at a much lower rate than the NICs and remain substantially agrarian in their economic base. Although declared by some to be "would-be-NICs" (Ranis, 1983), the high road to an urban-industrial future remains problematic in these countries. Malaysia has shown the greatest, and by some unexpected (McGee, 1982), rates of manufacturing growth, but a great proportion of this growth has been in the form of direct foreign investment into export processing zones (EPZs) in Penang, Kuala Lumpur and Johor (Salih, et al., 1987). Most of the remainder of the economy is still dependent on cash-crop production, mineral extraction, and, in the Klang Valley around Kuala Lumpur, import-substitution industrial growth. Indonesia, which has not embarked on an export zone policy, has its own problems stemming from the association of almost all of its manufacturing sector with the processing of oil and other natural resources that have experienced severe declines in international prices.

In each country of this third category, services and trade have been the mainstay of urban employment in most cities. Much of this employment, as with the manufacturing employment, is in very small-scale, low-productivity activities. As such, the specter of "urban involution," a process in which cities expand on the basis of low-productivity employment, squatter settlements, and high levels of basic needs poverty, continues to persist despite high rates of national economic growth.

The foregoing discussion should not be taken to imply that a rapid shift toward an urban-industrial society is either the only or even the best path for any of the agrarian economies of the Pacific Rim, especially if it were to be of the type followed in South Korea throughout most of the 1960s when rural development was virtually abandoned in that country. Accelerating rural development remains the most logical path to avoid the urban involution scenario in the agrarian countries. The issue is not, therefore, how to promote the growth of large-scale urban industries, but how to encourage rural industrialization to slow down rapid rural-metropolitan migration in situations of increasing rural population densities and low capacity of a few large cities to absorb rapid population increases.

As previously suggested, although low per capita GDP does not automatically translate into high levels of poverty, with regard to absolute poverty, i.e., poverty defined by access to basic goods and services, the association is apparent. Table 2 indicates that for the poorest countries, Indonesia, the Philippines and Thailand, from one-quarter to almost two-thirds of the national population is in absolute poverty. In these countries, providing basic services is made all the more difficult by the destitution of a large proportion of the population that can neither directly pay nor be indirectly taxed for them.

Nor are the NICs free of either squatter settlements or sweatshops with appalling working conditions or other forms of urban destitution. Another measure of poverty, the relative position of the lowest income groups vis-a-vis higher income groups, indicates that while average incomes may be increasing and basic needs poverty has been substantially reduced, perceived deprivation may be an important factor in the expression of dissatisfaction and political mobilization of lower income groups. In showing the ratio of the wealthiest 20 percent of households to the poorest 20 percent, Table 2 suggests, for example, that income distribution in Indonesia appears to be characterized by conditions of shared poverty rather than high inequalities between classes. The middle class in Indonesia is still small, and while the wealthy engage in high levels of conspicuous consumption, the great majority of the urban population has incomes that range within a relatively narrow band.

This situation stands in sharp contrast to Malaysia and Mexico, where the data suggest that the poorest households are receiving very small proportions of the economic benefits of development. In Malaysia, the inequalities, rather than absolute poverty per se, have been used by the government as prima facie evidence of the local Chinese dominance of the economy which in turn has been behind an overt policy to rapidly urbanize the Malay population and to establish target gains for Malay employment in high-level management and enterprise ownership. The anti-Chinese urban riots in 1969, which led to the adoption of an explicitly racist, pro-Malay national development plan, reflect the volatile nature of relative differences in income distribution. They also reflect the continuing historical legacies of a century ago, when Chinese labor was first imported in large numbers by British colonialists.[10]

The data presented have a number of obvious comparability and reliability problems and should therefore be viewed as suggestive of inter-country differences rather than proof of them.   Nevertheless, the figures raise important questions about the future of cities in different settings.   In the poorest countries, where as much as half of the population has no savings at all and spends 80 to 90 percent of income for food and shelter, who will pay for the provisioning of urban infrastructure and services? What low-cost and self-help approaches can be found as alternatives in these countries to the high-rise housing complexes of Korea, Hong Kong, Japan and Singapore?   Which will be more politically important with regard to future unrest in cities on the Pacific Rim, absolute poverty or relative deprivation?   What will be the role of the city government in ameliorating urban poverty?   As the discussion in Section 3 will indicate, financial pressures on urban governments everywhere have led to a profound redefinition of the role of the state in addressing these equity issues.

The fourth category has but one country, China.   From a demographic perspective similarities exist between China and Indonesia, and from the perspective of its economic structure, it shares similarities with other agrarian countries of the Pacific Rim.   But past experience and the political dimension preclude a joining of China with these countries.   Unlike most other medium- and low-income countries in Asia, for example, basic social and economic policies pursued in China over the past four decades have resulted in low levels in basic needs poverty, unemployment and income inequality.   Furthermore, the Chinese state has assumed powers over the mobility of capital and labor, the structure of industry and the distribution of social product and international trade which no other Asia country Pacific Rim country has contemplated.

The exercise of these powers, which included sending millions of urbanites to villages during the 1960s and 1970s, has placed China on an urbanization path and produced a set of urban issues which has significantly differed from other agrarian economies and the planning situations of most Pacific Rim countries.   Concentration levels of urban population in large cities have remained lower in China than anywhere else in Asia, and urban issues are focussing less on the consequences of rapid rural-urban migration and more on worker incentives, the relative distribution of responsibility over the provisioning of urban infrastructure, and the pace at which to introduce land pricing systems and cost-recovery measures in the delivery of urban services, including public housing (Douglass, 1988a).   Thus, even though labor absorption and the transfer of labor from agriculture are shared concerns of all agrarian countries, the types of policies, policy tools and political context for resolving perceived urban issues in China require a separate treatment of this economy from others.

What remains to be seen, however, is how far and how fast the new "Open Door" policy toward foreign investment and the many other reforms allowing for a flourishing of private enterprises, market incentives, and "letting some get rich first" will proceed in the coming years. On one hand, the officially-stated objective of current reforms is not to yield to the logic of capitalist development, but rather to allow for some degree of capitalist relations of production to rapidly raise the productive forces beyond the stage of "primary socialism" (Zhao, 1987).[11] But as the drive to expand China's exports to the Pacific Rim continues, the future of cities may well begin to reinforce the coastal-big city concentrations which state policies had been attempting to counter up to the mid-1980s. With the urban population of China expected to increase by more than 100 million people by the year 2000 (Table 1), the impact of new policies favoring coastal regions will be extremely important in countering the hyper-growth of very large metropolitan regions being witnessed in all other Pacific Rim countries.

The following section takes the discussion on national settings and urbanization processes to the international scale. The position is taken that the level and nature of participation of each national economy in the larger Pacific Rim economy will substantially affect the future of its cities. Participation is not, however, a one-way, international-to-local process of determination. Rather, the interplay between local and international political and economic forces will continue to direct the future of cities.

The Internationalization of Urbanization

In addition to helping explain contemporary differences in patterns of urbanization, a historical perspective on urbanization reveals a continuing enlargement of the spatial sphere of interaction between cities. Long-distance trade was an early stimulus of urbanization throughout the world, but the major forces guiding the daily life of cities on the Pacific Rim were, until well into the 19th century, largely contained within spatially restricted hinterland areas of each city.

The coming of European imperialism to Asia began to integrate cities on a more global basis, but even at the height of colonialism in the late 19th century, cities on the Asian perimeter of the Pacific were more closely linked with Europe than with each other. The Dutch colonial policy was to sink any and all non-Dutch ships, including those of the native Bugis, moving through Indonesian waters. Colonial cities in Malaysia, the new capital city of Bangkok in Thailand, and cities in Australia and New Zealand were linked to London. The rest of Indochina served French cuisine in its cities. Korea was still in its 500 years of seclusion as the Hermit Kingdom, and Japan, after 300 years of self-imposed isolation, only opened to the outside world with the arrival of Perry in 1858. China was perhaps the only territory to have a multiplicity of foreign linkages, but these, too, were mainly European.

A century later, as the world approaches the year 2000, primary transportation, communications, trade and investment linkages between cities on the Pacific Rim bear little resemblance to those of 1900. Interaction between cities is no longer contained within empires. Quantum advances in transportation and communications have greatly reduced the "friction of distance" between settlements, and developments in the world economy have integrated cities into networks that operate well above the level of the nation-state. The emergence of Japan as a major center of global capital accumulation, the rise of East Asian NICs and the re-orientation of the U.S. economy to the Pacific have been major factors in the internationalization of urbanization on the Pacific Rim.

This internationalization process has only recently begun to be incorporated into thinking about cities, and more particularly, the future of cities on the Pacific Rim. Received theory has tended to explain urbanization as a process taking place almost wholly within parameters set at the level of the nation-state. At the sub-national level, variations both in levels of urbanization and in the characteristics of individual cities have been seen as the outcome of regional variations in resources, factors of production and initial advantage as they interact with territorially limited markets. Although much utility can be made by assessing urbanization from national and sub-national development perspectives, when looking at either the process of urbanization or the types of responses being made to address a variety of contemporary urban issues, the need to bridge local and national perspectives with an international one becomes self-apparent.

At the international level, the dynamics behind the advent of the Pacific Age have been a product of two highly interrelated developments in the world capitalist system: the transnationalization of capital and the emergence of a new international division of labor. The transnationalization of capital, a process which has been accelerating since the early 1960s, involves the increasing concentration of production in the hands of large-scale enterprises producing commodities in more than one country. Recent estimates indicate that by the early 1980s there were approximately 10,000 transnational corporations with 90,000 affiliates producing and assembling commodities throughout the world (Stopford and Dunning, 1983: 10). Assets of transnational corporations in 1981 were eight times the level of the early 1960s. Overseas production of these enterprises in 1981 was valued at almost S1 trillion, and their combined worldwide sales totalled S2.7 trillion. Sales of only the top 500 transnational corporations accounted for 20 percent of the world GDP in that year (Stopford and Dunning, 1983: 51-3).

Other estimates suggest that the total share of all transnational corporations stands at 40 percent of the capitalist world economy (Douglass, 1988c).

These enterprises have used new technologies in production and communication to segment the labor process into a large number of discrete, simplified assembly operations with relatively low labor skill requirements which can be located in the low-wage regions throughout the world. Components can be made in one or several countries and be brought together for final assembly in another.[12] Rather than gravitating toward either the market or raw materials -- the two concerns of classical industrial location theory -- branch operations of transnational corporations can be located and quickly relocated depending on the wage, availability, quality, and reliability of supplies of labor, and the costs imposed by and stability of the host government.

The transnationalization of capital has both fostered and depended on the emergence of a new international division of labor (Froebel, et al., 1980; Cohen, 1981). Over the past two decades, the pre-existing division of labor, based on a global division between manufacturing in the North and primary sector employment in the South, has given way to the emergence of a single world labor market for industrial labor. This development has profoundly affected the structure of economies throughout the world, and has been the common factor in both the deindustrialization of high-wage economies, particularly the U.S., and an equally rapid rise of a limited number of NICs.

Four of the most dynamic NICs -- Korea, Taiwan, Hong Kong, and Singapore -- are on the Pacific Rim. Second only to the phenomenal economic growth of Japan, their emergence has become the hallmark of the new "Pacific Age" in the world economy. From poor, agrarian economies in the 1960s, they have become major world exporters of labor-intensive manufactured goods in the 1980s. A significant portion of the economic growth of these countries has resulted from joint ventures and direct foreign investments by U.S. and Japanese corporations searching for low-wage labor outside of their home countries.

The economic restructuring of national economies has already had observable impacts on patterns of urbanization and the internal structure of cities. One feature of the new urban patterns has been the building of a Pacific Rim network of cities to form a spatial sub-system of the world economy. The main centers of this urban network, such as Los Angeles, Tokyo, and Singapore, have gained new status as "world cities" in which transnational corporate headquarters and management functions, international financial institutions, and global service and communications industries have concentrated.[13] The magnitude and pace of change reflected in the emergence of this network is underscored by the observation that a mere 25 years ago none of these cities would have been candidates for such status.

At lower levels in the nascent Pacific Rim system of cities, the shift of labor-intensive production away from North America and Japan has led to the appearance of new manufacturing centers in East and Southeast Asia, particularly in the NICs. At the same time, in the agrarian economies key sectors of the domestic market for manufactured goods are in the hands of foreign investors who have gained near-monopoly positions in markets protected by import-substitution policies. Recent studies in Indonesia have shown that foreign enterprises are significantly more concentrated around the largest cities, and as such exacerbate the problems associated with the polarization of development in that country (Kelly, 1985).

The transnationalization of capital is not, however, simply a one-way movement outward from the major economies toward less-developed ones. Because it involves more than just production, including access to markets, oligopolistic competition for shares of markets rather than profits from individual operations, and switches into finance-related activities, the transnationalization process also includes cross-penetration of investments between, for example, U.S. and Japanese corporations in each other's home territory. This cross-penetration has, in fact, been a major feature of Japanese investment in the 1980s. In the mid-1980s, Japanese transnationals were investing more in production in the U.S. than in the individual low-wage economies of East and Southeast Asia, and Japanese have been principal investors in U.S. bond markets as well as urban land markets. In Australia, another high-income economy, foreign ownership accounts for 36 percent of the manufacturing sector, 55 percent of mining and of transport equipment, 62 percent of chemicals, 91 percent of oil refining, and 100 percent of automobile production (Wheelwright, 1980). As these trends proceed, transnational corporations originating in different countries are beginning to link together on a global basis. Automobile and electronics makers are leading the field in making these linkages, which involve, *inter alia*, Japanese automobile manufacturers producing parts in Taiwan and Mexico for U.S. companies (Douglass, 1986).

The ways in which the economic growth of cities on the Pacific Rim is being conditioned by supra-national forces can be seen from recent data on Pacific Rim trade, the location of transnational enterprises and their service and production units, the movement of international finance capital, and what is rapidly becoming a global real estate market. For example, a large part of the economies of such cities as Los Angeles, San Francisco and Seattle have increasingly come to rest on the role they play as major ports for channeling Pacific Rim trade into and out of the U.S. economy. Partly because of their geo-economic position, cities on the west coast of the U.S. have also received substantial direct foreign investments from Japan and other Pacific Rim countries in production, office buildings and land. California accounts for 70 percent of the U.S. employment in Japanese-owned manufacturing plants, mostly in automobile production and electronics. It is not surprising to find, therefore, that almost all Japanese automakers have established their U.S. headquarters in Los Angeles, and nearly 30 percent of all downtown office buildings are owned by foreign interests, again mostly Japanese.[14] Japanese firms have also made substantial investments in computer-related operations in the cities in and around California's Silicon Valley.

In the U.S., the processes described above have begun to generate a new bi-coastal pattern of urbanization still dominated by the Boston-New York-Washington megalopolis but being effectively challenged by the Los Angeles metropolitan area, now one of the most rapidly growing urban regions on the Pacific Rim. This new pattern has been paralleled by net population losses in many of the industrial cities around the Great Lakes, and has been tempered only by the relocation of assembly plants in southern states and the growth of border cities in Texas which serve as branch management centers for U.S. industries being relocated in Mexico (Sklair, 1987). In showing how international boundaries separating higher and lower income countries can generate the growth of border cities while cities in high-wage industrial heartlands, such as Detroit, begin to experience absolute population declines for the first time in this century, the emerging patterns of urbanization in the U.S. present perhaps the clearest picture not only of what Peet (1985) calls the geography of class struggle, but also of the international dimension of locational choices available to contemporary "captains of industry."

International linkages in production are an important element of the changing patterns in the U.S. and elsewhere on the Pacific Rim. The nature and importance of these linkages are partially captured by data showing the changing composition of exports in each of the four types of countries identified in the first section. Table 3 shows first the relative importance of exports in the economies of major Pacific Rim countries, and second, the changing sectoral composition of merchandise exports. The importance of exports, as measured by the ratio of exports to GDP, varies from lows of six and seven percent in the U.S. and China, respectively, to extremely high levels in the small island economies of Hong Kong (64 percent) and Singapore (128 percent).

Looking at the composition of exports, as expected the NICs and Japan stand apart from the others as exporters of manufactured goods. These densely-settled countries, each with a very small natural resource base, have been integrated into the Pacific Rim economy primarily on the

Table 3. Level and Major Sectors of Merchandise Exports, 1965 and 1982

Country	Exports 1982 $bn.	%GDP	Fuels/Min 1965	Fuels/Min 1982	All Primary 1965	All Primary 1982	Textiles 1965	Textiles 1982	Machinery[1] 1965	Machinery[1] 1982	Other Mfg. 1965	Other Mfg. 1982	Total 1965	Total 1982
U.S.	199	6	8	9	35	30	3	2	37	44	26	24	100	100
Japan	147	12	2	1	9	3	17	4	31	56	43	36	100	100
Canada	72	23	28	24	63	46	1	1	15	32	21	21	100	100
S. Korea	24	28	15	1	40	8	27	21	3	28	29	43	100	100
Hong Kong	22	64	2	2	13	8	43	34	6	19	37	39	100	100
Singapore	22	128	21	30	65	43	6	4	10	26	18	28	100	100
China	22	7	n/a	26	n/a	46	n/a	15	n/a	6	n/a	34	100	100
Australia	21	12	13	37	86	78	1	1	5	6	9	16	100	100
Mexico	21	11	22	78	84	88	3	1	1	5	13	7	100	100
Indonesia	21	22	43	85	96	96	1	1	3	4	1	2	100	100
Malaysia	14	48	35	35	94	77	1	3	2	15	4	4	100	100
Thailand	6	14	11	7	95	71	1	10	1	6	4	13	100	100
Philippines	5	11	11	12	95	50	1	7	1	3	3	6	100	100
N. Zealand	5	20	1	5	95	76	1	2	1	8	5	14	100	100
Pac. Rim	$601	10	12	16	40	33	8	5	23	36	26	26	100	100

Source: World Bank, *World Development Report*, 1985.
1. includes fossil fuels and minerals
2. weighted by the population of each country.

basis of their low labor costs which have been made even more attractive by very favorable foreign investment policies in these countries.

Japan, with 96 percent of its exports in manufactured goods, is shown to have moved away from its textile base of the early 1960s and into the export of electronic goods, automobiles, and, until recently, steel and ships. In the process much of the textile export industry in other Asian countries, notably in the East Asian NICs of South Korea, Taiwan and Hong Kong, was established through direct foreign investment by Japanese companies (Fujiwara, 1986; Takeo, 1985). The movement of labor-intensive production from high-wage economies to lower-wage economies via direct foreign investment is indicative of the way in which national economies are being restructured within the new international division of labor.

The exporters of manufactured goods face a common problem in the coming years that will profoundly affect the welfare of their cities. With the possible exception of Mexico, which has seen the relative international costs of its labor plummet with the fall of the peso, each is, in its own way, having to cope with rising labor costs vis-a-vis other countries. In Singapore, an explicit strategy has been adopted to accelerate the move into high-tech, high-wage manufacturing activities in direct competition with those in Japan and the U.S. An implicit objective is differentiate Singapore from other NICs and would-be NICs on the Pacific Rim. Yet Korea, where labor struggles have become intense, and Taiwan, a major recipient of Japanese investments in higher-technology production processes, cannot be far behind in pursuing a similar strategy.

Should such a strategy fail, due, for example, to the rise of protectionism against the import of these commodities in the U.S., there would be great difficulty in reconciling the drive for higher standards of living through higher wages and the need to continue to compete with other countries on the lower end of labor-intensive exports. Korea, Hong Kong and Taiwan face similar dilemmas. The only bright side of this issue, as pointed out by Lim (1987), appears to be that the increasing capital intensity of high-tech manufacturing has made its locational pattern somewhat less sensitive to wage differentials and more sensitive to labor skills and highly disciplined work habits, both of which the NICs appear at the moment able to offer in greater abundance than most other Asian countries.

Structural change in the composition of exports among the agrarian countries has not followed that of the NICs. The Philippines, Thailand, Malaysia, and China, although substantially shifting away from primary sector exports, still have more than half of their total exports in this sector. Mexico and Indonesia, two of the world's largest oil economies, saw the primary sector increase its share of GNP during the decade of high world oil prices following 1973. The subsequent fall in oil prices a decade later has severely damaged the capacities of both countries to sustain the pace of economic growth, to manage international debt payments, and, equally, to put together the finances needed to keep pace with their continuing high rates of urbanization. With Mexico City expected to be the largest city in the world by the year 2000, and the Greater Metropolitan Region of Jakarta (called Jabotabek) expected to have over 25 million inhabitants in that year, the capacity to finance the expansion of urban infrastructure and public services may fall well short of the needs in both countries.

China's integration into the Pacific Rim economy remains tentative from both a political and international economic point of view. If the past is in any way a guide to the future, grand swings in the style of public intervention cannot be ruled out despite what now appears to be a thorough rejection of the policies of national closure and self-reliance of the Maoist era in favor of integration into the capitalist world economy. Research by Wu (1987) on the impacts of foreign investment has concluded that although its relative importance in China is as yet extremely small, it has tended to concentrate in the very large coastal cities which have been the target of past anti-growth policies. Cities such as Shanghai have received particularly high concentrations of foreign investment. This raises the dilemma of trying to use foreign investment to assist in modernization without exacerbating what has been perceived as an imbalanced pattern of urbanization in the country. The very recent shift in government policy now favoring a coast-first strategy may have reconciled this contradiction, but not the underlying problems of regional disparities in the urbanization process (Douglass, 1988a).

Trade linkages on the Pacific Rim, either between countries or between production units and branches of transnational enterprises, presents another set of relations which have important implications for urbanization. At the top of these relations are two economies, the U.S. and Japan, which are simultaneously the territorial base for most of the transnational corporations on the Pacific Rim and also the largest markets for commodities produced by all Pacific Rim countries. In 1981 of the top 500 corporations in the world, 242 were U.S-headquartered. Japan-based transnationals, with a much lower number of 62 out of the top 500, nevertheless had the second-highest level of sales volumes (Stopford & Dunning, 1983).[15]

Table 4 indicates that both countries are either the principal or second destination for exports from almost every Pacific Rim country. In many instances, the proportion of total exports going to either Japan or the U.S. is in excess of 50 percent and as high as almost 90 percent.

Equally revealing is the dichotomy which results from linking each country with its principal destination. The U.S., which has become the largest market for world manufacture of consumer goods, is most closely linked with the NICs. Japan, on the other hand, has had a very low level of imports of manufactured goods and, as a resource-poor country, has been most closely linked with the primary product exporting countries of the Pacific Rim. Japan has at the same time become increasingly oriented toward the U.S. market in its own export expansion. By 1983 almost half of Japan's exports to Pacific Rim countries was destined for the U.S. This re-orientation is itself part of the structural change in this region which has seen many of the former exports to East and Southeast Asia, notably textiles, move offshore from Japan along with the assembly under Japanese makers' names of commodities such as electronic machinery in the NICs. Domestic industries in these same countries have also become increasingly competitive in the mainstay Japanese consumer durable export activities.

The implications for urbanization to be drawn from this summary of patterns of trade are threefold. First, and most generally, cities are linked to each other through a complex set of economic relationships that have become internationalized. These relationships deeply affect the future of each city and have made cities more competitive across national boundaries for the location of industries and jobs, for financing urban programs and projects through private banking and related institutions, and for markets for locally produced goods and services.

Second, decisions about the structure and development of the built environment of cities are increasingly being made by non-local interests, many of which are extra-national and unresponsive to the application of territorially defined and limited policies. For example, such instruments as taxation have low levels of effectiveness in the face of transfer pricing and related techniques; they also risk chasing away scarce investments altogether.[16] Urban land use and land prices, especially in central areas of world cities, are increasingly being determined not by local needs for housing, parks or amenities, but by international investors for international functions.

Third, the prosperity of cities in all countries will greatly depend, either directly or indirectly, on the prosperity of U.S. cities and their inhabitants. A key question therefore is whether, in the face of very limited increases in real expendable incomes, the U.S. can provide the requisite expansion of markets to continue to absorb the ever-increasing export capacity of other Pacific Rim countries. Gluts in many of the major manufactured exports, from video tape recorders to automobiles and ships, have already appeared in major markets. And recent protectionist moves in the U.S. and continuing high levels of protection of markets in Japan and other Pacific Rim countries raises the possibility of severe limitations on trade in the near future.

Table 4. Share of Exports to Pacific Basin Countries, 1975 and 1983 (%)

(A 1975)

Exporter	Destination								
	Japan	U.S.	Canada	Aust/NZ Pac. Is.	China	ASEAN	E. Asia NICs	Other	Total
Japan	0	39	4	8	8	21	19	1	100
U.S.	23	0	52	6	1	8	10	1	100
Canada	9	87	0	1	2	1	1	0	100
Australia/NZ/Pac. Is.	41	17	4	14	4	11	6	3	100
China	38	4	2	3	0	18	34	1	100
ASEAN	39	25	1	4	1	22	7	1	100
Brunei	84	8	0	0	0	6	2	0	100
Indonesia	52	31	0	0	0	12	4	0	100
Malaysia	22	25	2	4	2	39	6	0	100
Philippines	49	38	1	2	1	4	4	0	100
Singapore	15	20	1	10	1	37	11	4	100
Thailand	40	16	0	2	1	25	14	2	100
E. Asia NICs	22	45	5	5	0	12	9	2	100
Hong Kong	11	45	5	9	1	20	7	2	100
Korea	36	43	5	2	0	4	7	3	100
Taiwan	18	47	5	4	0	13	12	0	100
Other¹	47	11	1	16	4	10	9	1	100
PACIFIC RIM	19	32	18	6	3	12	10	1	100

Source: IMF, *Directions of Trade Yearbook* 1977 and 1984
1. Includes Burma, Kampuchea, Laos, Macao, Papua New Guinea, Vietnam, North Korea

(B 1983)

Exporter	Destination								
	Japan	U.S.	Canada	Aust/NZ Pac. Is.	China	ASEAN	E. Asia NICs	Other	Total
Japan	0	48	4	6	5	17	19	1	100
U.S.	24	0	42	5	2	11	15	0	100
Canada	6	88	0	1	2	1	2	0	100
Australia/NZ/Pac. Is.	37	16	2	14	3	12	12	3	100
China	32	12	2	2	0	8	41	4	100
ASEAN	32	22	1	3	1	31	9	1	100
Brunei	70	8	0	0	0	14	8	0	100
Indonesia	52	23	0	2	0	19	5	0	100
Malaysia	27	18	1	2	2	40	11	0	100
Philippines	26	48	2	3	1	10	11	0	100
Singapore	11	21	1	6	1	48	11	2	100
Thailand	26	26	1	3	3	24	16	1	100
E. Asia NICs	20	50	4	3	5	10	7	1	100
Hong Kong	6	46	4	4	16	16	4	3	100
Korea	23	54	4	3	1	9	7	0	100
Taiwan	28	49	3	3	0	7	9	0	100
Other[1]	42	17	0	6	4	13	18	0	100
PACIFIC RIM	17	37	12	5	3	14	13	1	100

Source: IMF, *Directions of Trade Yearbook* 1977 and 1984
1. Includes Burma, Kampuchea, Laos, Macao, Papua New Guinea, Vietnam, North Korea

Should protectionist efforts be strengthened, the impacts will not, however, be as straightforward as international trade theory might suggest. Rather than impeding the transnationalization of capital, they would be more likely to accelerate it as transnational enterprises are compelled to set up production units in the protected markets. Evidence of this can already be observed in the case of Japanese investment in automobile production in the U.S. which has, at least in part, been a response to "voluntary" quotas limiting the number of cars that can be exported from Japan to the U.S. each year. Paradoxically, local governments, which are now engaged in extremely heavy competition against each other for the huge investments that accompanying the setting up of Japanese operations in the U.S., have turned protectionism on its head by offering special "enterprise zone" status to, for example, Toyota in California -- a status which exempts the import of car parts from tariff duties. Thus the main impact of protectionism is more likely to be a reduction of investment in countries with small domestic markets rather than the expected expansion of local enterprises in the U.S. or other key consumer economies.

In the agrarian countries, where even very high rates of growth in the now small manufacturing sector will be incapable of absorbing the annual increases in the labor force over the next decade, the export-oriented industry development path may be of limited short- and medium-term bene-fit. For example, excluding cottage industries, Indonesia has less than eight percent of its labor force in manufacturing. Even with an unusually high annual employment growth rate this sector cannot begin to absorb the majority of the 1.3 million annual increase to the labor force, and this says nothing about the plight of low-productivity and low-income workers already counted as the "working poor." Especially in the coming years of expected slow world economic growth and threats of protectionism, addres-sing concerns about the future of cities in the agrarian economies of Asia will require rural-based solutions in addition to the more widely advocated export-oriented industrialization approaches.

International factors have not, of course, acted independently of national political and economic relations. Indeed, one of the more obvious, if paradoxical, outcomes of recent revolutionary changes in international transportation and communications technologies has been the heightening of the importance of social, political and economic difference between Pacific Rim countries in the locational decisionmaking of transnational corporations. The rising importance of "socially-produced" spatial differences in patterns of industrial location has radically restructured the industrial landscape of the Pacific Rim, and along with it the cities of this region.[17]

The relationships between international, national and local levels of social, political and economic organization point to a major problem which is likely to prevent concerted efforts to deal with emerging urban problems. Although growing international interdependencies clearly suggest that cities will have an increasingly intertwined and shared destiny, the wide variations in the local contexts of urbanization also suggest that agreement on appropriate responses to common concerns will be extremely difficult to achieve. This is compounded by the ways in which the hyper-mobility of transnational capital can play territorially fixed cities against each other in the competition to win scarce investments. The absence of effective means for cities to cooperate at international levels may be their own undoing. An every-city-for-itself game seems to be in the making which ultimately threatens the well-being of all.

Policy Issues

Cities, as habitats for future generations of the world's population, have entered a historical period in which the maintenance of their own economic and social welfare will depend on the resolution of global as well as national and local issues. For purposes of discussion, these issues have been organized under three sub-headings below: resources to sustain the urban habitat; employment for the urban labor force; and financing the provisioning of infrastructure and public goods and services.

Resources for the Future of Cities

The theme that the future of cities on the Pacific Rim is a shared one is portrayed by the increasing scale at which cities must find resources to sustain them and extra-local -- increasingly international -- sites to dispose of their refuse and waste. City governments are not, however, accustomed to viewing many of these issues, such as food, as either urban questions or issues that they have any responsibility to resolve. Yet cities as a collective term for populations that no longer produce food or are actively involved in the maintenance of the larger natural environment, will begin to confront them as the world passes the year 2000 and more than half its population becomes urban.

Three resources, food, energy and water, are likely to gain increasing prominence in the future of cities on the Pacific Rim. In addition, disposal of refuse and garbage has already become a pressing issue.

Food. Standard definitions used throughout the world to distinguish "urban" from "rural" invariably take as axiomatic the proposition that cities, unlike villages or other rural settlements, do not engage in agricultural production. The corollary which follows is that cities do not produce their own food, but must rely on rural populations to do so. This basic concept of the city immediately raises two issues. One is that as societies become 70 or 80 percent urban or more, who will produce food for the city? The second is that as cities expand geographically and other factors lead to the depletion of agricultural land, where will food be produced? Both questions are nested within a world-wide rather than a local set of relationships. Cities now depend on locations remote from their own hinterlands for food supplies which are produced by fewer numbers of people and mediated through a world economic system by a handful of oligopolistic agribusinesses and trading houses.

In the 1980s the world's food supply, if equitably distributed, would be sufficient to feed the world's population (GAIA, 1984). There would appear to be, therefore, little cause for concern. But five points may serve to put the current glut of farm production into a longer-term perspective. First, the reasons for these surpluses are also reasons for concern: without price support programs and other non-market mechanisms, individual farmers risk losing most when all farmers are successful and market prices fall. The huge numbers of farm failures in the U.S. in recent years reflect, in part, the contradictions of successful farming.

In this context, one of the most significant features in the global supply of basic food is that five countries -- the U.S., Canada, Australia, Argentina, and France -- account for about 80 percent of all the world's cereal exports. In 1979 the U.S. alone accounted for slightly more than 50 percent of all cereal exports, making world prices substantially determined by the successes and failures of production in a single country. In the U.S., urbanization has meant a fall in the farm population from 15 percent of the total population in 1950 to 2.4 percent in 1984. In the mid-1980s 3.6 million farmers and farm workers were meeting half of the world's food deficit.

The second point is that growth rates in per capita food production in both the NICs and the agrarian countries have, after a period of "green revolution" successes, started to fall. Early successes in the green revolution, based on new seeds and high inputs of fertilizer and water, gave hope that the required growth rate of four percent per year in food production during the UN's Second Development Decade of the 1970s could be met and sustained. But by the end of the 1970s, rates of growth dropped, and for the decade as a whole the actual rate achieved was 3.2 percent.[18]

As a result, imports of grain into developing countries increased to a record 100 million tons in 1981 compared to 30 million in 1972 and 50 million in 1977 (Aziz, 1982: 4).[19]

For East and Southeast Asia, highest land yields in grain production were generally reached at the end of the 1970s and early 1980s when Korea, Malaysia, and later Indonesia reached food self-sufficiency for the first time in modern history. Nearing the end of the 1980s, it appears that these efforts are not being sustained at previous rates and are beginning to reap diminishing returns.[20]

Compared to 1974, tonnage of cereal imports in 1983 were almost double in Indonesia, Korea, Malaysia, the Philippines, Singapore and Thailand, and were triple in Mexico, the home of the first great success in the green revolution (World Bank, 1985: 185). The evidence suggests that cities in these countries may be returning to previous patterns of importing grains rather than relying on domestic sources.

The third point is that the concentration of the world's marketed food supplies in the hands of a few large enterprises raises serious concerns about distribution. Five of the world's largest transnational grain trading companies handle all of the grain exports from the U.S. The question for cities to ask is whether or not this dependency on a small number of producers and an even smaller number of distribution channels will secure their basic food requirements in a rapidly urbanizing future. Markets, especially international oligopolistic markets, cannot be expected to accomplish the social objective of providing every territory with its own basic supplies of food.

Nor do markets work to deliver food to those in the cities which may be in most need. There are an estimated 470 million people in absolute poverty who do not receive the money entitlements to purchase sufficient food in the market. Changes in food prices in these conditions have a ripple effect around the world that threatens the very survival of millions of its inhabitants, an increasing number of whom are the urban poor without access to even the smallest piece of land on which to grow any type of food.

The fourth point is that there are a number of disquieting global trends in the physical conditions surrounding food production. One involves changes in the world's environment. The depletion of the ozone layer protecting the earth from the sun's radiation is one of the most serious changes, and is already reportedly causing S2 billion in reduced crop yield in the U.S. every year, an amount expected to increase as the temperature of the earth continues to rise.[21] The depletion of the equatorial forests that cool the earth is also expected to increase environment-related damages to agricultural production. These global environmental changes have been linked to recent droughts in the world and around the Pacific Rim where, in 1988, crop failure in the U.S. alone were credited with causing significant increases in the cost of living.

Other factors leading to a worldwide decline in the expansion of land used for food production include uncontrolled soil erosion in many rural regions, the encroachment of cities into prime agricultural land, and cropland toxification from industrial as well as agricultural pollution. Together they result in an estimated annual world-wide loss of 11 million hectares of agricultural land (GAIA, 1985: 40). Between 1975 and 2000 the world is expected to lose 275 million hectares, or 18 percent of its arable land. In addition, desertification results in the loss of seven million hectares of grassland per year.[22]

Loss of prime agricultural land to cities is a classic problem of urbanization throughout the world for the simple reason that many of today's largest cities first appeared in rich agricultural regions. In the U.S., between 1967 and 1975 the encroachment of cities resulted is the loss of 2.5 million hectares of agricultural land (Brown, 1985: 25). In Canada the difference between land quality around cities and in more remote locations has meant that it takes 2.4 hectares of new land in the western provinces to replace one hectare lost to urban expansion in the east.

A fifth point concerns inputs into agriculture. Intensification of agricultural production has relied on massive increases in the use of chemical fertilizers and pesticides. Just to meet the requirement to double the amount of food produced in the years 1980-2000 to feed the world's population will call for an estimated 380 percent increase in commercial energy use. During the period of very high oil prices of the late 1970s, the World Bank estimated that the energy-intensive nature of increasing agricultural production could result in a doubling of food prices in real terms between 1980 and 2000. This would result in a rise of the number of malnourished people from 500 million in 1975 to 1.3 billion in 2000 (Soedjatmoko, 1981). None of these projections take into account ecological damage under stringent production conditions or severe droughts or floods which have become recurring features in the developing world.

The conclusion to be drawn from the preceding discussion is that there are a number of reasons suggesting that cities in many Pacific Rim countries will have to begin to consider the possibilities of redefining the age-old concept of a city as a non-agricultural entity by including agricultural production as a basic part of their regional economy.

Energy and Fuel. The Pacific Rim accounts for almost half the total commercial energy consumed in the world. Between 1965 and 1983 the per capita consumption of energy more than doubled in several countries of the Pacific Rim. Although the U.S. alone accounts for more than half of the Pacific Rim's share, as the growth rate of consumption in this and other post-industrial countries has begun to level off, it has accelerated in the rapidly urbanizing countries of East and Southeast Asia (Table 5).

At least two types of issues are related to energy. One concerns the side effects associated with the intensity of energy use; the second concerns access to energy resources. Beginning with the first, Table 5, which shows the tonnage of energy used per square kilometer of land, displays a wide variation in energy intensity around the Pacific Rim, ranging from a low of 12 tons per km^2 in Australia to 20,000 tons per km^2 in Singapore. Since most energy is consumed in or near cities, the Australia and Singapore comparison obviously overstates the real differences in degrees of areal concentration of energy use. Nevertheless, in comparison to the low population density countries, high density ones such as Japan, Korea and Taiwan, as well as Hong Kong and Singapore, have very small territorial areas within which very high levels of energy are used. The NICs also currently have the highest rates of increase in per capita energy consumption on the Pacific Rim.[23]

How these and other countries cope with the side effects of energy use, including environmental pollution and toxic waste, will be critical to the future of their cities. Since almost all urban and industrial energy now in use in the world is derived from the conversion of oil, coal or natural gas, the use of energy has been associated with very high levels of residue discharged into the air, land and water. Finding alternative sources of energy, whether solar power or super conductors, is very much an urban issue.

The side effects of energy use will be especially important in the world's megacities where the automobile has become the mode of urban transportation and commuting times to work may average more than one hour on congested motorways. The use of fossil fuels to power motor vehicles chronically pollutes the air of most of these cities. Emissions from automobiles account for half of the annual 450,000 tons of lead being dumped into the air by the human use of fossil fuels. In Los Angeles, where temperature inversions for several months each year prevent pollutants from escaping, photochemical smog produced largely from automobile emissions has caused extensive damage to surrounding forests and plant life (GAIA, 1984). A similar situation exists in Tokyo, where schools are closed by smog alerts and loud speakers atop ward offices daily warn people to stay indoors and avoid exertion every summer. Other megacity governments simply do not warn their citizens of the daily health risks.

The second issue, that of access to energy, has a territorial as well as a social dimension. The territorial one is straightforward: urban-industrial growth in the energy-poor countries of the Pacific Rim, especially the NICs, will require ever-increasing, globally-extensive supplies of energy. Given that these countries must also depend on global sources for basic food supplies, much of the production of cities will be used to pay for the import of these two commodities, which do not include the other raw

Table 5. Consumption of Commercial Energy 1965 and 1983[1]

Country/ Territory	Total 1983		% Share 1983		Growth Rate 1973-83		Per Capita[2]		Rate/yr. 1965-83	GDP/CAP Rate/yr. 1965-83
	Mn. tons	tons/ km²	Pac Rim	World	Prod.	Consum.	1965	1983		
Australia	92	12	2.4	1.1	4.5	2.5	3.3	4.8	1.7	1.7
Canada	239	24	6.2	2.8	1.4	2.0	6.0	8.8	1.8	2.5
China	629	66	16.2	7.4	5.7	5.4	0.2	0.5	4.6	4.4
Hong Kong	10	10,000	0.3	0.1	n.a.	5.8	0.6	1.6	4.7	6.2
Indonesia	38	20	1.0	0.4	2.7	7.8	0.1	0.2	3.7	5.0
Japan	404	1,086	10.4	4.7	5.0	0.4	1.5	2.9	3.1	4.8
Malaysia	13	39	0.3	0.2	15.9	7.1	0.3	0.7	3.8	4.5
Mexico	130	66	3.4	1.5	17.0	8.7	0.6	1.3	3.5	3.2
New Zealand	12	45	0.3	0.1	4.3	1.5	2.6	3.8	1.7	1.2
Philippines	16	53	0.4	0.2	20.8	2.3	0.2	0.3	2.1	2.9
South Korea	58	592	1.5	0.7	4.6	8.8	0.2	1.2	7.5	6.7
Singapore	12	20,078	0.0	0.0	n.a.	4.9	2.0	4.8	4.0	7.8
Taiwan	41	1,139	1.1	0.5	n.a.	n.a.	n.a.	2.2	n.a.	n.a.
Thailand	17	33	0.4	0.2	13.7	5.4	0.1	0.3	5.7	4.3
United States	2,175	232	56.1	25.5	0.1	-0.4	6.6	7.0	0.3	1.7
Pacific Rim[3]	3,886	91	100.0	45.4	n.a.	4.6	n.a.	2.4	n.a.	n.a.
WORLD	8,524	56	(45.6)[1]	100.0	n.a.	n.a.	n.a.	n.a.	n.a.	n.a.

Sources: World Bank, *World Development Report 1985*; *The 1987 World Information Almanac*

1. In oil equivalents based on apparent consumption of coal, lignite, petroleum products, natural gas, and hydro, nuclear and geothermal electricity

2. In thousands of kilogram oil equivalents

3. Weighted by the population of each country

4. Pacific Rim share of world consumption

materials needed to maintain their economic base. Table 6 shows the extent to which countries of the Pacific Rim are dependent on food and energy imports. In the case of Japan and the Asian NICs, the figures are striking. Sixty-two percent of Japan's imports in 1982 were composed of food and energy; for Singapore and South Korea the level was 42 percent.

Table 6   Food and Energy Imports, 1965-1983

Country/ Territory % Imports	Cereal Imports (mn. tons) % Δ			Food as % Imports		Fuel as % Imports		Food & Fuel	
	1974	1983	74-83	1965	1982	1965	1982	1965	1982
Australia	7.2	4.2	-41	6	5	8	14	14	19
Canada	1.5	0.4	-70	10	8	7	10	17	18
China	9.2	19.2	109	N/A	23	N/A	1	N/A	24
Hong Kong	0.7	0.9	38	26	14	3	8	29	22
Indonesia	1.9	3.0	56	6	7	3	21	9	28
Japan	19.6	25.3	29	23	13	20	50	43	63
Malaysia	1.0	1.8	76	27	12	12	15	39	27
Mexico	2.9	8.5	194	5	10	2	12	7	22
New Zealand	0.1	0.1	-3	8	7	7	17	15	24
Philippines	0.8	1.3	64	20	10	10	26	30	36
South Korea	2.7	6.4	137	15	12	7	30	22	42
Singapore	0.7	1.5	113	24	8	13	34	37	42
Thailand	0.1	0.2	132	7	5	9	31	16	36
U.S.	0.5	0.6	29	20	8	10	27	30	35
Pacific Rim	48.7	73.3	51	N/A	N/A	N/A	N/A	N/A	N/A
World	174.1	265.8	53	N/A	N/A	N/A	N/A	N/A	N/A

Source: World Bank, *World Development Report* 1985.

Given that most energy resources currently being used are not renewable and may soon be exhausted, the search for alternatives would appear to be a prudent course of action. At current rates of consumption, for example, known reserves of oil will be exhausted within 30 years (GAIA, 1984: 112). The counter-position has been that, as was evidenced following the OPEC-initiated price increases in the 1970s, when prices for one form of energy increase, the market will find cheaper alternatives. Some of these options, notably nuclear energy, have already proliferated, but rising costs and loss of public faith in the safety of nuclear power stations has kept its share at about two percent of total world commercial energy use. The increasing concentration in the control over all types of energy by a handful of global corporations also raises serious questions about the ways in which the "market" will identify and develop alternatives.[24]

In addition to the question of the spatial distribution of energy, there is another energy crisis that has not received as much publicity. It is the lack of access to fuel by the urban poor, and ranges from the elderly people who freeze to death in unheated apartments on a wintry night in U.S. cities to the steady depletion of "non-commercial" fuel resources, such as wood, in cities and rural regions throughout East and Southeast Asia. In either type of location, meeting basic energy and fuel needs is most expensive for the poorest people and often proves to be an impossible task.[25]

In the agrarian economies, the depletion of fuel resulting from such wood-using activities as brickmaking and household fuel gathering in forest reserves around cities is accelerating, particularly around large cities, and the costs of gathering basic fuel for cooking and warming homes have often increased dramatically (Sachs, 1981; UNEP, 1986). In more peripheral forest areas, timber extraction is still treated as a mining operation despite regulations and laws requiring implementation of reforestation programs by businesses that are granted logging concessions. In many countries the depletion of potentially renewable local resources is out of control. The concern is not about commercial energy supplies; it is about energy for survival in the city, and some say the world.

Water. People in the cities of the high-income countries tend to take water as a ubiquitous commodity that requires little attention. This is true even though rivers in these countries are severely polluted and such cities as Los Angeles have long since completely exhausted their own local water supplies and now depend on sources hundreds of miles away.

In lower income countries such as Indonesia, water is never taken for granted. In the *kampong*, slums and squatter settlements that comprise most residential areas of Jakarta, piped water is rare and the water from the rivers, stagnant many months of the year, is undrinkable. Only 40 percent of the urban population has access to safe drinking water (ADB, 1986). Most of the food cooked and beverages made and consumed in the city use water that is, by official standards, unsafe to drink. Furthermore, the average cost of obtaining water of any kind may account for as much as ten percent of a poor household's income, a substantially higher percentage than that borne by wealthy urbanites.

Cities have not only polluted their own water supplies; they are also in competition with agriculture and agro-industry for access to water. The applications of high-energy chemicals in agricultural, an escalating process, requires steady and plentiful supplies of water. Rural-urban competition for water in lowland areas and fertile plains where cities have emerged is already severe. The processing of agricultural products, especially cassava, is one of the primary factors in the depletion of ground water under the Bangkok metropolis, which is sinking as much as 20 centimeters per year and is annually flooded for several months. Jakarta is also beginning to sink as both the city and agriculture use groundwater. The irony is that using water causes flooding (Douglass, 1988d).[26]

Resource in, Refuse out. The corollary of high resource use is high waste production. Slum and squatter settlements in many lower income countries of Asia sit on and gain meager incomes from vast unprocessed garbage heaps. In China cities are beginning to surround themselves with what some observers have called "Great Walls" of garbage that are increasingly mixed with refuse which, unlike the past, cannot be recycled by rural households (Whitney, 1988). The picture at the other end of the income spectrum is of a different order, but the crisis is coming nonetheless. By 1992 at least one-quarter of all U.S. cities will be completely out of landfills for refuse dumping (*U.S. News & World Report*, May 4, 1987). This and other factors doubled the per ton cost of burying refuse between 1980 and 1984, and costs are expected to double again by 1990 (Brown, 1985: 242).

In other more densely-settled countries, the increasing intensity of energy and industrial chemical use may well bring very high social costs. In Japan approximately three-quarters of all industries were, in the 1970s, concentrated near Tokyo, Osaka, Nagoya and North Kyushu. The intensification of industrial production in these river delta regions in the 1960s led to heavy pollution destroying most of the coastal fishing, a large number of deaths from PCB and cadmium contamination, and high incidences of respiratory disease (Bennett and Levine, 1976; Douglass, 1988b).

In lower-income countries the capacity of governments to effectively enforce pollution and dumping regulations is often lacking. Without sufficient refuse services, private citizens, rich and poor, dump wastes directly into rivers, which run only in the rainy seasons, down ravines and on public land. In addition, there is a perception, usually unvoiced, that a principal means of successfully competing for the siting of a transnational production unit is to maintain little or no effective regulation over industrial wastes. The longer-term effects on the toxification of ground water and soils are yet to be felt, but will be much more difficult to address than many of dishearteningly visible short-term side effects in many Pacific Rim cities today.

Yet the days in which the city could find rural governments and Pacific islands willing to accept its wastes, in addition to the practice of moving polluting industries from the North to the South, may be drawing to an end as awareness of the social and economic consequences spreads. Cities will have to begin to find their own means of recycling wastes, ultimately helping to change attitudes from one now accepting a throw-away material existence to a more resource-conserving one.

Toward Urban Resource Ecologies.   Trends in the use of the world's resources may well undermine the very basis for sustaining cities in the coming decades.   One response, still at a minor level, has been for cities to begin to create their own resource ecologies.   Some have allowed people to partially meet their food needs by allocating small plots to households wishing to grow their own fruit and vegetables.   Other possibilities include the novel use of hydroponics by Tokyo supermarkets to grow their own vegetables in the store.   Cities have also made tentative efforts to support solar energy, develop biomass energies, and recycle wastes.

Such resources as grain production are, however, unlikely to become urban activities.   Problems of urban encroachment on prime agricultural land, competition for water, and the limitations of the chemical-intensive solutions offered by agribusiness suggest that rural and urban development need to be placed in a common development framework within which they are made mutually supportive and sustaining.   Planning for cities will in many places require a territorial framework that overcomes the traditional rural-urban dichotomy (Friedmann and Douglass, 1978).   Cities will be increasingly pressed to renew themselves, provide food in their hinterlands, regenerate their resource base, and to recycle their own wastes. This may see an urban life that oddly revives the past -- composting, vegetable gardens -- while using the best of new technologies.

As populations become increasingly urban, national governments are likely to be pressed to formulate their own urban development strategies and policies to manage the use of resources in cities.   Resource issues will also have to be addressed at international levels through efforts to reach agreement on the exploitation of non-renewable resources and the environmental impacts of energy consumption and disposal.   In sum, efforts at all levels will be required to meet the needs and adjust to the constraints of renewing the resource and ecological basis for the future of cities.

Employment, Inequality and Access in the City

Since at least the days of Adam Smith, the city has been viewed as the fountain of economic opportunity, with urbanization and upward economic mobility perceived to go hand in hand. As more of the Pacific Rim's population resides and works in cities, the burden of living up to this image has become heavier. The widening gap between the economic performance of enterprises in a given economy and the welfare of the middle and lower classes has not only made conventional indices of national economic health misleading; it has also meant that getting a job in the city has, for the majority of people, become both more arduous and less rewarding. Providing productive employment for the urban labor force is likely to be the most important political as well as economic issue in the coming years, not only for employment itself but because working to earn a decent income is the pivot around which most aspects of economic inequality, poverty, and access to the public provisioning of goods and services turn.

Open unemployment has traditionally been seen as the major indicator of economic ills. In the U.S., although national unemployment levels have recently fallen to very low levels, they are persistently high among blacks and other minority groups who live in central urban areas. Elsewhere, such as in Australia and Canada, open unemployment rates have remained around the ten percent level or higher over the past five years. Even in Japan, where an image of full, lifetime employment has been projected to its own citizens and abroad, the rise in the value of the yen and the rapid offshore movement of Japanese companies has resulted in the highest unemployment rates since the early postwar years.[27]

In many economies, trends in the conditions of those who are working have become as important as unemployment and are also placing increasing burdens on city governments to take a larger role in providing welfare-related services. Real wages have fallen in recent years for full-time employees, and many other workers in these economies, including Japan, have been pushed into part-time positions with few, if any, health or retirement benefits. In the U.S., "contingent workers" -- those who work at home, temporarily for sub-contractors, or part-time -- have been steadily replacing full-time employees. Between 1980 and 1985 the number of these workers doubled to reach 17 percent of the U.S. labor force.[28] In Japan, as in the U.S. and Australia but at a much faster rate, married women have been rapidly brought into the labor force as part-time, low-wage workers leading the transformation of the Japanese labor market toward lower job security, benefits and incomes.

Within these overall trends there are of course important differences between national settings. Unlike Japan, for example, large cities in the

U.S. will continue to be plagued by high spatial concentrations of unemployment in the inner city. In most cities these high rates of unemployment will persist even with high rates of employment growth for the larger urban region as a whole. The situation in New York, where a net increase of 167,000 jobs between 1977 and 1981 occurred during a period when inner-city, minority unemployment rates continued to soar, illustrates this problem. Virtually all of the employment expansion was concentrated in white-collar service industries that either discriminated against or required different skills than those of inner-city populations (Kasarda, 1983).

This inner-city problem in the U.S. is the manifestation of a larger structural change taking place on the Pacific Rim that has moved labor-intensive manufacturing employment to low-wage countries and has transformed U.S. cities into information processing (and low-wage service) centers. The resulting rise in skill requirements for entry-level positions is partly behind statistics showing an unemployment rate of 38 percent for inner-city minority workers between 16 and 19 years of age in the U.S. in 1984. This compared to 16 percent for whites in the same age bracket.

As previously discussed, in the Asian NICs, urban employment prospects hinge very much on the health of the Pacific Rim economy, particularly the strength and openness of the U.S. domestic market. They also turn on the capacity of each NIC to remain competitive with other NICs. With such huge countries as China or Indonesia only marginally involved in the low-wage offshore assembly industries that are the mainstays of Korea, Taiwan and Singapore, maintaining an income sufficient to pay the high costs of housing and other goods and services in the NICs may prove difficult if they are forced to compete with the agrarian economies for labor-intensive manufacturing jobs. To the extent that the NICs can move on to the production of more sophisticated products or heavy industry, the export-oriented approach may continue to pay the way for rapid urbanization, but this again rests on sustaining the economy of the Pacific Rim economy as a whole, and the U.S. in particular.

But to the extent that export-oriented growth strategies depend on foreign investment, there are also a number of issues related to the choice of technologies and its impact on employment. A recent study by the ILO (1984) concluded that technologies used by branch operations of trans-national corporations are becoming more capital-intensive, and therefore less labor-absorbing. The main reason is that choice of technologies is part of world-wide systems of production contained within single corporations which are not made with concern for the needs of a particular host economy. Since long-term growth of the company is dependent on the "right" technology choice vis-a-vis competitors, this takes precedence over local employment impact considerations. The study further found that the policies of host countries have almost no effect on the technological choices of foreign investors.

In the agrarian economies urban employment markets are likely to remain highly segmented and characterized by a large proportion of the labor force in very low productivity work. The neglect of rural development will continue to lead to an expansion of low productivity employment in all sectors. Temporary, seasonal and permanent rural-urban migration has become a major component of rural household survival strategies in these countries (Hugo, 1984). A major reason for this is the continuing absolute increases in rural populations in situations of slow or even negative growth in agricultural employment, the absence of productive non-agricultural employment opportunities in rural areas, high levels of land concentration, and urban biases in the planning process.

At the same time, biases favoring large-scale national and transnational corporations are working to turn the once petty commodity producers in the "informal sector" in these economies into de facto low wage, self-exploiting sales agents for the large factory system. In Jakarta, for example, small shops that once made and vended their own ice cream now sell that made by large companies, accepting very low margins of profit and continuing to house the migrant-vendors in substandard conditions in the attics above the old shops. In other words, the penetration of large-scale producers, in a situation of high levels of surplus labor and overall low labor-absorptive capacity of leading growth sectors, works to reproduce rather than eliminate low productivity employment in the large cities of Asia (Douglass, 1983; Armstrong and McGee, 1985).

Although the largest numbers of destitute people reside in the agrarian economies, other countries are not immune from the problems of urban destitution. Massive structural change in the U.S., in addition to resulting in high rates of open unemployment, has produced a number of disturbing trends among those who are employed. The gist of these trends is that, first, the majority of new jobs in the economy are paying wages that yield poverty-level incomes, and second, as the middle class is squeezed in this process, income inequalities are increasing. The increasing dichotomy in the expansion of the urban service sector between high-wage producer-oriented services and minimum-wage "MacDonald's hamburger" low-skill services partly explains both the fall in wages and increasing urban income inequalities. Nearly 60 percent of all jobs created in the U.S. between 1979 and 1984 paid less than $7,000 per year (in 1984 dollars) compared to fewer than 20 percent in the previous six years (*Honolulu Star-Bulletin*, December 14, 1986). In 1987 real wages declined for the fifth year of the present decade (*Business Week*, August 12, 1986).

In the post-industrial economy of the U.S., rapid changes in urban labor markets, which brought minority populations to central city ghettos in the 1950s and 1960s and are now leaving them "structurally" unemployed, lie behind figures showing that between 1976-1982, the number of people below officially adopted poverty lines increased from 17 to 24 percent of the total New York City population (Fainstein & Fainstein, 1985: 199). In the winter of 1985 more than 20,000 people per night were sleeping in New York city shelters. During the same period, Manhattan received billions of investment dollars in office buildings occupied by transnational corporate headquarters, financiers, and insurance companies (Kirby, 1985).

These changes are affecting the design and form of cities as well. Observers have noted a new trend toward a fortressing of U.S. cities, of constructing brightly-lit corridors to bring the suburban commuters safely through danger zones to the office and back. The main features of these paths are smooth walls, no dark niches to hide or sleep in, and no benches to sit on -- a far cry from the convivial open spaces that fill the city of the mind's eye. Neighborhoods in all major cities are also becoming more clearly demarcated and differentiated by income classes (Eklund and Williams, 1978).

The issue of employment will be a central policy concern everywhere, but responses can be expected to vary according to the particular conditions in each nation, region and city. In the U.S. the response in some areas may be similar to Rhode Island's erstwhile Green House Compact, which sought to develop a state industrial policy that would identify and support new high growth industries and ease some of the worst negative employment effects of declining industries. It may also take the form of national legislation on plant closures with regard to compensation, job retraining and counselling services. And it may move toward new forms of enterprise ownership, including community and worker partnerships. In contrast, the policy question in Japan seems to center more on the debate between finding a new export base to replace its now high-wage electronics and automobile industries versus a more inward-looking, domestic market oriented approach. In Canada and Australia, the opportunities may be more related to resource-based activities.

In the NICs, urban employment may focus more on improving working conditions and the wage rather than creating jobs per se, although all of these issues are interlinked. Whether hours can be decreased from the ten hours a day, six-day work week common in factories in some of these countries, and whether real wage increases can keep pace with per capita GNP growth and, in the case of Korea, high housing costs, will be important public issues. At the same time, the vulnerability of these economies to fluctuations in the international economy, such as changes in exchange rates and energy prices, and potentially new sources of low-wage labor in other Pacific Rim countries, make predictions about the future of employment in the NICs very difficult to make.

In the agrarian economies, all of which are concerned with the high levels of concentration of urban growth in one or a few very large cities, the future of urban employment will, as previously argued, depend greatly on accelerating rural development. In the Philippines, the recently announced program of radical land reform combined with agriculture support packages for small farmers, in generating a broad rural-based alternative source of employment, could well have a greater impact on relieving urban problems than many of the more visible programs to expand urban industry. Likewise, in Indonesia, crop diversification and multiple-cropping strategies may be the best strategy for generating new jobs in cities in rural regions while maintaining the national goal of food self-sufficiency. In Thailand, the ending of the heavy rice tax may be a major avenue for generating both urban and rural growth in regions outside of Bangkok.

In China, the policy framework for providing urban employment has been posed as one of managing a set of contradictions in socialist development. Key among these is the contradiction between raising productivity by increasing the material incentives to work and achieving a just distribution on the basis of need rather than effort. In a spatial framework, the government has also set the contradiction as one of the high growth potential of large coastal cities versus the objective of decentralizing urban development away from these cities and toward smaller cities and towns.

Financing the Urban Future

Cities everywhere have been experiencing severe constraints on their financial capacity both to maintain existing infrastructure and services and to meet their growing needs. As with other factors, in many countries this trend is the local translation of a larger one taking place at the international and national levels where government indebtedness has combined, with the ascendancy of conservative governments at the center that have moved to cut national spending on social and economic development programs.

Increased indebtedness of nations has become an issue of principal concern everywhere. Although most prominently noted in such countries as Mexico and the U.S., even a country enjoying extraordinary trade surpluses, namely Japan, has a public debt almost equal to that of the U.S. and has recently announced substantial cuts in central subsidies to local governments (Douglass, 1988b). In other countries the lingering effects of the rise in oil prices or, conversely in the case of Indonesia, the fall in oil prices, has created both acute and chronic problems in state financing.[29]

The exact impact of declining central support to urban governments varies.   In most of the post-industrial countries, local governments are empowered to directly or indirectly tax their residents and accrue debt.   In these countries increased local taxation has been a major trend which, until the mid-1980s, worked fairly well to fill in budgetary gaps. By 1986, however, the varying effects of slow economic growth, a fall in commodity prices and a decreasing tax base resulted in urban governments moving back into deficit spending.[30]

In most developing countries of Asia, where even at national levels the mechanisms to collect direct income taxes are largely ineffectual, urban governments do not have the revenue collecting powers available to the post-industrial countries.   All are almost wholly dependent on central government grants for routine and developmental expenditures, and cutbacks in central subsidies have had debilitating impacts on cities in these countries. With no fallback position, the already huge deficits in such basic infrastructures as roads, drainage, power supplies, and piped water are likely to increase, especially outside the capital cities where urban infrastructure and services invariably receive low priority.

International factors have compounded the problems of urban finance.   The transnationalization of capital and a new international division of labor have worked to intensify the competition between cities for the location of industry and, therefore, the maintenance of their economic (tax) base. The most dramatic impact has arguably been in the high-wage countries of the Pacific Rim where concessions and subsidies to large-scale enterprises are in extreme contrast to the days of more territorially-restricted enterprises of the 1960s.[31] They have included tax abatements, land assembly and site preparation, the provision of economic overhead capital, relocation of entire neighborhoods, low interest financing, outright grants, the adoption of "right-to-work" laws forbidding closed union shops, job training and even the construction of new city amenities such as museums to satisfy the economic as well as social requirements of new industrial managers. As summarized by Bluestone and Harrison (1982: 209):

> The expansion of international competition and the new technological breakthroughs that make rapid capital mobility possible have produced a set of conditions under which government can no longer coerce the private sector to cooperate in the regulatory process or to provide the necessary revenue for the provision of public goods and social redistribution. When financial

capital and even real plant and equipment can be moved with relative ease, jobs can be held hostage, thus forcing people to choose between industrial growth accompanied by unhealthy water and air, and environmentally wholesome but desolate ghost towns.

The impact has also been high in other Pacific Rim countries. The only difference between the post-industrial countries and the NICs in this regard may be that the latter have been making many of these concessions for decades. Although these countries would appear to be the prime beneficiaries of the deindustrialization of the U.S. and Japanese economies, they too are in competition with each other and have been compelled to offer more concessions. Singapore, for example, recently increased the tax holiday for foreign investors from five to ten years and has increased access to low-cost long-term loans as a means of countering generous grant schemes being offered in other Asian countries. Even in China, which has only just begun to seek foreign investment, the government has recently served warning to the managers of the huge, and as yet still largely empty, economic zones to stop competing through unsanctioned subsidies and extensions of tax holidays to foreign investors.

All of these competitive efforts suggest that as Pacific Rim countries, rich and poor, turn to the EPZ approach toward attracting transnational capital, the financial benefits to the host countries may deteriorate. Recent studies have indicated, for example, that while employment generation may be in some cases significant, incomes generated from taxes in the EPZs do not cover the costs of constructing and operating them.[32] Furthermore, a major reason for the shutting down and relocation of branch operations away from export zones has been the ending of tax holidays.[33]

The concessions and subsidies used to gain new industries have not, in the main, alleviated the third source of the crisis in financing urban development, namely, the pervasive increase in low-income, often public aid dependent, populations. This has a two-sided edge which cuts away at the capacity to maintain the urban habitat. The first is the decline in taxable incomes needed to pay for services; the second is the increasing demand for such services.

A disturbing trend in industrial relocation in the U.S. has been the tendency to adopt labor-saving technologies in new plants, leading to a net decrease in the number of employees needed to produce a given commodity. As a result, with every relocation the total number of jobs in that particular activity in the economy tends to decline. In many cases, of course, the relocation is completely out of the country. While this improves labor productivity and "competitiveness" of American labor, it also appears to be generating longer unemployment lines. General Motors, for example, which announced the wholesale dismissal of more than 30,000 U.S. workers at the end of 1986, was at the same time making arrangements to import under its own name more than 100,000 cars per year made by Japan's Toyota, Isuzu and Suzuki automakers in assembly plants located in Taiwan and Mexico.

Conclusion

Looking at the international, national and urban scales, the foregoing discussion can be summarized by three points. First, international forces appear to be increasingly antagonistic to efforts to maintain basic levels of urban financing. Cities on the Pacific Rim are entering a period of intensive, perhaps debilitating competition to maintain and/or capture new a basis for their economic survival.[34] Second, competition to gain industrial activities is requiring a shift in the balance of expenditures away from social programs in favor of the provisioning of economic overhead capital for industry. Third, national governments have become less rather than more active in mediating international and local relations.

How have cities coped with these changes? First of all, as discussed above, all but a few of the key world cities on the Pacific Rim have been compelled to lower their claims on the private sector and to finance economic and social programs through increased taxes on consumption, user fees, and borrowing. In this regard, one of the most telling indicators of the way in which cities in rich as well as poor countries alike are being urged to follow a single solution for their economic ills is the widespread adoption of the free trade zone strategy in the U.S. and other high-income countries. Called "free enterprise zones" in the U.S., where at least 26 states have adopted legislation giving special tax exemptions to firms locating in these zones, these attempts to make inner city minority workers competitive with Korean, Taiwanese or Singapore labor paid a fraction of the U.S. minimum wage seems on the surface patently absurd. So far the limited success of these zones seems to bear out this initial impression.[35] It also points out the fallacy of trying to find a single general solution for the economic problems facing Pacific Rim cities.

Other cities have simply refused to take on the role of guiding the local economy or providing a social safety net. An extreme example is Houston, Texas, which, in becoming the headquarters of 34 out of 35 of the largest U.S. petroleum companies, is in one of only four states without any income tax on corporate incomes and one of six states with no personal income tax.[36] In other instances the local state has attempted to construct its own strategy to counter the capacity of transnational corporations to play off one area against another. California's unitary tax, which attempted to tax industries and the basis of their worldwide profits was a major effort in this direction. In the face of so many more hospitable locations, however, California was unable to effectively maintain this tax.[37]

Perhaps the more pervasive solution is the turn toward cost-recovery programs and privatization of public services. As cornerstones in the ideologies of conservative governments in such countries as the U.K., U.S. and Japan, these approaches have also become a major thrust in the international lending practices of USAID and the World Bank. Cities are encouraged to sell off public assets, even profitable ones, and to withdraw from funding welfare programs as a means of both reducing financial outlays and giving greater play to market forces in allocating goods and services to cities and their inhabitants. In the U.S., as concessions and give-backs to business increase, the poor are put into a pay-as-you-go world of health, housing and social welfare. Indonesian cities, even relatively small ones, are being encouraged to fortress themselves with toll roads and charge user fees to even the poorest groups for access to village standpipes.

Many of these efforts, particularly those which work to reduce subsidies to the wealthy, may have merit, but taken together they represent a fundamental redefinition of the role of the state in maintaining a minimum standard of welfare in society and of shoring up failures of the market to secure these standards. In more specific terms, it redefines the concept of equity away from one having a redistributive dimension to one based on the principal that users and beneficiaries should pay for services received. This change in political philosophy is profound, yet it does not yet seem to be on the urban agenda for public debate.[38]

Other pressures on urban financing are related to the increasing dependency ratio, i.e., the ratio of working to non-working population, of the urban population. In high population growth countries, such as Mexico, the problem is manifested in terms of the number of children per family. In high-income, slow-population growth countries the problem is the rapidly growing number of retired workers and senior citizens. In Japan, a country with few pension programs and almost no public or private institutions for the elderly, one-fifth of the population will be over age 65 in the year 2000, making the financing of health care and housing for the elderly one of the most pressing issues in the future of this highly urbanized society. In the U.S., as massive corporate buyouts and takeovers result in the cancellation of former retirement benefits, the issue is also becoming compelling.[39] All of these events put increasing pressure on the state to provide more, rather than less, financial outlays for the commonwealth.

Suggestions abound for addressing the problems of financing the future of an urban world. They range from obtaining community and employee compensations from companies closing plants without sufficient warning, to unitary taxes, city-private sector partnerships, negotiations with new industries concerning types of jobs that will be offered (e.g. full-time versus temporary employment) and infrastructure to be provided by the companies. It is hoped that these and other efforts will bear fruit, but the nature of the dilemma remains unchanged: how can cities successfully compete with each other to attract internationally mobile economic activities and, at the same time, sustain the financial and institutional capacity to improve the social and the environmental integrity of their habitats.   International, national and local political processes cannot be expected to produce outcomes that move in a concert toward a resolution of this dilemma. Given the scale and velocity of economic and technological forces moving on the Pacific Rim, as well as the magnitude of the impacts they are having on daily life in the city, the issues surrounding it will undoubtedly provide the slogans and banners of many of the struggles that will be witnessed in the construction of the future of cities on the Pacific Rim.

Notes

1.   In Asia, Africa and Latin America more than nine-tenths of the population continued to live in rural settlements up to the end of World War II. The acceleration in the pace of urbanization in these countries following World War II and national independence is indicated by projections showing increases in the proportion of population living in cities from 13 percent in 1950 to 43 percent by the year 2000 (Roberts, 1978).

2.   The size of the urban population was already higher in the Third World by 1980 when estimates showed 834 million urban residents in the more developed countries and 972 million in those less developed (Armstrong and McGee, 1985, Table 1.1).

3.   As coined by Friedmann (1973), hyper-urbanization may be statistically defined as a rate of population growth equal to or greater than 3.5 percent per year, the rate at which the population will double every 20 years.

4.   From a total of 26 in 1980 there will be 60 cities with populations larger than five million in the year 2000.   These 60 cities will provide shelter, food, water, refuse collection, and energy for some 650 million people.

5.   Based on current levels of economic interaction, the countries of the Pacific Rim include those of North America (Mexico, the U.S. and Canada), East Asia (Japan, South Korea, China, Hong Kong and Taiwan), Southeast Asia (Indonesia, Malaysia, Philippines, Singapore and Thailand), Asia, Australia and New Zealand.

6.   Excluding China, which is as yet weakly integrated into the Pacific Rim economy, the proportion was almost 58 percent in 1986 and would reach 65 percent in 2000.

7.   In Beijing alone there are an estimated 1.5 million temporary workers (Douglass, 1988a).

8.   Slum areas do exist in Japan's major cities, but not on the scale of New York or Los Angeles. It should also be noted that Japan has long had a group of outcasts, the so-called *burakumin*, who have

been kept in urban ghettos for centuries. Korean populations are also concentrated in such cities as Osaka and Nagoya.

9.   Even where megacities have not yet appeared, the growth of large cities with over 500,000 inhabitants has been advancing over that of smaller cities. In Australia, for example, five cities account for two-thirds of the nation's urban population. Nine cities in Canada account for a similar proportion. In South Korea, seven cities account for 77 percent of the urban population.

10.   Malaysia is almost 40 percent Chinese, with most of the Chinese now residing in cities. The island of Penang, one of Malaysia's most rapidly growing export-processing areas, was until very recently about 80 percent Chinese.

11.   As concluded by Cohen (1988: 535), even current reforms allowing for the expansion of capitalist relations of production are within a mode of "authoritarian modernization" that have a high degree of historical continuity stretching back at least a century.

12.   One of the most telling indicators of the way in which transnational systems of production are integrating cities and sub-national regions on the Pacific Rim is recent trade data showing that intra-firm shipments of electronic components produced in the U.S., assembled abroad, and returned to the U.S. for domestic sales now comprise the largest share of U.S. exports to and imports from Southeast Asia (Lim, 1986).

13.   As defined by Friedmann (1985), world cities are the "'basing points' for global capital" (p. 2) in the "spatial organization and articulation of production and markets" (p. 5). They are not only points of concentration of the control and management functions of global capital, but also serve as centers of ideological penetration of capitalism through the "dissemination of news, information, entertainment and other cultural artifacts" (p. 10). See also Cohen (1981) and Hymer (1972).

14.   Eighty-two percent of California's total trade goes to 12 Pacific Rim countries. As further evidence of a Pacific re-orientation of the U.S. economy, the value of imports and exports in Los Angeles increased by 83 percent from 1980 to 1985 to reach S64 billion;

for San Francisco the amount went from S19 to S27 billion, a 42 percent increase. For New York, however, the increase in combined import-export value was only S1 billion during the same period, albeit reaching a higher grand total of S84 billion (*U.S. News & World Report*, January 19, 1987).

15.   Determining the amount of trade being conducted between branch operations of transnational corporations is not possible under current national accounting methods. For example, the U.S. categorizes parts made by U.S. corporations operating in Taiwan as Taiwanese-rather than American-made.

16.   Japan's Finance Ministry has noted an increase in the number of Japanese corporations setting up offices overseas as a means of tax evasion. For purposes of avoiding taxes in Japan, some 10,000 Japanese companies and 300 banks have offices in the tiny tax-free Cayman Island in the Caribbean (Douglass, 1988b).

17.   "Socially-produced differences" cover those related to differences in labor quality and costs, the costs imposed and subsidies given by the state, and the quality of the built environment (Smith, 1984; Harvey, 1982).

18.   Per capita world grain output, which had increased at a rate of 1.2 percent per year between 1950 and 1973, fell to 0.3 percent between 1979 and 1984 (Brown, 1985: 8).

19.   To feed the six billion people who will inhabit the earth in the year 2000, food production would have to increase at a minimum rate of 2.7 percent per year between 1980 and 2000 (Soedjatmoko, 1981).

20.   This technological fix to a dire food problem was controversial from the outset. The uniform use of a single seed variety over vast areas made crops highly susceptible to disease and pest infestations. The latest varieties of corn, for example, have been bred to be resistant not to pests, but to pesticides, reflecting the increasing toxicity of chemicals being used to sustain existing levels of agricultural production.

21.   According to NASA's Goddard Institute of Space Studies, the temperatures, which are rising much faster than predicted ten years ago, may produce by the year 2000 temperatures which have not existed on earth in 100,000 years (*Honolulu Star-Bulletin*, April 26, 1987).

22.   Soil erosion in the U.S. is causing an estimated one-third of the cropland, or 50 million hectares, to have already begun a marked decline in long-term productivity.   GAIA (1985: 40) global estimates of agricultural land loss include 150 million hectares lost due to conversion to non-agricultural use; 50 million from soil erosion; 50 million from toxification, and 25 million due to desertification.

23.   By way of comparison with less densely-populated countries, in 1970 Japan's GNP production per hectare of level land was $18,000; in the U.S. it was $1,500 -- less than ten percent of Japan's level (Bennett & Levine, 1976).

24.   Eight companies control the processing and marketing of more than half the crude oil production and refining, as well as gasoline and natural gas sales, coal production, and Btu energy production in the U.S. (Freeman, et al., 1976: 231).

25.   In the U.S. the poor (under $2,500 annual income in 1982) spent 15 percent of their income on energy.   The amount consumed was less than half of that of the wealthiest (more than $24,500), who spent four percent of their income on energy (Freeman, et al., 1976: 119).

26.   Flooding cost $5 billion per year in damages in the U.S.   A rising proportion of flood losses is being inflicted on cities, especially via urban expansion onto flood plains in areas around Houston, Tulsa, Chicago, St. Louis, Hartford, Tampa, Phoenix (Platt, 1986).

27.   Contrary to the image exported abroad, only about one-quarter of Japan's labor force enjoys lifetime employment (Woronoff, 1985).

28.   If voluntary part-time workers are included, the total would reach 25 million, or 25 percent of the labor force.   3.8 million part-time workers are actively searching for more work; part-timers earn an average of $4.17 per hour versus $7.05 for full-time workers.   Part-

timers accounted for 40 percent of the employment growth in retail sales occupations in the U.S. over the past 12 years to comprise one-third of all retail employment in 1985. 70 percent of part-timers have no employer-provided retirement plan, and 42 percent have no health insurance coverage (*Business Week*, December 15, 1986).

29.   The external debt in the Philippines is almost three times the value of the country's exports (ADB, 1986). In Indonesia, South Korea, and Thailand it is between 1.2 to 1.5 times the value of exports. Increases (1975-1984) in the debt/export ratio have been most dramatic in the following countries: Malaysia from 31 to 62 percent; Philippines from 88 to 294 percent; and Thailand from 45 to 151 percent.

30.   In 1983 three-quarters of the states raised taxes in an effort to catch up with combined effects of 1978 grassroots tax revolt, recession, and steep cuts in federal grants. This created large surpluses in many states in 1984, but these were quickly eaten away; the 1985 recession showed tax revenues increasing only one percent after adjustment for inflation. Meanwhile, federal grant-in-aid in 1986 was about six percent below the 1985 level (*Fortune*, May 12, 1986). Between 1981 and 1986 the federal government also cut spending on education, nutrition and health programs by $36.5 billion (*Newsweek*, February 6, 1986).

31.   In a plant relocation decision, the Goodyear radial tire plant in 1979 stated the following conditions: a place large enough to provide a skilled labor force of 1,400, but small enough to be unlikely to attract any other Fortune 500 company that might want to come and bid up wages, and no unions. Competitive bidding among townships was then initiated to find the best offer, with the winner agreeing, *inter alia*, to move an interstate highway, build access roads, and change school district boundaries (Bluestone and Harrison, 1982: 183).

32.   In Asia in 1982 there were 26 EPZs in eight countries, with an equal number or more in planning stage. The extreme, Singapore, has more than one-third of its total employment in EPZs.

33.   Twenty of 68 firms in the Bataan EPZ (Philippines) ceased oper-
        ation in 1970s. The two main reasons cited by the enterprises for
        moving to other locations were increases in wages and ending of
        the tax holiday.

34.   "Survival" may sound extreme, but the case of a suburban town of
        Clairton calls for no other descriptor. In 1985, this town, located
        15 miles south of Pittsburgh, laid off its entire police force and fire
        department personnel and was left with S1,000 in the bank after
        revenues from U.S. Steel Corporation declined by 50 percent
        (Japan Times, December 3, 1985).

35.   Incentives include income and sales tax breaks, tax credits for local
        employment generated and tax abatements available only to very
        large-scale enterprises.   In Missouri, for example, the enterprise
        zone package was made available only to corporations willing to
        invest S500 million or more in the zone.   Of 26 current state
        programs 16 offer sales tax breaks, 15 give income tax reductions,
        13 allow tax credits for employing enterprise zone residents and ten
        offer property tax abatements (Walton, 1982).   Of 15 large-scale
        investors in "ghetto factories" in the mid-60s, nine have closed;
        inner-city unemployment went up from 15 to 25 percent during the
        1960s-1980s.

36.   Houston itself has no zoning laws and very limited city planning.
        In the words of Bluestone and Harrison (1982: 84), the city is "in
        a mess," with severe levels of poverty amid affluence, high crime
        rates and deteriorating public services.   In addition, Texas has one
        of the lowest levels of worker's compensation and unemployment
        insurance.

37.   Fujitsu, a large Japan-based computer company, expressly located
        its U.S. plants in Seattle to avoid California's Unitary Tax.
        Japanese companies spent several million dollars in lobbying efforts
        which eventually led to the exemption of non-U.S. companies from
        the tax (Douglass, 1986).   Twenty-four states were moving to adopt
        unitary tax in the early 1980s, but most have now abandoned their
        efforts.   Only Alaska, Montana and North Dakota still had tax on
        foreign-owned enterprises as of September, 1986.   The new exemp-
        tions for foreign enterprises from the unitary tax in California are
        estimated to cost the state S83 million in lost taxes.

38.   Bluestone and Harrison (1982) argue that most of the major redis-
        tributive programs in the U.S. began at local levels and were only
        later adopted by the federal government. Many cities have tried to
        keep the original definition of equity alive by such policies as those
        adopted in Concord, California, which impose impact charges on
        developers of non-residential projects to be used to finance day-care
        centers (*Land Use Digest*, March 15, 1987).

39.   The withdrawal of the private sector from contributing to pension
        schemes is now a widespread phenomenon in the U.S. As reported
        by *Business Week* (December 8, 1986), "In one of the greatest
        waves of corporate restructuring ever, companies are laying off
        thousands, reneging on promises of benefits of retirees, and asking
        those who remain to finance more of their retirement out of their
        own pockets." Some of largest pension fund insurers are going
        bankrupt from having to pay benefits for massive layoffs in, for
        example the steel making industry. Meanwhile, the number of
        people aged 65 and older in the U.S. will double by 2020, resulting
        in a paring of benefits from Social Security funds.

References

Armstrong, W. and T.G. McGee (1985) *Theatres of Accumulation: Studies in Asian and Latin American Urbanization.* New York: Methuen.

Asia Development Bank (ADB) (1986) *Key Indicators 1986.* Manila.

Aziz, S. (1982) Can we eradicate hunger by 2000? *Development, 4,* 3-5.

Bennett, John W. & Solomon B. Levine (1976) Industrialization and social deprivation: Welfare, environment and the postindustrial society in Japan. In Hugh Patrick (Ed.), *Japanese Industrialization and Its Social Consequences,* 439-492. Berkeley: University of California Press.

Bluestone, Barry & Bennett Harrison (1982) *The Deindustrialization of America.* New York: Basic Books.

Bronger, Dirk (1985) Metropolitanization as a development problem of Third World countries: A contribution towards a definition of the concept, *Applied Geography and Development,* 26:71-97.

Brown, Lester, et al. (1985) *State of the World.* New York: W.W. Norton.

Chandler, Tertius and Gerald Fox (1974) *3000 Years of Urban Growth.* New York: Academic Press.

Cohen, Paul (1988) The Post-Mao Reforms in Historical Perspective, *The Journal of Asian Studies, 47*(3), August, 518-540.

Cohen, R.B. (1981) The new international division of labor: Multinational corporations and urban hierarchy. In M. Dear and Allen J. Scott (Eds.) *Urbanization and Urban Planning in Capitalist Society,* 287-318. London: Methuen.

Douglass, Mike (1983) *Regional Integration on the Capitalist Periphery: The Central Plains of Thailand.* The Hague: Institute of Social Studies.

Douglass, Mike (1984) *Outline Urban Strategy.* Jakarta: National Urban Development Strategy Project, GOI/UNCHS.

Douglass, Mike (1986) Structural change on the Pacific Rim: Perspective on Japan. Vancouver: Simon Fraser University, Dept. of Geography, Discussion Paper No. 1.

Douglass, Mike (1988a) Urbanization and Urban Policies in China, International Conference on Urbanization in China, Tianjin, August 16-20.

Douglass, Mike (1988b) "Transnational capital and urbanization in Japan," Conference on Transnational Capital and Urbanization on the Pacific Rim, UCLA Center for Pacific Rim Studies, March 26-28.

Douglass, Mike (1988c) Transnational capital and urbanization on the Pacific Rim, *International Journal of Urban and Regional Research,* September.

Douglass, Mike (1988d) "Land use and the environmental sustainability of the extended metropolis." Paper presented at the Conference on the Extended Metropolis in Asia, East-West Center EAPI, September 19-23.

Eklund, Kent & Oliver Williams (1978) The changing spatial distribution of social classes in a metropolitan area, *Urban Affairs Quarterly, 13*(3), 313-339.

Fainstein, Susan and Norman Fainstein (1985) Urban social movements, *Urban Affairs Quarterly*, December, 187-206.

Freeman, S. David, et al. (1976) *A Time to Choose: America's Energy Future.* New York: Ballinger.

Friedmann, John (1985) *The World City Hypothesis.* Los Angeles: University of California Los Angeles/SAUP.

Friedmann, John, and Mike Douglass (1978) Agropolitan development: Toward a new strategy for regional planning in Asia. In F. Lo and K. Salih (Eds.), *Growth Pole Strategy*, 163-192. Oxford: Pergamon.

Froebel, F., J. Heinrichs & O. Kreye (1980) *The New International Division of Labor.* Cambridge University Press.

Fujiwara, Sadao (1986) Foreign trade, investment and industrial imperialism in postwar Japan, 1951-1985. Yamaguchi: Economic Society of Yamaguchi University, Paper Series 3.

GAIA (1984) *An Atlas of Planet Management.* Anchor Books.

Harvey, David (1982) *The Limits to Capital.* University of Chicago Press.

Hauser, Philip and Robert Gardiner (1982) Urban future: Trends and prospects. In P. Hauser, R. Gardiner, A. Laquian and S. El-Shakhs, *Population and the Urban Future*, 1-58. Albany, New York: SUNY Press.

Hay, Richard, Jr. (1977) Patterns of urbanization and socio-economic development in the Third World. In Janet Abu-Lughod and R. Hay, Jr. (Eds.), *Third World Urbanization*, 71-102. Methuen.

Hugo, Graeme (1984) Structural change and labor mobility in rural Java. In G. Standing (Ed.), *Circulation and Proletarianization.* Croom Helm.

Hymer, Stephen (1979) The multinational corporation and the law of uneven development. In H. Radice (Ed.) *International Firms and Modern Imperialism*, 37-62. Penguin.

ILO (1981) *Employment Effects of Multinational Enterprises in Developing Countries.* Geneva.

ILO (1984) *Technological Choice and Employment Generation by Multinational Enterprises in Developing Countries.* Geneva.

Ito Tatsuo & Tanifuji Masafumi (1982) The role of small and intermediate cities in national development in Japan. In O. Mathur (Ed.) *Small Cities and National Development.* Nagoya: UNCRD.

Kasarda, John D. (1983) Entry-level jobs, mobility, and urban minority unemployment, *Urban Affairs Quarterly*, September, 21-40.

Kelly, Roy (1985) The Regional impact of direct foreign investment in Indonesia. Harvard University, unpublished Ph.D. dissertation.

Kirby, Andrew (1985) Nine fallacies of local economic change, *Urban Affairs Quarterly*, Dec., 207-220.

Lee Jeong-Sik (1988) "Regional development policies in Korea: Retrospect and prospects." International Conference on Urbanization in China, Tianjin, August 16-20.

Lim, Linda (1986) U.S. trade with Southeast Asia 1985, *Southeast Asia Business,* (11) (Fall), 56-59.

Lim, Linda (1987) Capital, labor and the state in the internationalization of high-tech industry: The case of Singpore, Conference on Transnational Capital and Urbanization on the Pacific Rim, UCLA Center for Pacific Rim Studies, 26-28 Mar.

McGee, T. (1982) Proletarianization, industrialization and urbanization in Asia: A case study of Malaysia. Flinders Asian Studies Lecture, 13, Adelaide, Flinders University.

Molotch, Harvey and John R. Logan (1985) Urban dependencies: New forms of use and exchange in U.S. cities, *Urban Affairs Quarterly, 21*(2), December, 143-169.

Peet, Richard (1987) The geography of class struggle and the relocation of United States manufacturing industry. In R. Peet (Ed.), *International Capitalism and Industrial Restructuring.* Boston: Allen & Unwin, 40-71.

Pernia, Ernesto (1982) The performance and prospects of small and intermediate cities in the Philippines. In Om Mathur (Ed.), *Small Cities and National Development.* Nagoya: UNCRD.

Platt, Rutherford (1986) Metropolitan flood loss reduction through regional special districts, *JAPA*, Autumn, 467-479.

Ranis, Gustav (1983) The NIC's, the near NIC's and the world economy, Conference on Patterns of Growth and Structural Change in Asia's Newly Industrializing Countries (NICs) and Near-NIC's in the Context of Economic Interdependence, East-West Center, Honolulu, Apr 3-8.

Roberts, Brian (1978) *Cities of Peasants; The Political Economy of Urbanization in the Third World.* Edward Arnold.

Sachs, Ignacy (1981) Energy, environment and development strategies, *Development, 2*, 3-10.

Salih, Kamal, Mei Ling Young, Rajah Rasiah & Hashim Bahari (1987) Transnational capital and local conjuncture: The semiconductor industry in Penang, Malaysia. Conference on Transnational Capital and Urbanization on the Pacific Rim, UCLA Center for Pacific Rim Studies, 26-28 Mar.

Sassen-Koob, Saskia, 1981, Towards a conceptualization of immigrant labor, *Social Problems, 29*(1), October, 65-83.

Sklair, Leslie (1987) Developmental effects of transnational capital: The cases of China and Mexico, paper presented at the Conference on Transnational Capital and Urbanization on the Pacific Rim, UCLA Center for Pacific Rim Studies, March 26-28.

Smith, Neil (1984) Deindustrialization and regionalization: Class alliance and class struggle. *Papers of the Regional Science Association, 54*, 113-128.

Soedjatmoko (1981) The food-energy pivot: Turning point in development, *Development, 2*, 20-24.

Soja, Edward, R. Morales, and G. Wolff (1983) Urban restructuring: an analysis of social and spatial change in Los Angeles, *Economic Geography, 59*(2), April, 195-230.

Southeast Asia Business (SAB) (1986) Policy News, 36.

Stopford, John M. and John H. Dunning (1983) *Multinationals; Company Performance and Global Trends.* London: Macmillan.

Taylor, Michael and Nigel Thrift (Eds.) (1982) *The Geography of Multinationals: Studies in the Spatial Development and Economic Consequences of Multinational Corporations.* London: Croom Helm.

UN (1969) *Growth of the World's Urban and Rural Population 1920-2000.* New York: United Nations.

UNEP (1986) *The State of the Environment.* Nairobi: UNEP.

Walton, John (1982) Cities and jobs and politics, *Urban Affairs Quarterly, 18*(1), September, 5-17.

Wheelwright, T. (1980) The age of the transnational corporation. In G. Crough, et al. (Eds.), *Australia and World Capitalism.* Penguin.

Whitney, J.B.R. (1988) The waste economy and Kotadesasi in China. Paper presented at the Conference on the Extended Metropolis in Asia, East-West Center EAPI, September 19-23.

World Bank (1985) *World Development Report 1985.* Washington, D.C.

Woronoff, Jon (1983) *Japan's Wasted Workers.* Tokyo: Lotus Press.

Wu, C.T. (1987) China's re-entry into the world system: Regional impacts of foreign investment, Conference on Transnational Capital and Urbanization on the Pacific Rim, UCLA Center for Pacific Rim Studies, 26-28 Mar.

Zhao Ziyang (1987) Advance along the road of socialism with Chinese characteristics, *Beijing Review*, November 9-15, 23-49.

THE NEW INTERNATIONAL DIVISION OF LABOR AND URBAN CHANGE: A NEW ZEALAND CASE STUDY

David C. Thorns
University of Canterbury

The paper reviews the debate about the extent and form of dein-dustrialization and restructuring taking place within advanced capitalist societies and the impact of this process on urban regions. The position advanced by the proponents of the New International Division of Labor is evaluated and contrasted with that developed by advocates of a more locality-focused approach. A New Zealand case study is developed as a means of testing some of the assumptions and arguments of these two approaches. The case study presents data on the changing occupational struc-ture and gender modifications within the work force, the degree of casualization, levels of unemployment and regional diversity and urban change. The paper concludes by drawing attention to the role played by the New Zealand State in setting the context for change and to the necessity for seeing restructuring as an ongoing process of continued modification and change to regions and urban centers.

There has been a continuing debate between explanations of change situated at the level of regions and localities within nation states and those set at the international level. The first set of explanations emphasizes the importance of particular historical and cultural configurations which mold the patterns of change, whereas the latter tend to assume a more universal pattern in which the regional and local consequences are simply derivative of the broad sweep of capitalist change. Both points of view have their advocates in the current arguments about the process of "deindustrialization and restructuring" which is taking place within most advanced industrial-capitalist societies.

The development of western capitalist societies since the 1920s has been characterized by a pattern of depression, recovery to a long boom and then the emergence of a further depression, which illustrates the present period of the 1980s. The booms and slumps constitute the long waves of capitalist development, illustrating how such a system is marked by cycles arising out of the inherent contradictions within its structure (see Gamble, 1979; Mandel, 1975; Wallerstein, 1974; Offe, 1984).

During the 1920s and 1930s all of the major capitalist industrial nations experienced rising unemployment and falling profitability to capital as a result of a slump in sales within both the domestic and international economies. These conditions spread from Western Europe and the U.S. to affect equally severely both Australia and New Zealand. In both cases, demand for agricultural products slumped, leading to a sharp decline in the pastoral sector with its consequences for urban servicing and processing industry.

The recovery from depression conditions of the late 1920s and early 1930s was brought about by a combination of a restructured capitalism, reshaped by improved technological efficiency, attacks on real wage rates achieved by higher levels of unemployment and pressure on workers to accept lower wage rates; second, government initiatives in the area of public works and the growth of the welfare state; and third, the Second World War. The war created an increased demand for production and affected patterns of trade and marketing, encouraging the development of import substitution manufacturing activity. The collective impact of this series of changes was to lay the basis for a sustained period of economic growth in the 1950s and into the 1960s. The 1960s saw the emergence of a new set of "crises" and contradictions which began to be manifest in "stop go" cycles of economic growth and short fluctuations between growth and decline within the economies of western capitalist nations (Rose, Vogler, Marshall and Newby, 1984).

Within the general process of change, however, there have been important variations between nation states which reflect their historical location within the world capitalist system and their particular pattern of development. Recent discussion, for example, has pointed to a variety of "trajectories of development" that can be identified varying from Germany which was seen as the ideal-typical case of capitalist development, to Sweden which has a system more strongly organized from below through activities of its labor movement (Lash and Urry, 1987). This variety points to the necessity of developing analyses which explore both the inter-national and the intra-national context of change (Feagin and Smith, 1987).

The main lines of discussion can be grouped around two sets of approaches. The first is that of the New International Division of Labor (NIDL) thesis developed by Froebel, et al. (1980) at the Max Planck Institute in Germany in the late 1970s. The second in contrast is focused at the level of localities where empirical studies have been used to develop theories of change. Such an approach has led to a re-emergence of both case studies of change (Pahl, 1984; Castells, 1983), and studies which have been concerned with exploring the interplay between macro-level changes and the local setting, with a view to exploring the way the local context, its history, social organization and "culture" provide both a facilitator of change and a base for local opposition and resistance (Gregory and Urry, 1985; Giddens, 1981; Massey, 1984; Cooke, 1982, 1985, 1986; Smith and Feagin, 1987).

In New Zealand these two lines of approach have also commanded research attention. For example, the work of Armstrong (1980) and McMichael (1980) has attempted to explain the shape of New Zealand development through an analysis of the nations' place within the International Division of Labor. Armstrong, for example, sees New Zealand along with Australia, Canada, and Uruguay as comprising a group of nations with a common path of development centered around providing a limited range of primary commodities for European markets. In New Zealand's case export income has relied on the production of such primary products as wool, meat, butter, and cheese. Other writers have also argued that the internal structure of economic and social relations has been the result of the drive for accumulation within the world capitalist system giving little recognition to locally generated social structures or influence of the state (Bedggood, 1980; Pearce, 1987).

In contrast to this approach, other work has focused on the particularities of New Zealand's development and the way that local social structures emerged over time as the society moved from bush clearings to towns and cities (Pearson, 1980; Hamer, 1980). A recurring weakness in much of the work has been a limited attempt to integrate analyses of the macro context with regional and local level changes. It has therefore been difficult to evaluate the competing claims of the rival explanations. The present discussion attempts to clarify the issues to be addressed and begins the task of presenting data which allows exploration of New Zealand's economic and social development at national, regional and local levels.

New International Division of Labor

The thesis of a New International Division of Labor derives from both dependency theory (Frank, 1971) and World Systems Theory (Wallerstein, 1974). The thesis builds on these analyses of the reorganization of capitalism into a more global system, based on new multi-national companies operating within global rather than national markets. Production thus becomes more internationalized and new forms of linkages occur across national boundaries. An example of this process would be the Ford Motor Company's production of its cars in a "world factory" with components being manufactured in a large number of nations and then assembled (Hill, 1985). Such moves are identified as one response by multi-national capital to the problem of falling profitability. To ensure continued profits they have moved production to cheaper labor markets, thus shifting from the older industrial and well-unionized areas of the U.S. and Europe to the newly industrializing areas of Europe, such as Spain, Portugal, and Italy and to the newly industrializing nations, such as Central and South America, the Philippines, and Southeast Asia.   In the U.S., for example, this process began in textiles and has now spread to electronic products such as semiconductors, indicating the growing range of products and the increasing extent of this process (see Grunwald and Flamm, 1985).

The increased mobility of capital has consequently been a dominant characteristic of the most recent period of change.   The result of the changes is to create a new division of labor across nation states and provide new forms of inter-dependency.   It also opens up new strategies of control to capital and a weakening of the power of organized labor.   Labor under this analysis is much less mobile than capital, is organized locally rather than globally, and often is unaware of the interconnections between the local production plant and the multi-national company.

The theory develops two models of the change process.   The first envisages a single division of labor across the world with the establishment of a single occupational hierarchy and system of specialization.   Industrial nation states become relatively unimportant within a system driven by the needs of capitalists for the accumulation of profit.   Capitalists' drive for profit leads them to locate where labor laws are not well developed, there is inadequate or no planning, development or environment controls, wage rates can be kept low and profits can be repatriated to tax havens and shelters.

The second model emphasizes the internationalization of production capital with vertically organized and integrated activities spanning a number of nation states.   In this model micro chips might be manufactured in the U.S. but shipped to Taiwan to be assembled into the final product, as the labor costs would be much lower.   Thus, for example, in 1980, one third of all imports into the U.S. were from off-shore plants of U.S. companies (Bluestone and Harrison, 1983, 1986).

The work set in motion by the NIDL thesis concentrated attention on the impact of the move to internationalize production on the older industrial "cores" of developed capitalist nations.   Such areas were seen to "deindustrialize" with substantial declines in local employment in the manufacturing sector, especially in areas of traditional male employment (e.g. steel production, engineering, mining and ship building).   In the U.K., for example, between 1961 and 1976 there was a net loss of 857,000 jobs for males within the economy and a net increase of 1.5 million jobs for females (Thorns, 1982).   Changes on such a scale reflect a substantial fall in the manufacturing, mining and agricultural sectors and a strong increase in the service sector. However, the service sector growth has been disproportionately of female employees, with a million extra jobs between 1971 and 1976 for women in the service sector, compared to only 268,000 for men. This movement provides a major shift in the gender composition of the work force as it became more heavily tertiarized.

By 1981 60 percent of all wives of employed men were employed, 40 percent of the labor force was female and 90 percent of part-time work was done by women (Pahl, 1984). The consequences of these changes are profound for the composition of households and their income and consumption power. Clearly by 1981 dual earning households had become a majority and the gap between such households and single- or no-income households had widened.

The impact of these changes has not been evenly spread across the regions but has rather been concentrated in the regions which were first to industrialize turning them into areas now often called "rust bowls." In the U.K., the West Midlands is one such region. This area was one of the most significant regions during the industrial revolution and subsequent development in the 19th century of the iron, steel and metal trades, and engineering. In the 20th century the region became the center of the British motor manufacturing industry which in its turn stimulated a range of component parts production. Collectively these changes led to the area being one of the major capital and consumer goods producing regions within the U.K., having until the 1950s a per capita income second only to the South East and virtually no unemployment in the postwar period through the end of the 1950s. By 1981 the region had changed to the extent that it had the lowest gross domestic product of any region in England and an unemployment rate of 17 percent. This rate compared with a national rate in 1984 of 13.5 percent. The vulnerability of the area to the reorganization of motor car manufacture which shifted the balance to Japanese and American production led to the progressive decline in the area's industrial base leading to amalgamation and mergers, rationalizations of plants and closures, resulting in labor shedding and rising unemployment. The companies that have survived in the region have done so by changing their products, intensifying their labor process, establishing stronger control over the labor force and reinforcing their market position by acquiring profitable companies (Flynn and Taylor, 1985; Maguire and Smith, 1985).

The U.S. shows a similar pattern of change with a growing rust bowl in the older, industrial Midwest states where jobs have been lost in the textiles, steel and engineering sectors of the manufacturing economy (Bluestone and Harrison, 1983, 1984). The move of capital overseas from 1975-82, for example, displaced 170,000 workers in the garment and textiles industry alone and a further 75,000 in the electrical industry (Grunwald and Flamm, 1985). This new-found capital mobility provided by new technology shifted the bargaining power toward capital and allowed management to push for favorable local taxation regimes and cuts in wages and additional payments. The job losses sustained in the private sector were between 450,000 and 650,000 in both the manufacturing and non-manufacturing sectors. The flow-on effects, however, of the job losses are much greater, and possibly as many as 32 million jobs were affected (Bluestone and Harrison Part 11, 1983, 1986). The impacts of this level of deindustrialization have been extensive at the level of the communities where the workers were resident. There has been a loss of income, a loss of family wealth, and impacts on the physical and mental well-being of the workers, families and communities (Smith and Feagin, 1987).

The other side of the deindustrialization process was the growth areas or the sunbelts where new forms of business activity grew, stimulated by the application of new technologies creating the high-tech industries. For example, in the U.S. employment and production in the high technology industries since 1970 have expanded to make the Greater Los Angeles area the world's largest "technopolis" (Soja, et al., 1983, 1986; Castells, 1985). The area now contains more engineers, scientists, mathematicians and technological specialists than any other region in the U.S. In the U.K. a similar high-tech development has occurred producing a pattern of regional development centered along the M4 corridor from Bristol to London and up to East Anglia encompassing Cambridge. Sixty percent of the new jobs created in Britain since the 1960s have been located in this area (Hall, 1985). The physical quality of the local environment, a labor market based around individual skill and specialized knowledge, and a link to the defense and military complex as they are among prime funders of the high-tech development sectors appear to be important factors in these regional changes in this area.

The deindustrialization and reindustrialization process creating the rust bowls and sunbelts and bringing with it a recomposition of the labor force by skill, wage level, gender and location leads to a process of urban restratification. Although much attention in research has been focused on the distinctive regional nature of change, it is also important to appreciate that many of the same changes are occurring within regions, albeit at a lesser scale. Clearly, to identify the components of such changes, detailed empirical study is required at the level of particular localities, whereas much of the "new international division of labor" debate has been set at a much higher level of generality (Cooke, 1985; Dickens, 1985).

The result of the research stimulated by the NIDL thesis has drawn attention to five key areas of change. First, there is a substantial shift in the occupational structure with the balance between manual and non-manual work moving in favor of non- manual employment and a decline in the skilled section of the manual working class. The identification of such changes is of course not unique to the NIDL position but has also been identified in mobility studies from the work of Blau and Duncan in the

1960s to that of Halsey and Goldthorpe in the 1980s (Blau and Duncan, 1967; Halsey, et al., 1980; Goldthorpe, 1980). Changes in the structure of work and occupations are the product of the introduction of new technologies into industrial production, such as computer-aided design, and computer-aided manufacturing, robotization and other types of technological innovation which produce a de-skilling of work, and of the growth in the service sector of the economy.

The second change is a substantial gender modification of the employed work force (Walby, 1986). There has been growth in the numbers of both full and part-time female workers into both manufacturing and service employment. Research has pointed to the rise of female workers in the service sector at the same time that male employment in the manufacturing and primary sector of the economy has been falling.

The third change has been a casualization of a significant sector of the work force with the expansion of sub-contracting and the use of temporary, usually female, labor. This revival has meant the predicted trend toward the disappearance of the informal sector with the advance of capitalism has not occurred in either the developing or the developed countries (Portes and Sassen-Koob, 1987). The principal function played by the informal sector is that of by-passing the formal regulated labor market covered by legislation under which wages and conditions are legally stipulated. The growth of unregulated "sweatshop businesses" has been substantial. Over the 1970s and 1980s it is estimated that 6,000 were opened in New York, Los Angeles and Chicago, employing 85,000 workers (Feagin and Smith, 1987). The informal workers employed in these businesses are, as unregulated and often illegal migrants, open to exploitation and the payment of much lower wage rates. This provides an improved return to capital and indicates why so little pressure is mounted in the U.S., for example, to stem the flow of illegal workers from south of the border (Cohen, 1985).

The increased level of subcontracting and industrial home-working in the advanced capitalist societies is in many ways a re-enactment of their industrial past and is characteristic of 19th century practice. Growth in this sector has been documented for the U.S., Spain, Italy and the U.K. (Portes and Sassen-Koob, 1987). The shift to greater casualization brings to capital the advantages of decentralized production permitting the use of the cheapest available labor markets, more flexible labor practices and lower overhead costs as many of these can be transferred to the sub-contracting workers. In many of these changes capital has been assisted by the state sector through non-enforcement of regulations and controls or through more active measures such as the deregulation of the labor market and the inhibiting of trade union organization and thus opposition.

The fourth change has been the rising rate of unemployment, a trend apparent in all O.E.C.D. countries. The rates across this group of nations vary, as does the extent to which unemployment is effectively measured, but the trend is similar. The average for European countries in the 1980s is around ten percent, with Spain having the highest rate at 20 percent.

The fifth change is the growth in regional disparities in employment and wealth. The emergence of rust bowls and sunbelts have become typical features as new technologically based employment grows and traditional manufacturing declines.

Critique and Comment

The NIDL thesis appears to be a plausible and powerful analytical tool for understanding the widespread changes occurring within contemporary industrial capitalist societies. There are a number of significant problems, however, with both the theory and the way that it has been used.

The thesis has functionalist tendencies set within it as it ascribes all change within the economic and social structure to a master process, that of capitalist accumulation. The process of causation is one way, from the core industrial nations to the periphery, from the decisions of multi-national capitalists' board rooms to the local plants. A consequence of this emphasis is that it fails to explain actual patterns of development and change and much of the comment and analysis generated has remained at aggregate levels. The empirical verifications attempted have focused on aggregate statistical material to chart the changes within the division of labor of the nation states being observed. This does not usually permit the analysis of changes between sectors or, equally important, within sectors. The service sector, for example, although it has increased in size, is quite diverse. A growing gap has opened up between those employed in low-paid service jobs such as routine clerical work, cleaning offices, domestic work, and work in the tourist, restaurant and entertainment areas and those employed in the newer higher paid sectors linked into the high-tech and corporate business sectors of the economy. There is a need, therefore, in any analysis, to be able to distinguish between the older services and the newer more skilled and higher paid ones. A further useful distinction can be made between services set within the "public" sphere and those in the private, which allows the changing balance between these spheres to be explored (Urry, 1986; Lash and Urry, 1987).

The NIDL thesis has a further range of problems which relates to the disappearance of usually important aspects of analysis. The nation state disappears as a central actor in the process of change and the working class disappears as an important social force shaping change; it becomes simply a reactive force (Skocpol, 1979; Smith and Tardanico, 1987). Such limitations arise because of the focus on global economic determination in the form of capital accumulation within a world capitalist system. Explanations taking such a mono-causal form do not allow the thesis to take adequate account of the context of change being considered and the contingent nature of change. Just as the nation state is less evident so also is the working class as a movement producing modification and changes. The proletariat has undergone a major reconstruction with the decline in the old industrial heartlands, severely depleting the traditionally strong centers of union militancy in manufacturing and mining. The newly emerging areas of working class activity have been in the white collar and service areas of the economy. The process of proletarianization of these occupational groups has in some cases produced greater militancy. However, the more dispersed nature of these areas of employment and gender composition have had a considerable impact on the nature of the working class response to change (Crompton and Jones, 1984).

Morgan and Sayer (1983) for example, in their recent study of the electronics industry, point out that concrete forms of capital accumulation are influenced by technological developments in ways that require empirical investigation as the consequences are not always identical. They show the use of female labor to be simply one strategy available to capital to affect the costs of production and in the case of the electronics sector, the employment of female labor has dropped, not increased, with 96 percent of the jobless in this sector between 1971-1981 being female. Similarly they show that the debate about "de-skilling" also requires close empirical attention as again, it is a "contingent" question as to whether "de-skilling" or "re-skilling" is dominant, especially as within the debate the definition of what constitutes skill is so often poorly defined. They suggest that in the electronics industry during the 1970s the proportion of skilled workers has in fact increased. Such variations point to the need for close empirical study of the processes of change taking place in national and local contexts.

Locality-Based Approaches

The approaches identified earlier focus more on the localities within which the changes are taking place. Further, they are based more firmly on a commitment to empirical study of the actual process of change. They thus reflect the critique of the NIDL that it operates too much at an aggregate level and disregards the contingent nature of the changes to employment structures, household organization and local social and political resistances. The theoretical attention has, therefore, been directed toward whether localities are simply convenient bases for observing macro processes of change or whether localities have significance in their own right. A number of writers have taken up the discussion of "locale" as a suitable theoretical category through which to explore the place-specific features of change (Giddens, 1981; Gregory and Urry, 1985; Dickens, 1985; Saunders and Williams, 1987; Smith and Tardanico, 1987).

Local Ethnographies

The impact of uneven regional development over the past decades has brought with it quite marked differentiation between local areas, bringing into greater prominence spatial variations and thus the need for locality based research. Within the localities affected by change there is considerable divergence between those in the sunbelts where there has been job growth and expansion and in the declining areas where the local economy has shrunk. These variations in turn have an impact on the nature and consciousness of the working class, increasing the level of internal fragmentation as the sections advantaged in terms of jobs and income are increasingly separated both spatially and socially from those in declining industry and regions (Newby, et al., 1985).

Patterns of paid work have changed, bringing modifications to domestic work and household organization. Pahl (1984) notes that if a period of history somewhat longer than the last decades is inspected, the most striking result is that unemployment and limited opportunities become the more usual state for working class communities. Certainly in the New Zealand case the long boom from the late 1930s to the mid-1960s is the exception rather than the rule and even within this boom period full employment was characteristic only of the post-World War II period (Rosenberg, 1986; Pearce, 1987). The world of work has thus always operated as both an arena of paid employment in the formal economy and an arena of domestic work where self-provisioning occurs (Redclift and Mingione, 1983). This can include work done by household members both for the household itself or in the form of exchange relations with other households where tasks are done for each other on either a monetary or exchange basis (Pahl, 1986). Clearly fluctuations in these patterns of household organization are important in building any understanding of resistances and reactions to deindustrialization within localities.

The regional and uneven nature of the processes of change has a further important consequence which has become illuminated through local based study: the growth of consumption sector cleavages (Saunders, 1984, 1986; Dunleavy, 1980, 1985; Pahl, 1984, 1986). The work of this group of writers points to the changes brought about within localities to household economies, to the gender composition of the labor market, and to the levels of unemployment. Within the U.K., evidence indicates that the distribution of incomes has become less equal during the 1970s, with some groups seeing real income rises whereas those on the lowest incomes have seen declines in real income. A similar trend is also found in the U.S. (Sassen-Koob, 1985).

Regional disparities together with the increased proportion of dual earning households have created a move toward a sharply divided society, but one divided not on traditional class lines. The divisions among those with dual incomes in the growing sectors and those on single incomes in the declining sectors are one such division; another is between those working and those dependent on the state for income in the form of benefits. These changes are sufficient to create the conditions likely to lead to a pattern of restratification within advanced capitalist societies and reshaped working-class politics fragmented by consumption sector cleavages rather than those arising solely from the productive system. The fragmentation and the development of consumerism further moves the responses to change in the direction of individualism rather than collectivism (Marshall, et al., 1985).

Local Area Case Studies

A second group of writers has seen the impact of localities as much less important to shaping change, preferring to see the localities as simply settings in which to observe wider processes of change (Massey, 1984). The most extensive research in the U.K. adopting this approach is that initiated through the Economic and Social Research Council's research programme on the changing Urban and Regional System. This program focuses on a range of localities to assess how macro changes are mediated through local social structures (Cooke, 1986, 1987).

The work of these researchers points to a growing localism within Britain and other advanced capitalist societies and an associated fragmentation within national politics. Such changes lead to a re-emergence of a politics of place and an ideology of localism (Kilmartin, et al., 1985). This ideology of localism has been associated with radical movements of both the left and the right in the 1970s and 1980s. The left has argued for local state autonomy as a means by which control could be regained and the destructive forces of capitalist social reorganization combated through local resistances. For the right, decentralization is a way of reducing the burden of state expenditures and of central state activity within the welfare arena. Consequently, a return to community and individual provision is suggested which would provide greater consumer choice and improve the accountability of services to users.

The range of research questions explored here has included the regional and local implications of the decentralization of production, the development of local class structures and political forms, and the ways in which local resistance to change have developed and have formed local social movements.

Case Study of New Zealand Experience

The general restructuring debate has now been reviewed, but further weaknesses with the present work need to be identified before moving to the substantive discussion of New Zealand material.

The current wave of empirical research examining the interrelationship of changes in the international division of labor and localities has not yet clearly articulated the links between these two arenas of activity, nor has it successfully theorized this relationship. In practice detailed case study material, largely empirical in nature, has been developed (see Cooke, 1986). Further, most of the research, apart from Pahl's study of Sheppey, has a relatively short time span. One problem with this approach is the tendency to see the last change as the most crucial in shaping the locality. The growth of the industrial centers of Britain, now facing rapid deindustrialization ideally needs to be traced at least from the mid-19th century when many were created as part of the first wave of the Industrial Revolution.

A further problem has been that something of an ambiguity has existed in much of the discussion about the role of the state in the processes of change observed and documented, and the links between the central and local elements of the state. In part this arises out of the varied patterns of national and local government control across different European societies and the U.S. These differences give rise to debates about the significance of local state action and the possibilities of building local socialism in a period of dominance at the level of the central government by parties of the political right. The focus on capital accumulation processes and state structures has left many of the studies paying little attention to the role of worker action. The class dynamic has not always been present, yet over the present century the shaping of both national policy and the structure of work relations in many European and Australasian societies can be attributed to the power of organized labor or lack of it (Lash and Urry, 1987; also Harvey, 1987a and b).

The final area of concern is the tendency in the rediscovery of localities to attach to "local culture" an explanatory power which may be inappropriate. The results of detailed empirical work on various localities, as, for instance, in the U.K. has begun to demonstrate variations in patterns of work, union organization, local political organization, etc. (Cooke, 1987).

However, the extent to which any of these can be explained as a consequence of local culture (i.e., local values and beliefs) is still debatable and needs to be rigorously examined so that the notion of local culture does not become a convenient catch-all explanation.

One way to clarify and explore the various explanations offered within the debate is to examine, over a long time frame, the connections between the national, regional and local levels and how these have shaped the experiences, political action and organization of workers and others. The case study to be reported has begun such an exploration. The task is threefold. First some identification of the overall patterns within the New Zealand economy as a whole is required, then the regional level needs to be explored and finally specific localities. The study examines the restructuring process since 1920 and how this has affected the major urban centers within New Zealand. The key questions revolve around the structure of employment and income and whether these in combination produce varied consumption patterns and demands which lead to highly varied life styles.

National Context of Change

New Zealand as a white settler society has been in existence for just under 150 years. As a migrant society it has been composed primarily of settlers drawn from the British Isles, and thus has had a fairly homogeneous immigrant population. The economy of the society and thus its social structure has reflected its particular niche within the international system as a primary producing nation centered around a narrow range of commodities with the majority of the exports of the country going directly to the U.K. The restructuring of Europe into the E.E.C and Britain's membership, therefore had a major impact on the patterns of trade and led to the erosion of the power basis of the farming and pastoral interests, one of the dominant forces within New Zealand politics. The 1970s and 1980s have seen the rise of new factions within New Zealand's capitalist class to dominance. The new factions represent corporate, multinational capital and thus the last two decades have been characterized by rationalizations and closures of plants, mergers and takeovers and the formation of New Zealand-based multinational and multi-product companies which are now expanding their operations through the acquisition of companies in other parts of the world (Rosenberg, 1988; Feagin and Smith, 1987). For example, Fletcher Challenge, New Zealand's largest company, has over this period acquired interests in North America (40 percent of its assets and profits), Australia and Chile, thus internationalizing its production base and strengthening its bargaining power with respect to New Zealand labor.

The main periods within this transition are the last two decades of the 19th century through the 1920s, the Depression and recovery to the "long boom" in the post-war years to the mid-1960s, and from the mid-1960s to the present which have been years of restructuring and a return to depressed economic conditions in the mid-1980s (Fitzgerald and Thoms, 1987).

The late 19th century saw a number of important changes. The first was the triumph of the free-holding farming class over the squatters and large estate holders who in the middle of the century formed an incipient landed class (Eldred-Grigg, 1980). The Liberal Government, elected in 1890, had as one of its aims land reform to break up the large estates and open the way to the development of free-holding. The result was an owner-occupied family farming structure in the 20th century with little use of regular employed labor.

In the 1880s a further significant change occurred in the economic and social base with the development of refrigeration. The first shipment of frozen meat left New Zealand for Britain in 1882, beginning an important new chapter in the development of the colony. The following decades saw the rapid expansion of this trade and the establishment of processing plants. This led to the growth of small service towns centered around the freezing works and dairy factories and containing a range of support services for pastoral production such as stock and station agents to provide the finance, transport and marketing links for the producers.

In addition to land reform the state was a crucial actor during this period in the changes taking place through the policy adopted under Vogel of raising overseas loans to promote the development of New Zealand's infrastructure of transport. This led to the building of the main rail system and created the conditions which allowed the development of pastoral production. The 1920s saw New Zealand dominated by pastoralism with an export income derived almost entirely from wool, butter, cheese and frozen meat (mostly sheep meat), these four commodities contributing 80 percent of exports by value of product. The processing was in small-scale factories with only six percent of factories employing more than 50 people and fewer than four percent over 100 people. It was thus a small town-based society where people tended to have a strong attachment to the localities in which they lived, as well as local communal organizations such as lodges, churches, volunteer fire brigades, school committees, and sports clubs, especially rugby (Hall, et al., 1984). Role segregation was marked, as were gender divisions. New Zealand was seen as a "man's" country (Phillips, 1980).

The Depression led to changes within the pastoral economy. The first set of changes were those contained within a program of import licensing and import substituting domestic manufacturing stimulated by wartime shortages (Gould, 1982; Hawke, 1981, 1985; Rosenberg, 1986; Pearce, 1987). An additional pressure for change was the need to diversify the employment base after the failure in the 1920s of a pastoral-based economy to sustain employment (see Figure 1). The results of these changes were two decades of modest economic growth, low to insignificant levels of unemployment, a restructuring of employment across the economy into manufacturing for both men and women, an increased participation rate for women in the work force, strong growth in public service employment, and a movement to New Zealand of migrant labor from the Pacific Islands, accompanied by a greater degree of urbanization.

The period from 1936-66 established the structural conditions for a more broadly based economy and society. Thus, by the late 1960s New Zealand had become urbanized, industrialized in the sense that workers were increasingly employed in large-scale plants often part of multi-national companies, and proletarianized in the sense that 80 percent of the work force were salary and wage earners with petty proprietors virtually disappearing from the scene. The composition of the work force had, however, changed substantially from the 1930s, with a decline in the proportion of unskilled workers and a strong rise in non-manual employment. The dominant class imagery was one of equality rather than segregation fed on the belief in equality of opportunity through educational advancement and social mobility enabled by an expanding economic base. Local community life was still strong although signs of erosion in the institutional base were becoming evident, which have become apparent in more recent decades.

The mid-1960s marks the end of the "long boom" which began in the postwar years, and the next 15 years to 1984 are characterized by much less certain conditions. The period is one of cycles of expansion and recession which by the 1980s had moved toward a depression with unemployment emerging as in the 1920s and 1930s as a significant feature of the society. The external environment in which New Zealand traded changed in the late 1960s and early 1970s. Most significant were the formation of the E.E.C., oil price rises of the early 1970s which affected the profitability of an agricultural sector heavily dependent on transport services, and the limits that had been reached in technological innovation within New Zealand's pattern of agricultural production which inhibited further expansion. Both capital and the state sought solutions through restructuring their respective activities. Capital reorganized through mergers, takeovers and amalgamations, increasing the size of plants and changing the basis of ownership from individuals to one of interlocking company ownership with an increasingly large role played by the financial institutions such as insurance companies, many of which were owned overseas or by subsidiaries of overseas-based companies (Fogelburg, 1978; Pearson and Thorns, 1983). The state

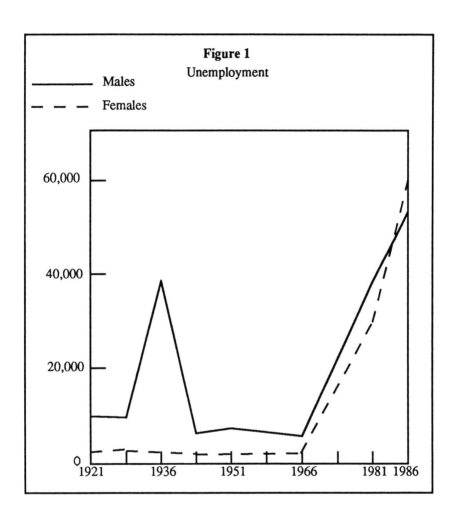

Figure 1
Unemployment

restructured through the development of a new energy based sector to the economy and through reductions in the welfare budget to provide funds for the new sector and for a raft of subsidies to both manufacturers and farmers. Part of this restructuring stimulated by the state, as in other advanced capitalist countries, was industrial reorganization and rationalization plans which led to job losses in traditional areas of manufacturing (e.g. textiles lost 11 percent of jobs within this sector between 1973-78) and agricultural processing faced change with the closure of older small plants in both the dairy and freezing industries with consequent impacts on the small service towns (Scott, 1980). The state played a further role in the restructuring by raising loans to underwrite the development of the new energy sector which involved capital-intensive plants in the areas of petro-chemical production, electricity generation, aluminum smelting, steel expansion, and forestry mills. The expected growth in the economy and employment which these new ventures was intended to stimulate did not eventuate and the government was faced with rising inflation, debts and unemployment.

The election of a Labor government in 1984 brought a dramatic break with the broadly social democratic welfare based economic development strategy pursued since the mid-1930s. The new form of economic management adopted was based around less overt governmental regulation of the economy and a commitment to a greater incorporation of New Zealand into the international economy through the phasing out of import licenses and control and the removal of exchange control on capital movements. The early acts of the new government, therefore, signalled the end of the raft of subsidies and support mechanism to farmers and manufacturers that had been built up over the previous 40 years. The result of this move to economic liberalism has been the initiation of a further and extensive reorganization of New Zealand capital, with further mergers, takeovers and the rise to prominence of a small number of multinational companies. The result has been plant closures and a steady rise in the unemployment rate through the 1980s. Not only has the restructuring occurred within the private sector but the state sector has also been extensively reorganized through a policy of corporatizing government departments which reorganize them along commercial lines and requires them to trade at a profit and pay taxes to the state. The departments were corporatized during the first term of the present labor administration from 1984-1987, and during the second term the government has moved to begin the sale of state assets and thus to privatize the newly formed corporations. The growing influence of the corporate sector of capital within the society can be seen in the formation of the business round table a small exclusive grouping of the directors of the large corporate businesses and the role these corporations are now playing in the purchase of state assets. For example, the state owned petro-corporation involved in the exploration and development of New Zealand's oil and natural gas resources has recently been bought by Fletcher-Challenge, New Zealand's largest company, when it was offered for sale under the government's assets sale policy.

New International Division Of Labor Hypotheses Examined

Table 1   Sectoral Distribution of Employment 1921-86

	Ag	Mfg	Const	Svcs	Ag	Mfg	Const	Svcs
		MALES				FEMALES		
	%	%	%	%	%	%	%	%
1921	32	15	8	37	7	16	0	61
1926	30	13	10	35	9	15	0	58
1936	29	14	8	34	4	15	0	56
1945	25	19	9	44	7	24	1	67
1951	22	24	11	41	6	24	1	69
1956	29	24	13	42	5	23	1	71
1961	18	25	13	43	4	23	1	70
1966	16	28	12	43	5	23	1	70
1971	14	26	12	47	5	22	1	69
1976	12	26	12	47	6	20	1	70
1981	14	25	9	48	7	19	1	69
1986	13	24	11	49	7	18	0	72

Changing Occupational Structures and Gender Composition

Table 1 provides data on the broad pattern of employment by sectors from the 1920s to the 1980s. Given the importance of pastoralism in the 1920s agriculture for males was a significant source of employment (around 30 percent), whereas manufacturing occupied only 15 percent of male employment. However, the largest single area is the service sector. This is partly a reflection of the requirements of pastoral production which necessitated high numbers of service workers in, for example, the transport industry (the largest single component of the service sector). However, of the total work force in 1921 only 23 percent was female, and only in the government sector did female workers outnumber male workers. The data overall does show that New Zealand's employment structure in the 1920s was strongly shaped by its tertiary sector with just under 50 percent of all workers employed here compared to 19.5 percent in agriculture and 15.5 percent in manufacturing.

By the end of the middle period of development in the mid 1960s the economy and employment structure had been considerably reshaped. Agricultural employment had halved in importance to only 16 percent of male work and manufacturing had almost doubled from 15 to 28 percent. However, the service sector was still the most important employment source, involving 58 percent of the total employed population. The participation of women in the work force had increased over the period from 23 to 27 percent, though they were still largely concentrated in the government sector of employment. The balance, however, between male and female workers within this sector had changed, with an increased number of male workers relative to female employed.

The final period from the mid 1960s to the 1980s can be divided into two sub-periods. During the first period the government attempted to add an additional capital-intensive productive sector to the economy through a series of energy related projects. These additions produced an increased demand in the construction industry and led to regional changes in income levels and employment bases. By 1981 manufacturing had shrunk as a source of employment for males to 25 percent and for females to 19 percent. The impact of this decline on the overall level of employment was limited through the growth of service employment. However, this was at a slower rate than the decline in manufacturing especially in some of the regional centers, as rationalizations occurred within the meat and dairy processing industry, as well as in textiles.

The final five years covered by the table indicate a further slight reduction in the manufacturing sector during the second period identified and a consolidation of the service sector as the major arena of employment.

An important issue raised by these movements is the extent of the compositional changes within the service sector over time. Analysis of the service sector has failed to adequately identify this diversity, what it contains and whether it is the "older" services such as domestic work and relatively unskilled tasks or the newer and more skilled areas. An alternative way of examining this change is that of distinguishing between publicly provided services and those provided by the private sector (Urry, 1986). The extension of publicly provided services across a range of areas such as education, health, housing and social welfare services with the development of the welfare state from the mid-1930s is reflected in the growth in community and governmental services. This growth expanded employment for both women and men in white collar occupations especially during the 1950s and 1960s. However, in the 1970s and 1980s with the state restructuring which has occurred this process has moved in the opposite direction with a reduction of government workers in the welfare areas of state activity and an increase in revenue collecting, with the introduction of a new scheme for indirect taxation (Goods and Services Tax, 1985). Such a change to government activity shifts the base of recruitment for public servants to those with skills in accounting rather than in social or administrative settings. The deregulation of the financial sector in 1984 has also led to employment growth in financial services over the past few years.

The gender composition of the work force has undergone considerable change since the 1920s. The New Zealand data show an increased level of participation of females in the full-time paid work force, from 23 percent of the total in 1921 to 27 percent in the 1960s and 34.3 percent in the 1980s. However, employment of women is still largely confined to particular sectors of the economy. In the 1920s it was largely in government and personnel services. During the 1950s and 1960s growth occurred in the numbers of women working in the manufacturing sector. However, in the most recent period of restructuring during the late 1970s and 1980s, manufacturing employment for women has shrunk more rapidly than for men.

Table 2 Ratio of Male to Female Employees
by Sector of Employment

Sector	1921	1936	1966	1986
Agriculture, etc.	14.3	24.3	8.1	3.8
Mining	247.2	177.4	58.9	13.1
Manufacturing	3.1	2.8	3.3	2.6
Construction	167.8	141.2	41.6	18.2
Power and Water	31.1	19.0	13.1	10.6
Transport and Comm	19.4	25.6	5.3	3.2
Commercial	2.6	2.9	1.7	1.7
Finance	4.1	4.7	1.6	1.1
Government/Com/Soc	0.3	0.3	0.7	2.1
Public Administration	1.2	1.3	1.0	0.9

Table 2 shows that the ratios of male to females in the various sectors of the economy have generally declined over the 60 years covered. However, in the key sectors of the economy the changes have not been that extensive. For example, in 1921 there were just over three men employed in manufacturing for each woman, compared with 2.6 in 1981. In the area of government, community and social services there has been a reverse move with male workers entering areas previously dominated by female labor. Even with these sectoral shifts, however, there still exist substantial differences in pay and conditions of employment between women and men.

Casualization of the Workforce

The statistical data that can be obtained for patterns of employment do not provide a reliable source of information on the extent of casualization. Data on this issue are, therefore, difficult to obtain. However, there does appear to be an increase in this area of employment. Studies of the construction industry have shown that in the most recent decades there has been a move towards subcontracting and the use of self-employed labor (Gallacher and Savage, 1987). Also in the transport industry delicensing of carriers has seen a gradual move to owner operators working on contract. There has also been some revival in home-based production of such items as hand-knitted woolens, particularly for the high-priced end of the domestic and export markets. This is an expansion and return to a traditional rural based form of enterprise within rural communities and farming families. The use of these forms of labor contract moves overhead costs to the workers from the employers and is thus part of the restructuring process of capital to improve its profitability during times of economic change.

The New Zealand state has been moving to increase the flexibility of the labor market over the past few years. The 1987 Labor Relations Act, for example, allows for regional pay rates and is designed to increase flexibility in wage bargaining. Such a move is likely to weaken the national award structure which has been central to the wage fixing system since the 1894 Industrial and Arbitration and Conciliation Act (New Zealand Planning Council, 1988) Any resulting reduction in the strength of union organization and bargaining power could result in downward pressure on wage rates, clearly to the advantage of employers rather than workers.

Unemployment

The pattern of unemployment over the 60-year period has two distinct cycles. As Figure 1 shows the first was in the late 1920s and 1930s when unemployment increased across all sectors of the New Zealand economy. The proportion of women identified in the official figures at this period substantially under-represent the effect of the Depression on female employment chances as they were largely unrecorded within the official figures. All sectors of the economy shed labor during the 1920s and 1930s and it was not until after the war in the 1940s that full employment returned.   The decades of the 1950s and 1960s through the mid-1970s generally saw negligible unemployment and labor shortages.   These shortages were largely solved through migration to New Zealand, the greater incorporation of women into the full- and part-time paid labor force and the urbanization of the Maori population.

The mid-1970s saw the beginning of a new wave of unemployment which has been uneven in its full impact on the country. By mid-1988 8.5 percent of the work force or 113,000 people were out of work.   The areas suffering the severest effects have been the small service towns and regional centers where reorganization of the processing industry and local manufacturing has resulted in substantial rises in unemployment, up to double the national average.   Only two areas of the country have experienced substantially lower rates: the urban centers of Auckland and Wellington, both having around five percent of their respective work forces unemployed in mid-1988.   The emerging regional variations in unemployment show that one of the consequences of the latest period of restructuring is a more diverse and unequal society.

Regional Diversity and Inequality

The four urban centers selected for more extensive examination are those considered to be the "main" urban centers within New Zealand. Auckland and Wellington are in the North Island and Christchurch and Dunedin within the South Island.   The North Island is the more populous, containing 62 percent of the population in 1921.   This dominance had become even more pronounced by 1986 when 74 percent of the population was in this island.

Further, in 1921 the four centers contained 35 percent of the total New Zealand population, with Auckland at 157,757 the largest, containing 12% of New Zealand's population. Wellington and Christchurch each contained eight percent and Dunedin was the smallest with six percent (72,255). By 1986 Auckland's urban dominance (809,142) was such that 60 percent of the main center population and 25 percent of the total New Zealand population lived within this urban area.   The restructurings identified have clearly led to a northward movement within New Zealand's population and a substantial increase in Auckland's national dominance.

Employment Structure

In the previous discussion shifts in New Zealand's employment structure were identified, especially the movement from the primary sector into manufacturing after the 1930s and the shift into the tertiary sector in the 1970s and 1980s. This movement affected male and female employment in different ways emphasizing the important impact of gender on employment. It is now necessary to explore the extent to which the four centers reflect a common path of change.

The broad patterns of change from 1921-86 show that agricultural decline has occurred in all cases and that manufacturing grew after the depression of the 1930s to constitute a major component within the occupational structure until the mid-1960s. From that time on manufacturing has declined in relative importance as a source of employment. However, a number of significant variations reflect the particularities of the four centers.

Table 3. Manufacturing Jobs in the Four Main Urban Centers

	1921				1966			
	male		female		male		female	
	no.	%	no.	%	no.	%	no.	%
Auckland	11,222	30.7	4,933	35.1	58,833	55.0	24,020	57.6
Wellington	11,110	30.4	2,914	20.8	12,888	12.2	5,285	12.6
Christchurch	8,145	22.3	3,212	33.0	24,036	22.7	8,522	22.7
Dunedin	5,980	16.4	2,918	20.9	9,846	9.32	3,842	9.3
TOTALS	36,457		13,977		105,603		41,669	

	1981				1986			
	male		female		male		female	
	no.	%	no.	%	no.	%	no.	%
Auckland	70,557	65.0	33,585	68.0	66,585	66.4	31,014	70.1
Wellington	6,240	5.7	3,090	6.3	4,950	4.9	2,187	4.9
Christchurch	24,258	22.4	9,321	19.1	22,506	22.4	8,685	19.7
Dunedin	7,203	6.6	2,814	5.8	6,306	6.3	2,331	5.3
TOTALS	108,258		48,810		100,347		44,217	

Percent change in manufacturing jobs 1966-86: Males -4.5%; Females 6.4%
Percent change in manufacturing jobs 1981-86: Males -7.3%; Females -9.4%

Source: Census of Population, 1921, 1966, 1981, 1986.

Auckland, for example, has become the urban center with the largest manufacturing sector (see Table 3).   In 1921 manufacturing comprised 22 percent of male and 24 percent of female employment.   This placed the city fourth in relative importance, behind Dunedin, Wellington and Christchurch. All four centers experienced growth in manufacturing during the 1940s and early 1950s such that by 1951 manufacturing accounted for around one-third of male and female employment in all but Wellington.   In Wellington's case growth in manufacturing was much less but growth in the service sector, particularly the area of government services was much stronger than in the other three centers, reflecting its position as a capital city.   From 1966 on manufacturing declined in relative importance in Christchurch and Dunedin, with the latter's decline much steeper (from 35 to 25 percent).   During the same period (1966-86) in Auckland, by contrast, there was an initial increase in the number of manufacturing jobs for both women and men but after 1981 a decline also occurred.   Manufacturing jobs within the four centers between 1921 and 1986 have become increasingly centered in Auckland, with the proportion increasing from 30 percent in 1921 (for males) and 35 percent for females to 66 percent and 70 percent respectively.   The pattern in the service sector, however, shows some interesting differences.   Wellington has progressively become dominated by its service industries in terms of employment, with the manufacturing sector declining in importance from 1956 on.   The city shed manufacturing to the surrounding urban areas, particularly to the Hutt Valley and Porirua and changed into a commercial, government service based city during the 1950s and 60s.   By 1981 the manufacturing section had shrunk to only 15 percent of male and 11 percent of female employment.   Clearly dominant, then, is the service sector.   Within this the three key areas are government administration, financial services, transport and commercial services (retailing and wholesale) for men, whereas for women community services are a more significant area of employment.   Since the 1920s there has been a dramatic reduction in the number of women working in domestic and personnel services, the dominant area of employment in 1921 constituting one-third of the work for women within this sector.   By 1981 this had declined to less than one percent.

The urban areas of Auckland and Wellington have exhibited stronger growth in the private rather than the public services area.   This differential growth has contributed to the growth in income differentials between the northern and southern urban areas.

The patterns exhibited from 1921 to 1986 show the progressive northward movement of employment, particularly in the manufacturing sector.   The relatively small size of Dunedin and its lack of growth over the years reviewed has resulted in its experience of change, reducing it more to the level of a regional center with a lower income structure, property price regime, rent levels and higher levels of unemployment in the 1980s than the other three main urban centers. However, Auckland and Wellington have more buoyant levels of activity than Christchurch.

The flow on effects of the changes in the employment sectors and the relative growth rates can be seen across a wide range of other aspects of the urban structures. Two crucial ones are urban property prices and household and individual income levels. Both link to issues of accumulation and the distribution of wealth and therefore are key factors shaping patterns of stratification and restratification.

New Zealand is an owner-occupied society with 72 percent of households living in this form of tenure in 1986. This is not a recent phenomenon; throughout this century over 50 percent of households have owned their homes (Thorns, 1984). Consequently, both the ideology and reality of home ownership are widely endorsed. Taking the last period of restructuring from 1970 through the mid-1980s important shifts in house and land values have occurred. During this period there have been three boom periods, from 1972-74, from 1979-81, and from 1984-86. During these periods prices rose steeply around the country but increasingly during each boom a more pronounced regional pattern emerged. Over the last of the boom periods national sale prices moved from around S55,000 to S86,000 for a house. These shifts represent a 56 percent rise in price for a house (in three years and 109 percent for building sections). However, these rates of increase have not been even across the country. Auckland and Wellington have produced the most rapid increase in house prices, with Auckland moving from $87,413 (1983) to S190,000 (December, 1987), a rise of 117 percent in just four years. This compares with a rise in Wellington of 92 percent from S68,644 to S132,157; Christchurch of 67 percent from S50,733 to $84,773; and Dunedin of 55 percent from $38,691 to S59,997. The relativities between the four centers in property prices have changed such that in 1988 a Dunedin property would only buy 31.5 percent of the average Auckland house, in Christchurch 44 percent and in Wellington 70 percent.

The size of these differentials indicates the high costs associated with movement from one urban center to another for workers who are made redundant as part of restructuring brought about by the reorganization of manufacturing and service activity. The movement of capital is much easier and in the most recent restructuring process the mobility of capital has been significant. The movement of workers is, however, expensive and difficult, both because it causes social dislocation and because they are tied into the areas in which they live through their ownership of domestic property. The house they own is the worker's major investment and one tangible asset. Consequently many workers have used severance payments not for mobility but to freehold their house and further reinforce their immobility. The result has been disproportionately increasing rates of unemployment rising to 15 percent in a number of the regional service centers. The main centers have not been immune to increases in unemployment, with rates in Christchurch rising to 8.3 percent and Dunedin 10.9 percent. However, the two North Island centers have had markedly lower rates of unemployment, with 5.3 percent for the Auckland area and 4.5 percent for Wellington in 1988.

Over the past 25 years the pattern of income distribution has changed with an increasing number of high income earners in Auckland and Wellington. In the 1960s workers' incomes were centered around the average income levels. The 1970s, however, were an important decade of change in the distribution of incomes. There was growth in dual income households as a result of the increased participation of female workers in the economy, albeit often in a part-time capacity. The decade saw the establishment of the one plus income household as the normal pattern, so providing a mechanism for households to withstand pressures on their purchasing power brought about by high levels of price inflation (Easton, 1983). Without this increase in numbers of earners per household the impact of falling real wages would have been more severe on the purchasing power of the majority of households. A result of the increased numbers of dual earning households has been to further extend the distribution of incomes and create growing levels of income inequality between those with high and low incomes (Penhale and Wigbout, 1982). The composition of income is clearly an important factor and for low-income households the additional earnings of other household members are a more significant component of the household income than they are in high-income households (Hall, 1987).

The changes noted for the 1970s have resulted in greater variation in income distribution between the four centers, with Wellington and Auckland emerging as higher income areas than Christchurch and Dunedin. These trends have become further entrenched in the 1980s.

In the 1980s male and female income distributions have come closer together as a result of structural changes to the composition of the work force, especially the increase in the service sector. In Wellington, 47 percent of male and 40 percent of female workers received incomes of between $10,000 and $20,000 in 1981, a much smaller discrepancy than in any of the other main centers. In Auckland the variation was 51 percent of male to 37 percent of female workers and for Christchurch and Dunedin 51 percent and 33 percent. Further, both male and female incomes in the North Island centers had higher overall distributions by 1986 and Wellington has emerged as the highest of the main centers. However, at the upper end of the income distribution the contrast between male and female incomes is still quite stark. Less than one percent of female earners in the four cities received incomes of $40,000 or more, compared with between eight and 16 percent of males. Also over the last decades there has emerged an identifiable group in poverty (see New Zealand Planning Council, 1988).

The income distributions identified are an important consequence of the employment shifts documented earlier and have produced significant effects on household consumption patterns and life styles, contributing to the development of more clearly visible and distinctive consumption sectors within the cities.

These changes within the structure of the four main centers have impacted on the life chances and life styles of the residents. The four cities have become more diverse and distinctive. The variation in employment patterns and rates of growth produced different patterns of in-migration, creating ethnically more diverse urban centers in the 1970s and 1980s, especially in the case of Auckland and, to a lesser extent, Wellington.

The collective impact of changes in work, demography, migration, income and tenure have, therefore, created cities of much more diverse patterns of consumption as exhibited by the growth of such features as restaurants and commercial entertainment for the new wealthy sections of the urban population with their greater discretionary income. The greater variation in income arises from the segmentation of the work force into areas of growth and decline and the increase in dual income households in the 1970s and 1980s. There is then some evidence to support the view that a restratification process is taking place within the urban centers.

Retrospect and Prospect

In the initial critique of the NIDL attention was drawn to the issue of the degree of independence possessed by individual nation states and, therefore, the degree to which the internal structures of a particular nation are simply the reflection of the process of global capital accumulation. New Zealand, even in the 1920s, did not have a great deal of control over the wider economic and trading environment within which it operated as a nation. It was dependent on pastoral production for its export income and consequently was vulnerable to fluctuations in commodity prices. The depressed state of the world capitalist economy in the late 1920s and early 1930s led to primary product prices falling which brought to New Zealand the first of the depressions. The way that New Zealand responded and restructured its economy and society in the post-Depression years indicates, however, that the state was a social institution of some importance in shaping the path of change adopted in the late 1930s and into the post-war years.

At each subsequent period of restructuring identified, state action was important in shaping the context of change. The disappearance, therefore, of the state which appears in some versions of the NIDL thesis would clearly result in an inappropriate framework for understanding the development of New Zealand society from the 1920s to the 1980s. The state initiated changes in the 1930s which provided a context within which capitalist activity expanded through the import controls and licensing policies, enabling local manufacturing activity to expand and replace imported commodities. The action of the national government in the 1970s through the promotion of the Think Big energy-related strategy led to capital switching, new overseas loans and a new pattern of regional investment. Finally, after 1984 the move to a more liberal market-oriented regime of economic management has led to further capital and state reorganization with extensive impacts on employment and regional development.

The greater use of "market forces" and the "user pays" principle are now being advocated as the ways to regulate economic decision making and consumer choices. These moves by the state have taken New Zealand's economic and social policies much closer to those of other western capitalist economies and away from the social democratic policy path of economic management and government controlled social welfare planning that had characterized New Zealand from the 1930s.

The data presented here, therefore, challenges the notion that the state is an unimportant actor in shaping change; rather it suggests that state initiated activity has been one of the agencies shaping the context within which change has occurred.

The relationship between capital, labor and the state which has characterized New Zealand over the past 60 years has evolved from small town capitalism in the 1920s and 1930s to an urban-based, more corporately-owned capitalism in the 1980s (Pearson and Thorns, 1983). The 1920s and 1930s were decades of small, privately owned companies and family-owned farms, whereas the 1970s and 1980s have been dominated by takeovers and mergers which have created large, publicly owned, multiproduct companies, increasingly multi-national in their operations. These changes affect the relative importance of the state, varying factions of capital and labor and thus the composition of the dominant class. Over time the center of social and political activity has shifted from the provincial towns and rural areas to the main urban centers. The data presented demonstrates that restructuring is not a one-off process but has been continually occurring over the past 60 years. The experience of change varies depending on the location of the workers concerned both spatially and sectorally. The four main centers have not proceeded along identical paths, but do demonstrate important and significant variations leading to the necessity for research to be sensitive to local level change. The final issue which requires further attention is that of the extent to which the 1970s and 1980s have brought about a restratification process resulting from the tertiarization of employment and the greater incorporation of women into the full and part-time paid work force. The growth of dual-income households, the greater regional disparities in income and wealth noted have created a much greater variation in life style both within and between the four main centers. The long-term impact of such movements needs to be further examined and their impact on the class structure assessed. Is, for example, a new form of stratification developing based not on labor market position but on consumption sector cleavage such as has been suggested by some recent writers (e.g. Saunders, 1986)? The evidence thus far does not support the view that the changes are consumption led. Rather, they are the product of modifications within the employment structure which are producing the fragmentation observable within the class structure. Fragmentation is not a new phenomenon, it is simply the latest phase in an ongoing process of class formation and change.

The NIDL thesis has been a valuable stimulus to debate and research, leading to a focus of attention on the structural changes taking place in employment within western capitalist economies. However, it is severely limited if the particularities of development are ignored. It is essential that the examination of structural change move beyond both the limited time frame used by many within this debate and the restricted level of analysis adopted. The way that national, regional and local levels of structural change interrelate and how these in turn shape and are shaped by the experiences and actions of workers, households and residents of localities is the continuing challenge at both a theoretical and empirical level.

Future analysis, therefore, should combine the identification of structural change and the detailed case study through the further development of local studies. When attention is paid to this locality level it becomes much more difficult to ignore the dynamics of class relationships and the role that organizational forms play in shaping both the facilitation of and the resistances to change.

References

Armstrong, Warwick (1980) Land class, colonialism: The origins of dominion capitalism. In W.E. Willmott (Ed.), *New Zealand and the World*. Christchurch: University of Canterbury.

Bedggood, David (1980) *Rich and Poor in New Zealand*. Sydney: Allen and Unwin.

Blau, Peter and Duncan Otis Dudley (1967) *The American Occupational Structure*. Chichester: Wiley.

Bluestone, Barry and Bennett Harrison (1986) *The Great American Jobs Machine: The Proliferation of Low-Wage Employment in the U.S. Economy*. Washington, DC: United States Congressional Joint Economic Committee.

Bluestone, Barry, Bennett Harrison and Larry Gorman (1984) *Storm Clouds on the Horizon: Labor Market Crisis and Industrial Policy*. Brookline, MA: Economic Education Project.

Bluestone, Barry and Bennett Harrison (1983) *The Deindustrialization of America*. New York: Basic Books.

Castells, Manuel (1983) *The City and the Grassroots*. London: Edward Arnold.

Castells, Manuel (Ed.) (1985) High technology, space and society, *Urban Affairs Annual Review, 51*(28). Beverly Hills: Sage.

Cohen, Robin (1985) Policing the frontier: Regulating the supplies of migrant labour. Paper presented at the Conference on the *Urban and Regional Impact of the New International Division of Labour*, Hong Kong.

Cooke, Philip (1982) *Theories of Planning for Space*. London: Heineman.

Cooke, Philip (1985) The changing urban and regional system in the United Kingdom. Paper presented at the conference on the *Urban and Regional Impact of the New International Division of Labor*, Hong Kong.

Cooke, Philip (Ed.) (1986) *Global Restructuring, Local Response*. London: Economic and Social Research Council.

Cooke, Philip (1987) Individuals, localities and postmodernism, *Society and Space, 5*(4).

Crompton, Rosemary and Gareth Jones (1984) *White Collar Proletariat: Deskilling and Gender in the Clerical Labour Process*. London: Macmillan.

Dickens, Peter (1985) Industrial restructuring, social change and "locale." Paper presented at conference on the *Urban and Regional Impact of the New International Division of Labor*, Hong Kong.

Dunleavy, Patrick (1980) *Urban Political Analysis*. London: Macmillan.

Dunleavy, Patrick (1985) Socialized consumption, political change and economic development, *International Journal of Regional Research, 9.*

Easton, Brian (1983) *Income Distribution in New Zealand* (Paper 28). Wellington: New Zealand Institute of Economic Research.

Eldred-Grigg, Stephan (1980) *A Southern Gentry.* Wellington: Reed.

Feagin, Joe R. and Michael Peter Smith (1987) Cities and the new international division of labor: An overview. In Michael Peter Smith and Joe R. Feagin (Eds.), *The Capitalist City: Global Restructuring and Community Politics.* Oxford: Basil Blackwell.

Fitzgerald, Kath and David C. Thorns (1987) *Locality Impacts of Economic and Social Change.* Christchurch: University of Canterbury, Department of Sociology.

Flynn, Nigel and Andrew Taylor (1985) Deindustrialization and corporate change in an "industrial heartland." Paper presented at the conference on the *Urban and Regional Impact of the New International Division of Labor,* Hong Kong.

Fogelburg, Graeme (1978) Changing patterns of shareownership in New Zealand's largest companies. *Research Paper No. 15.* Wellington: Victoria University, Department of Business Administration.

Frank, Andre (1971) *Capitalism and Underdevelopment in Latin America.* Hardmondsworth: Penguin.

Froebel, Folker, Jurgen Heinrichs and Otto Kreye (1980) *The New International Division of Labor.* Cambridge: Cambridge University Press.

Gallacher, Ian and John Savage (1987) Supply aspects of housing 1985-86 to 1988-89. *Research Paper 87/1.* Wellington: National Housing Commission.

Gamble, A. (1979) *The Decline of Britain.* London: New Left Books.

Giddens, A. (1981) *A Critique of Historical Materialism.* London: Macmillan.

Goldthorpe, John (1980) *Social Mobility and Class Structure in Modern Britain.* Oxford: Clarendon Press.

Gould, John (1982) *A Rake's Progress.* Auckland: Hodder and Stoughton.

Gregory, Derek and John Urry (Eds.) (1985) *Social Relations and Spatial Structure.* London: Macmillan.

Grunwald, Joseph and Kenneth Flamm (1985) *The Global Factory.* Washington, DC: The Brookings Institute.

Hall, Georgie (1987) *Two Income Families in New Zealand*, Research Series No. 6. Wellington: Department of Social Welfare.

Hall, Peter (1985) Technology, space and society in contemporary Britain. In Manuel Castells (Ed.), *High Technology, Space and Society.* New York: Sage.

Hall, Robert, David C. Thorns, and William E. Willmott (1984) Community, class and kinship: Bases for collective action within localities, Environment and Planning D, *Space and Society, 2*, 201-215.

Halsey, A., et al. (1980) *Origins and Destinations.*   Clarendon: Oxford Press.

Hamer, David (1980) Towns in nineteenth century New Zealand.   In D. Hamer (Ed.), *New Zealand Social History.*   Auckland: University of Auckland.

Harvey, David (1987a) Flexible accumulation through urbanization.   Paper presented at the *Urban Change and Conflict Conference,* University of Kent.

Harvey, David (1987b) Three myths in search of a reality in urban studies. *Society and Space, 5*(4).

Hawke, Gary R. (1981) The growth of the economy.   In W.H. Oliver and B.R. Williamson (Eds.), *Oxford History of New Zealand.*   Oxford: Oxford University Press.

Hawke, Gary R. (1985) *The Making of New Zealand.*   London: Cambridge University Press.

Hill, Richard Child (1985) The global factory and the company town: The changing division of labor in the international automobile industry. Paper presented at the conference on the *Urban and Regional Impact of the New International Division of Labor,* Hong Kong.

Kilmartin, Leslie, David Thorns and Terry Burke (1985) *Social Theory and the Australian City.*   Sydney: Allen and Unwin.

Lash, Scott and John Urry (1987) *The End of Organized Capitalism.* London: Polity Press.

Maguire, Michael and Dennis Smith (1985) *Dimensions of Restructuring in S.W. Birmingham,* Mimeo.   Birmingham: Aston University.

Mandel, Ernest (1975) *The Generalized Recession of the International Capitalist Economy.*   Brussels: Imprecar.

Marshall, Gordon, David Rose, Carolyn Vogler, and Howard Newby (1985) Class, citizenship and distributional conflict in modern Britain, *British Sociological Review, 36*(2), 257-84.

Massey, Doreen (1984) *Spatial Divisions of Labor.*   London: Macmillan.

McMichael, Phillip D. (1980) Settlers and primitive accumulation foundation of capitalism in Australia, *Revue, 42,* 307-34.

Morgan, Kevin and Andrew Sayer (1983) The international electronics industry and regional development in Britain.   Working Paper #34, *Urban and Regional Studies.*   Brighton: University of Sussex.

Newby, Howard, Carolyn Volger, David Rose, and Gordon Marshall (1985) From class structure to class action.   In R. Finnegan, et al. (Eds.), *New Directions in Economic Life.*   Manchester: Manchester University Press.

New Zealand Planning Council (1988) For richer or poorer: Income and wealth in New Zealand. Wellington: New Zealand.

Offe, Claus (Ed.) (1984) *Contradictions of the Welfare State.*   London: Heinemann.

Pahl, Ray (1984) *Divisions of Labour.*   Oxford: Basil Blackwell.

Pahl, Ray (1986) The restructuring of capital, the local political economy and household work strategies.   In D. Gregory and J. Urry (Eds.), *Social Relations and Spatial Structures.*   London: Macmillan.

Pearce, Geoffrey (1987) *Where is New Zealand Going?*   Ph.D. Christchurch: University of Canterbury.

Pearson, David (1980) *Johnsonville.*   Sydney: Allen and Unwin.

Pearson, David and David Thorns (1983) *Eclipse of Equality.*   Sydney: Allen and Unwin.

Penhale, Esther M. and Max Wigbout (1982) An exploration of differences between one and two income families in New Zealand, *N.Z. Population Review, 8*(2).

Phillips, Jock (1980) Mummy's boys: Bakeha men and the male culture in New Zealand.   In P. Bunkle and B. Hughes (Eds.), *Women in New Zealand Society.*   Sydney: Allen and Unwin.

Portes, Alejandro and Saskia Sassen-Koob (1987) Making it underground: Comparative material on the informal sector in western market economies, *American Journal of Sociology, 93*(1), 30-61.

Redclift, N. and Enzo Mingione (Eds.) (1983) *Beyond Employment.* Oxford: Basil Blackwell.

Revell, P. and P. Brosnan (1986) New Zealand labour force participation: The 90 years to 1988, *New Zealand Journal of Industrial Relations, 11,* 77-89.

Rose, D., C. Vogler, G. Marshall, and H. Newby (1984) Economic restructuring: The British experience, *Annals of the American Association of Political and Social Sciences, 475,* September, 137-57.

Rosenberg, Bill (1988) *Transnationals Dominate Top 20 Companies: The Rise of New Zealand Transnationals.*   Watchdog no. 59, 5-15.

Rosenberg, Wolfgang (1986) *The Magic Square.*   Christchurch: Caxton Press.

Sassen-Koob, Saskia (1985) Notes on the incorporation of Third World women into the wage labor through immigration and off-shore production, *International Labor Migration Review, 14*(4), 1144-67.

Saunders, Peter (1984) Beyond housing classes, *International Journal of Urban and Regional Research, 8,* 202-227.

Saunders, Peter (1986) *Social Theory and the Urban Question,* 2nd Edition. London: Heinemann.

Saunders, Peter and Peter Williams (1987) The constitution of the home: Towards a research agenda, *Housing Studies 3*(2), 81-93.

Scott, Claudia (1980) *Regional Development: Objective and Policies: An Appraisal*, Report No. 7. Wellington: New Zealand Planning Council.

Skocpol, Theda (1979) *States and Social Revolutions.* New York: Cambridge University Press.

Smith, Michael Peter and Joe R. Feagin (Eds.) (1987) *The Capitalist City: Global Restructuring and Community Politics.* Oxford: Basil Blackwell.

Smith, Michael Peter and Richard Tardanico (1987) Urban theory reconsidered: Production, reproduction and collective action. In Michael Peter Smith and Joe R. Feagin (Eds.), *The Capitalist City: Global Restructuring and Community Politics.* Oxford: Basil Blackwell.

Soja, Edward (1986) Taking Los Angeles apart, *Society and Space.*

Soja, Edward, Morales, Rebecca and Wolff, Goetz (1983) Urban restructuring: An analysis of social and spatial change in Los Angeles, *Economic Geography, 59*(2), 195-230.

Thorns, David C. (1982) Industrial re-structuring and change in the labour and property markets in Britain, *Environment and Planning 14,* 745-763.

Thorns, David C. (1984) Owner-occupation, the state and class relations in New Zealand. In Chris Wilkes and Ian Shirley (Eds.), *In the Public Interest.* Auckland: Benton Ross.

Urry, John (1986) Services: Some issues of analysis. Working Paper #17, Lancaster Regionalism Group, University of Lancaster.

Walby, Sylvia (1986) *Patriarchy at Work.* Oxford: Polity Press.

Wallerstein, Immanuel (1974) *Modern World Systems.* New York: Academic Press.

THE POLITICAL ECONOMY OF TECHNOLOGICAL TRANSFORMATION IN HONG KONG[1]

Jeffrey Henderson
University of Hong Kong

Contrary to what much development theory led us to expect, a number of newly industrializing societies, particularly in East Asia, have successfully restructured their economies to achieve high rates of growth and rising standards of living. Part of the restructuring process has involved the technological transformation of manufacturing industry. This has been especially the case in electronics production and has resulted in the emergence, over the past eight to ten years, of a regional division of labor among the developing countries of East Asia, with its own cores and peripheries. Focusing particularly on the semiconductor industry, this paper explores the processes that have created Hong Kong as one of the cores of this regional division of labor. While giving due weight to the role of foreign and local capital, the paper argues in particular that historically the social and technical reproduction of the labor force has been central to this development, and that state intervention in the reproduction process (by the Hong Kong government) and the indirect provision of wage subsidies (by both the Hong Kong and Chinese governments), have been crucial. The discussion of these determinants, however, is couched in relation to two other phenomena: the economic and geo-political relation of Hong Kong to the changing world system; and the socio-spatial dynamics associated with the growth of a largely locally-owned electronics production complex in the territory. The paper concludes with an assessment of the likely trajectory of electronics production in Hong Kong in light of the territory's changing internal and external political economies.

When leading social scientists from both the right and left of the ideological spectrum agree that recent economic growth in the "newly industrializing" countries (NICs) of East Asia have placed them on markedly different trajectories from other members of the developing world (Berger, 1986; Harris, 1987), it is time to sit up and take note. Whatever the ideological tone of our preferred explanation for the spectacular economic success of the East Asian NICs, it is clear that attention to the technological transformation of their manufacturing sectors is necessary. This paper is an attempt to provide some of that attention. It deals not with what is called the "gang of four"[2] as a whole, however, for I have engaged with them elsewhere (Henderson, 1989a). Rather it deals with Hong Kong, and particularly with an important branch of its manufacturing sector, semiconductor production.

Semiconductor production in Hong Kong originated with U.S. investment in 1961. From that time the labor processes implanted and developed in the territory were much the same as those that emerged in South Korea, Taiwan and Singapore in the mid-1960s, and in Malaysia, the Philippines, Thailand and Indonesia in the early 1970s. Thus, while the most capital- and skill-intensive parts of the production system (R and D, wafer fabrication, final testing and mask-making), together with corporate managerial control, remained firmly embedded in the U.S. or to a limited extent Western Europe (particularly true of wafer fabrication), Hong Kong and the rest of East Asia "specialized" in the largely unskilled, labor-intensive assembly of transistors, diodes (generically, "discretes") and integrated circuits (ICs). Until the mid- to late 1970s, then, the spread of semiconductor labor processes across the developing countries of East Asia was as depicted in Table 1, for a selection of U.S. companies.[3]

Within ten years, however, the situation had changed drastically. As Table 2 indicates, while semiconductor plants in Malaysia, the Philippines, Indonesia, Thailand, South Korea and Taiwan continued to concentrate substantially on assembly functions (albeit with some automation of the process and the addition of testing facilities here and there),[4] those in Singapore and Hong Kong had been technologically restructured. By the mid- to late 1980s the plants in those territories had specialized in some of the more capital- and skill-intensive labor processes such as circuit design and final testing. Additionally, a number of corporations had set up regional headquarters in one or another of those city-states. The implication of this restructuring was that Hong Kong and Singapore had emerged as the cores of a specifically regional division of labor (RDL) within the semiconductor industry of developing East Asia (Henderson, 1986a, 1989a: Chapter 4; Scott, 1987). As such they had begun to subject the "peripheries" of the RDL to material and corporate control decisions additional to those to which they were subject anyway, as a result of their dependent status within the industry's overall international division of labor.

This paper explores the reasons why Hong Kong has emerged as a core of this regional division of labor in semiconductor production. Its argument is cast in terms of the articulation and historical evolution of the external (world system) and internal political economies of the territory. It begins, therefore, with a brief outline of the world system factors (both economic and geo-political) which influenced the territory's initial industrial-

Table 1. U.S. Semiconductor Production in the Developing Countries of East Asia: Selected Companies, Circa 1976-79

Company	Nature of Operation and Labor Processes							
	S. Korea	Taiwan	Hong Kong	Singapore	Malaysia	Philippines	Thailand	Indonesia
Motorola	a		a, m			a		
National Semiconductor			a, m	a, m		a	a	a
Fairchild	a		a, m	a		a		a
Texas Instruments		a		a, m	a	a		
General Instrument		a			a			
Hughes			(a)			(a)		
Siliconix		a	a					
Teledyne			a	a				
Advanced Micro Devices				a	a	a		
Silicon Systems			a	a				
Sprague		a				a		
Zilog					a			

Key: a - assembly;   m - marketing center;   ( ) - operation under sub-contract arrangement

Sources: Interviews with company executives; company reports; trade press; Siegel, 1980; Scott, 1987; UNCTC, 1986; Hong Kong Productivity Centre *Electronics Bulletin* (various issues); Scottish Education and Action for Development (1984).

Table 2. U.S. Semiconductor Production in the Developing Countries of East Asia: Selected Companies, Circa 1985-88

Company	Nature of Operation and Labor Processes							
	S. Korea	Taiwan	Hong Kong	Singapore	Malaysia	Philippines	Thailand	Indonesia
Motorola	a		d, t, r, m			a		
National Semiconductor		a	a, t, m	t, d, m, r	w, a, t	a	a, t	
Fairchild	a, t	d	t, m	a, t, m		a		a
Texas Instruments		a		a, t, m		a		a
General Instrument		a, t			a			
Hughes			(a)			(a)		
Siliconix		a	a, t, d					
Teledyne			a, t					
Advanced Micro Devices			m	t, m		a	a	
Silicon Systems				d, a, t				
Sprague		a	r, m, t			a		
Zilog			d, r, m			a, t		

Key: w - wafer fabrication   a - assembly   d - design center
       r - regional headquarters   m - marketing center   t - final testing
       ( ) - operation under sub-contract arrangement

Sources: Interviews with company executives; company reports; trade press; Henderson, 1987; Scott, 1987; Ehrlich, 1988; Hong Kong Productivity Centre, *Electronics Bulletin* (various issues).

ization in the late 1940s and early 1950s. Having assessed the significance of the manufacturing sector, particularly electronics, to the territory's economic growth, paid attention to foreign control in the sector, and discussed the empirical evidence for technological transformation, the paper concentrates on the determinants of these developments. At this juncture it focuses separately and in combination on labor force formation and state policy. Subsequently, it turns once more to technological transformation in the semiconductor industry and introduces a spatial determinant, the emergence of a local complex of semiconductor and electronics production activity. The paper concludes with a comment on the future trajectory of electronics production in Hong Kong in light of changes in its internal and external political economies.

Hong Kong and the World System

From its inception as a British colony in 1841, Hong Kong has increasingly been incorporated into the world economy. Until the mid-20th century, however, its incorporation was largely based on its role as an East Asian entrepôt center. Hong Kong, in other words, was a trans-shipment point for largely British exports to China (and, to a lesser extent, other parts of the region) and for Chinese commodity and financial transactions with the core economies of Europe and the U.S. In spite of the massive disruption of the entrepôt trade occasioned by the Japanese occupation of the territory in 1941-45 and the raging civil war on the Chinese mainland, as late as 1951, two-thirds of Hong Kong's exports (overwhelming re-exports) were to China (Phelps Brown, 1971: 2).

The manufacture of commodities developed relatively early in Hong Kong. At least since the early 1930s, traditional carved wood furniture had been produced for both domestic consumption and export (Cooper, 1981), and basic cotton clothing was made for export to other parts of the British Asian empire, particularly Malaya (Mok, 1969). Such products, however, were made in the traditional manner, using skilled artisan labor, and were never more than a small fraction of the territory's exports.[5]

The beginning of the industrial production of commodities in Hong Kong from the early 1950s was a result of a combination of three factors: the restructuring of the world economy after World War II; geo-political considerations associated with the Chinese Revolution of 1949 and the Korean War of 1950-53; and internal (to Hong Kong) social changes consequent to the Chinese Revolution. If we can accept the over-accumulation/under-consumption theory of economic crisis (see Baran and Sweezy, 1966), then the Second World War, by absorbing surplus capital and physically eliminating surplus capacity, provided the basis for new rounds of accumulation subsequent to 1945. The post-war rejuvenation of the economies of the U.S. and (after the Marshall Plan) Western Europe led to increased real incomes in those core economies and hence consumer demands, at least from the early 1950s. While much of the rising demand for manufactured commodities was satisfied by production from within the core economies themselves, from about the mid-1950s on, this was not the case with the demand for cheaper cotton textiles and clothing in Britain. For a variety of structural reasons (see Gregory, 1985), the Lancashire cotton industry did not recover its pre-war dominance of the British market. There developed an increasing shortfall between the demand for cotton products and the Lancashire industry's capacity to meet that demand at a low price. For reasons which will be reviewed later, part of that demand was met by Hong Kong's newly established textile industry.

The geo-political context in which Hong Kong was located by the end of the 1940s resulted in two inter-related economic and social consequences for the territory: the virtual elimination of the entrepôt trade with China and the migration of both labor and industrial capital and expertise from the Chinese mainland. The first of these developments was a direct consequence of the growing obsession of the U.S. government and its allies with the supposed "Communist threat" subsequent to the dissolution of the wartime alliance with the Soviet Union and the military triumph of the Chinese Communist Party over its Kuomintang opposition in 1949. With the outbreak of the Korean War in 1950 and Chinese support for its North Korean ally, in rapid succession the U.S. government placed an embargo on all goods of Chinese origin and the UN prohibited the export of essential materials and strategic goods to China (Szczepanik, 1958; Riedel, 1972; So, 1986). These political initiatives, together with the Chinese government's switch to the USSR as its principal trading partner (Lin, et al., 1980: 3), resulted in the virtual elimination of Hong Kong's entrepôt trade with the mainland which by 1952 had collapsed to barely one percent of the territory's exports (Phelps Brown, 1971: 2). In its wake came unemployment of the order of 15 to 34 percent (Lin and Ho, 1980: 5).

The collapse of the entrepôt trade would have resulted in serious economic crisis had it not been for the fact that since the late 1940s Hong Kong, as already mentioned, had begun to be the recipient of "...refugee capital and refugee labor that provided the impetus for (its) industrialization..." (So, 1986: 244). Of particular significance was the transfer of industrial capital and managerial expertise in textile production from Shanghai. By the 1930s Shanghai had already developed a "modern" cotton textile industry. By the late 1940s, with the declining military fortunes of the Kuomintang, many of its textile "barons" had begun to transfer capital to Hong Kong, and to re-direct there new production machinery which otherwise would have been installed in their Shanghai plants (Mok, 1969; Wong, 1979). Within a relatively short time of arriving in Hong Kong, the Shanghai textile barons were able to set up modern factories combining the latest production equipment with cheap refugee labor. Though they did not have the trading networks necessary for export purposes (for the Shanghai firms had supplied the Chinese domestic market), they benefitted from the existence in Hong Kong of some 1,000 to 1,500 trading houses which previously had been involved in the entrepôt trade and as a consequence, had long established links with the British and other export markets (Szczepanik, 1958). By the mid-1950s, because of the problems associated with domestic cotton textile production, British department stores and clothing chains began to seek out cheap foreign supplies of cloth and garments. Encouraged by Commonwealth preferential import tariff arrangements, they not only placed contracts with Hong Kong manufacturers, but also directly assisted them in developing their production capacity and improving the quality of their output (Phelps Brown, 1971: 12). From this point, it was but a short step to foreign (again, initially British) direct investment in the territory's textile industry, though it should be emphasized that foreign investment has *never* been a major feature of this sector's development.

It was thus in these ways and for these reasons that Hong Kong began to develop an industrial economy. While textiles and garments remain the principal industrial sector, in terms of employment and value of output through the present day,[6] the latter part of the 1950s saw the beginnings of industrial diversification associated with the production of plastic commodities (initially flowers and other decorations, but subsequently kitchenware as well) wigs, and importantly, electronic products. While the entrepôt trade revived once more in the 1950s, its supremacy in the Hong Kong economy was increasingly challenged by manufactured domestic exports. Throughout the decade, industrial productivity increased by an average of 20 percent annually and by 1959 manufactured exports had surpassed the value of the entrepôt trade (Cheng, 1985: 125). By the early 1960s Hong Kong had become the largest supplier of manufactured commodities in the developing world (Lin and Ho, 1980: 2).

Growth of the Electronics Sector

Subsequent to the invention of the transistor in 1947 and the liberal licensing arrangements forced on major U.S. producers such as AT&T (Bell), General Electric and RCA by the federal government, Japan was able to develop its own semiconductor industry from the early 1950s. Operating behind high tariff barriers, the bulk of output fueled Japan's own consumer electronics industry and led in particular to Sony's introduction of the transistor radio in 1955 (Okimoto, et al., 1984: 14). By the late 1950s, competition from U.S. and domestic producers and rising wages in Japan resulted in Sony's partial internationalization of radio assembly. They developed a joint-venture operation in South Korea (a Japanese colony until 1945) in 1958, and by 1959 had begun to assemble radios in Hong Kong under a subcontract arrangement. Hong Kong's first electronics company, the Champagne Engineering Corporation, was soon assembling over 4,000 radios a month for Sony (Chen, 1971). By 1960, Champagne and two other companies had begun to produce their own radios even more cheaply than the Japanese (because of lower labor and overheads costs). The result was that Hong Kong radio exports to the U.S. increased fifteen-fold during 1960-61, effectively undercutting their Japanese competitors at the cheaper end of the market. By 1961, 12 firms were producing radios in the territory, of which two were joint-venture operations with U.S. companies. The successful competition with Japanese producers resulted in a Japanese government ban on the export of transistors to Hong Kong in 1962. They were replaced by imports from Britain, and also from the U.S. (Chen, 1971: Chapter 2).

The early development of Hong Kong as an offshore location for radio assembly by Japanese and U.S. manufacturers, together with the rapid development of an indigenous production capability, provided the *immediate* context for investment by U.S. semiconductor houses. Fairchild became the first semiconductor firm to develop production facilities anywhere in the Third World, which they did by setting up a transistor and diode assembly plant in Hong Kong in 1961. By 1966, when they moved to new premises in the territory's then most important industrial area, Kwun Tong, Fairchild had become by far the largest electronics firm in Hong Kong, employing about 4,500 workers (Chen, 1971). Since that time, Fairchild has been joined by nine other U.S. semiconductor firms (which currently include National Semiconductor, Teledyne, Siliconix, Motorola, Sprague, Commodore, Microsemiconductor), two European (Philips and Ferranti) and two Japanese producers (Hitachi and Sanyo).[7]

Before examining the determinants of the development of Hong Kong's semiconductor industry and the issues surrounding its recent emergence as a "core" of the regional division of labor, some sense of the electronics industry's significance in the local economy and the extent of its dependence on foreign control, markets and the like needs to be conveyed.

Manufacturing in the Hong Kong Economy

To gauge the economic and social significance of the electronics industry to the territory's development, we first need to indicate, in terms of

Table 3. Industrial Structure of Hong Kong:
Changing Contribution to Gross Domestic Product (at factor cost)
1961-86 (percent)

	1961	1970	1971	1972	1973	1974	1975	1976	1977	1978	1979	1980	1981	1982	1983	1984	1985	1986
Ag. and Fishing*	3.7	2.7	1.9	1.7	1.6	1.6	1.5	1.4	1.4	1.3	1.1	1.0	0.9	0.9	0.8	0.6	0.7	0.6
Manufacturing	23.6	30.9	28.1	26.9	26.6	25.8	26.9	28.3	27.2	26.9	27.6	23.9	22.8	20.6	21.9	24.1	21.9	21.9
Construction	6.2	4.2	4.9	5.3	5.5	6.1	5.7	5.4	6.0	7.0	7.3	6.7	7.5	7.3	6.0	5.3	5.0	4.5
Electricity, Gas, Water	2.4	2.0	1.9	1.7	1.8	1.8	1.7	1.4	1.5	1.1	1.1	1.3	1.4	1.9	2.0	2.5	2.7	3.0
Financial Services	10.8	14.9	17.5	20.5	19.2	17.6	17.0	17.9	19.6	20.7	21.4	22.9	23.8	22.5	18.8	15.9	16.3	17.0
Other Services	53.3	45.3	45.7	43.9	45.5	47.1	47.1	45.3	44.4	42.6	41.5	44.2	43.6	46.8	50.5	51.6	53.4	53.0
Totals	100.0	100.0	100.0	100.0	100.0	100.0	100.0	100.0	100.0	100.0	100.0	100.0	100.0	100.0	100.0	100.0	100.0	100.0

* Plus very limited mining and quarrying

Sources: 1961: *Report on the National Income Survey of Hong Kong.* Hong Kong: Government Printer, 1969.
1970-86: *Estimates of Gross Domestic Product.* Hong Kong Government.

Data for 1961-83 adapted from Y.P. Ho (1986: 172)

some general indices, the contribution which manufacturing industry as a whole has made. Table 3 conveys a sense of the contribution manufacturing industry has made to GDP relative to the contributions of other industries. Of particular note is that manufacturing reached its zenith, in terms of its contribution to GDP, in the early 1970s (31 percent in 1970); since then it has gradually declined to its present level of around 22 percent. During the same period the contribution of the service sector expanded significantly. This expansion was due partly to the growth in tourism (which now constitutes the second most important contributor to GDP after manufacturing), and partly to the emergence of Hong Kong as a major international financial center since the early 1970s.

Table 4. Changes in the Distribution of the Hong Kong
Labor Force by Industry, 1961-87 (percent)

	1961	1971	1976	1981	1983	1984	1985	1986	1987
Ag and Fishing*	8.1	4.2	2.7	2.0	1.2	1.2	1.7	1.6	1.5
Manufacturing	43.0	47.0	44.8	41.2	36.6	37.8	35.2	34.5	33.3
Construction	4.9	5.4	5.6	7.9	8.3	7.9	7.7	7.8	8.1
Elec, Gas, Water	1.1	0.6	0.5	0.7	0.6	0.5	0.6	0.7	0.7
Services	42.9	42.8	46.4	48.2	53.3	52.6	54.8	55.4	56.4
Totals	100.0	100.0	100.0	100.0	100.0	100.0	100.0	100.0	100.0

* plus very limited mining and quarrying

Sources: 1961: *Report of the 1961 Census*; 1971: *Hong Kong Population and Housing Census: 1971 Main Report;* 1976: *Hong Kong By-Census, 1976*; 1981-87: *General Household Survey.* Labor Force Characteristics Data for 1961-84 adapted from Y.P. Ho (1986: 173).

Turning to the contribution manufacturing industry has made to employment, we can see from Table 4 that it was proportionately the lead-

Table 5. Export Contribution of Hong Kong's Manufacturing Industries 1961-87 (percent by value)

	1961	1963	1965	1967	1969	1971	1973	1975	1977	1979	1981	1983	1984	1985	1986	1987
Clothing/Textiles	52.1	53.0	51.9	48.6	47.1	49.9	50.4	54.0	47.4	43.3	41.8	39.7	40.1	43.0	43.2	43.7
Electronics	2.5	4.0	5.8	8.8	10.1	11.2	13.5	14.0	15.5	15.7	17.6	20.8	22.8	22.1	22.7	22.6
Watches, Clocks, Precision Instruments	0.7	0.8	0.8	1.3	1.7	2.0	2.5	3.9	6.6	9.4	10.3	9.2	7.8	8.8	9.1	8.7
Toys and Dolls	4.6	5.5	7.5	8.3	8.5	8.6	7.7	6.5	8.0	7.5	8.1	7.7	7.7	7.6	7.6	6.5
Plastic Products	6.8	6.6	5.9	4.9	4.0	3.4	3.5	1.8	2.1	1.9	1.6	1.7	1.8	1.7	2.0	2.1
Handbags/Travel Goods	0.7	0.8	0.9	1.2	1.4	1.7	2.1	2.0	2.0	2.2	2.0	1.7	1.5	1.2	1.0	0.9
Footwear	3.5	3.8	3.0	3.3	2.8	2.6	1.4	1.1	1.0	0.9	1.0	0.7	0.8	0.8	0.8	0.7
Others	25.1	21.9	21.1	20.7	21.7	18.2	16.3	14.0	14.5	16.5	15.1	16.2	15.3	14.8	13.6	14.8
Totals	100.0	100.0	100.0	100.0	100.0	100.0	100.0	100.0	100.0	100.0	100.0	100.0	100.0	100.0	100.0	100.0

Sources: *Hong Kong Trade Statistics* (various issues) and *Hong Kong Review of Overseas Trade* (various issues). Data for 1961-84 adapted from Y.P. Ho (1986: 180).

Table 6. Establishments and Employment in the
Hong Kong Electronics Industry, 1961-1987

	Establishments		Number of Employees			
Year	Number	Average size (by employment)	M	F	F%	Total
1961	3	36.0	31	77	(71.3)	108
1962	14	62.9	262	619	(70.3)	881
1963	18	67.7	308	910	(74.7)	1,218
1964	29	101.4	621	2,320	(78.9)	2,941
1965	29	149.9	1,142	3,205	(73.7)	4,347
1966	39	278.8	1,897	8,976	(82.6)	10,873
1967	63	313.5	3338	16,410	(83.1)	19,748
1968	100	231.3	4,308	18,825	(81.4)	23,133
1969	114	274.2	6,573	24,686	(79.0)	31,259
1970	173	211.3	8,500	28,052	(76.8)	36,552
1972	280	146.6	10,525	30,531	(74.0)	41,056
1974	382	143.7	12,881	42,002	(76.5)	54,883
1976	680	88.4	12,948	47,161	(78.5)	60,109
1975	387	108.5	10,731	31,240	(74.4)	41,979
1977	711	98.7	19,057	51,131	(72.8)	70,188
1978	793	93.0	21,439	52,297	(70.9)	73,736
1979	1,041	74.6	19,294	58,369	(75.2)	77,663
1980	1,104	81.4	28,066	61,773	(68.8)	89,839
1981	1,216	73.1	28,609	60,312	(67.8)	88,921
1982	1,305	65.9	27,605	58,341	(67.9)	85,946
1983	1,351	70.1	31,430	63,201	(66.8)	94,631
1984	1,441	73.9	35,866	70,547	(66.3)	106,413
1985	1,284	63.9	27,712	54,283	(66.2)	81,995
1986	1,090	69.0	26,334	48,844	(65.0)	75,178
1987	1,180	66.6	27,892	50,670	(64.5)	78,562

Sources: 1961-70: Hong Kong Labor Department *Annual Reports*

1972-81: *Electronics Industry Data Sheets*, Hong Kong Productivity Centre (various issues).

1982-87: *Report of Employment and Vacancies Statistics*, Census and Statistics Department, Hong Kong Government.

ing provider of jobs during the 1960s and early 1970s (47 percent in 1971) and has since been progressively overtaken by the service sector, including government employment. In aggregate terms, manufacturing industry provided about 512,000 jobs in 1961, rising to a high of 990,500 in 1981 and falling by 1986 to about 918,000 (BBDO, 1987: 3). In spite of its relative decline as an employer vis a vis other industries, Hong Kong still provides more jobs, in proportional terms, through manufacturing than any other country in capitalist East Asia.[8]

Hong Kong, like Singapore, but unlike South Korea and Taiwan, never went through a phase of import-substitution industrialization. Its manufacturing base from the beginning was built almost entirely on production for the world market. Table 5 indicates the changes in the relative contributions of the various manufacturing sectors to Hong Kong's export performance. It is immediately clear that Hong Kong's continuing development as an industrial society, at least in terms of its export performance, is narrowly based on two sectors, electronics, and clothing and textiles, dominated by clothing with 33.9 percent of all manufactured exports, compared with 6.3 percent for textiles in 1984 (Y.P. Ho, 1986: 180). These two sectors accounted for about two-thirds of the territory's domestic exports in 1987. While the contribution of the clothing and textile sector declined from 52 to about 44 percent of exports between 1961 and 1987, the contribution of electronics has grown dramatically over the same period, from 2.5 to nearly 23 percent of exports (see Table 5).

The narrow base on which Hong Kong's industrialization rests will be referred to later in the paper in the discussion of the implications of the changing world economy for development prospects in the territory. We turn now to an investigation of the electronics sector in more detail.

Electronics

The electronics sector has, in the last 20 years, established itself as the second most important contributor to domestic exports (Table 5). It is important to examine its contribution to employment creation and the broad outlines of its control structures and markets before dealing directly with the semiconductor branch.

Table 6 provides data on the growth of the territory's electronics industry since the early 1960s. Within 20 years of its emergence as a subcontract assembler of cheap transistor radios, the sector had grown to encompass the production of a vast range of consumer items (TVs, VCRs, tape recorders, hi-fi equipment, computers, etc.) as well as components, such as semiconductors, capacitors, condensers, transformers, etc. By the late 1980s the industry was spread across nearly 1,200 factories employing over 78,000 people.[9]

There are perhaps two items of particular interest about the data in Table 6. First, the table shows that by the late 1960s, the industry was organized in terms of medium-sized factories of 200 to 300 employees. The rapid proliferation of factories during the 1970s and 1980s, however, coincided with a significant reduction in average size. This development has undoubtedly been associated with a proliferation of the subcontract assembly of particular parts of the products to small (often no more than ten workers), family-run firms (Sit, et al., 1979), as well as a major growth in undocumented informal sector subcontracting (Sit, 1983). Second, Table 6 indicates that the electronics work force in Hong Kong is overwhelmingly female, ranging from a high of 83 percent of the total in the late 1960s to about 65 percent at present. The gender composition of the electronics work force in Hong Kong, then, is very similar to that of the industry in other parts of both the developing and the developed world (Siegel and Markoff, 1985; Henderson, 1989a).

Let us now examine the extent of foreign control over the territory's electronics industry. From the data in Table 7, it is clear that throughout the period 1971-87, electronics has received more direct foreign investment than any other manufacturing sector. Indeed, by 1987 electronics was receiving nearly four times as much direct investment as the next most significant sector, construction. In spite of this relative growth in foreign direct investment in electronics, it has not resulted in significant job creation. On the contrary, while aggregate employment resulting from foreign investment has remained fairly stable, or even increased, proportionately it has declined relative to other sectors. Thus, while in 1971 foreign investment in electronics created 52.7 percent of all manufacturing employment created by foreign direct investment, this had dropped to 39.0 percent by 1976, and to 30.1 percent by 1983. By 1987, though, it had increased again to 37.3 percent (see Table 7). If for the sake of comparison we look at the territory's principal manufacturing sector (in terms of employment and value of exports), and until 1985 the second most important recipient of foreign direct investment, clothing and textiles, we find a very different picture. While foreign investment in textiles has been proportionately reduced by two-thirds between 1973 and 1987, aggregate employment created by that investment more than doubled over the same period. In proportion to total manufacturing employment created by foreign investment, though, it has remained relatively stable, fluctuating only between 19.4 and 21.9 percent over the 1971-83 period (derived from Table 7). The significance of these changes in the electronics sector will be discussed later in the paper; however, it is interesting to note here that the data in Table 7 may suggest that capital deepening has occurred in the foreign-owned electronics com-

Table 7a. Foreign Direct Investment in Hong Kong's Manufacturing Industry 1971-78

	1971			1972			1973			1974			1975			1976			1977			1978		
	A	B	C	A	B	C	A	B	C	A	B	C	A	B	C	A	B	C	A	B	C	A	B	C
Electronics	61	34.9	29,773	60	31.7	29,122	51	21.8	31,538	56	35.6	34,656	61	34.7	24,146	65	30.7	24,552	61	26.1	29,620	68	24.8	29,803
Clothing, Textiles	65	21.2	10,942	68	20.8	12,673	51	22.0	10,676	61	13.7	12,054	71	15.0	12,372	82	13.7	13,539	87	15.8	17,176	95	15.0	17,748
Chemicals	5	1.5	80	5	1.3	154	8	8.9	608	11	5.8	633	11	5.7	639	12	13.1	739	13	11.9	587	19	12.2	817
Electrical Products	6	2.1	1,145	10	2.3	1,337	8	3.6	1,719	11	5.7	1,769	14	5.7	3,847	18	5.0	4,203	21	10.2	4,918	25	9.7	5,217
Printing, Publishing	5	3.0	763	5	3.7	910	6	3.1	1,151	8	3.7	1,207	8	3.6	1,182	8	3.1	1,182	9	7.1	1,777	10	6.7	1,857
Watches, Clocks	12	3.4	3,186	13	3.2	4,032	12	13.2	4,649	17	10.9	4,643	20	11.1	5,391	23	9.8	5,577	25	6.8	4,894	27	6.5	5,024
Metal Products	10	2.6	1,852	9	2.2	725	9	1.8	928	12	3.0	1,071	12	2.9	1,434	17	2.9	1,815	26	4.8	2,215	30	4.7	2,215
Toys	12	3.8	7,034	9	3.6	9,241	8	5.3	5,856	7	3.5	5,857	8	3.4	4,412	8	3.0	4,412	10	3.1	5,392	11	3.2	5,742
Food	6	0.7	215	7	6.8	1,115	5	4.2	1,184	6	3.6	1,206	6	3.5	1,533	8	3.9	1,657	14	3.7	1,632	17	5.8	1,967
Constr'n.	NA	NA	NA	5	2.2	226	6	2.3	545	4	3.1	545	4	3.1	333	5	2.8	453	5	1.7	613	5	1.6	613
Others	60	25.8	1,529	58	22.2	1,735	51	13.8	1,342	54	11.2	1,697	55	11.3	4,318	65	12.0	4,871	65	8.8	5,943	79	9.8	7,153
Totals	242	100	56,519	249	100	61,270	221	100	61,216	247	100	66,338	271	100	59,602	339	100	63,000	386	100	74,758	386	100	78,330

A = Number of establishments

B = Proportion of total foreign manufacturing investment by sector (percent);

C = Number of employees

Sources: 1971-75: Hong Kong Department of Industry

1976-78: Hong Kong Department of Trade, Industry and Customs, *Annual Statistical Reviews*

Table 7b. Foreign Direct Investment in Hong Kong's Manufacturing Industry 1979-86

	1979			1980			1981			1982			1983			1984			1985			1986		
	A	B	C	A	B	C	A	B	C	A	B	C	A	B	C	A	B	C	A	B	C	A	B	C
Electronics	72	23.0	30,891	75	21.6	28,889	57	38.0	27,676	64	36.5	29,114	78	35.9	29,630	82	35.5	34,824	99	36.1	33,731	115	32.1	32,254
Clothing, Textiles	100	15.7	18,553	105	16.3	22,089	87	12.4	19,242	95	11.6	20,234	103	11.5	21,946	89	9.7	17,205	105	10.2	19,737	105	8.6	16,625
Chemicals	22	13.2	1,144	23	12.0	1,167	21	7.2	1,312	23	10.5	1,445	24	6.6	1,381	23	7.0	1,625	26	6.8	1,676	27	4.9	2,004
Electrical Products	29	9.0	5,587	34	10.6	6,094	29	7.5	8,878	32	6.3	8,333	34	6.1	8,546	38	8.0	9,569	39	7.7	9,619	32	6.2	6,991
Printing, Publishing	12	6.7	1,982	12	6.2	2,029	11	2.6	1,538	11	2.4	1,532	12	2.4	1,560	15	5.8	2,018	15	5.7	2,092	18	7.3	2,202
Watches, Clocks	33	7.3	6,267	41	7.1	7,228	35	5.7	8,864	41	5.1	9,125	47	5.0	8,778	30	4.8	4,086	35	5.1	4,352	32	5.1	4,142
Metal Products	32	4.5	2,385	34	4.1	2,478	30	3.6	2,337	33	3.32	2,337	33	3.6	2,900	44	4.8	3,651	42	4.7	3,724	42	4.5	5,361
Toys	12	2.9	6,058	11	2.6	5,853	13	3.3	6,337	13	1.8	4,738	13	1.6	4,738	11	0.9	3,090	12	1.0	3,190	12	1.1	3,347
Food	17	5.3	2,376	18	4.8	2,384	19	5.5	3,169	23	5.1	3,169	23	5.9	3,667	19	7.2	3,559	21	7.0	3,607	20	5.2	3,658
Constr'n	5	1.5	613	5	1.4	613	10	2.7	985	12	10.5	985	13	10.1	1,495	9	7.6	1,429	11	7.4	1,503	8	13.6	1,059
Others	93	10.9	7,526	102	13.4	8,476	83	11.5	9,801	91	11.1	11,476	105	11.3	11,495	82	8.7	7,977	91	8.3	8,349	98	11.4	8,783
Totals	427	100	83,382	460	100	87,282	395	100	90,229	438	100	92,803	486	100	96,046	442	100	89,033	495	100	91,580	509	100	86,426

A = Number of establishments

B = Proportion of total foreign manufacturing investment by sector (percent)

C = Number of employees

Sources: 1979-83: Hong Kong Department of Trade, Industry and Customs, *Annual Statistical Reviews*. 1984-87: Report on the Survey of Overseas Investment in Hong Kong Manufacturing Industries.

Table 8. Foreign Control of the Electronics Industry
in Hong Kong: 1972-87

	Number of Establishments	Proportion Foreign Owned (%)	Total Workforce	Proportion Working in Foreign-Owned Establishments (%)	Average Size of All Establishments	Average Size of Foreign-Owned Establishments
1972	280	21.4	41,056	72.4	146.6	488.1
1974	382	14.7	54,883	63.1	143.7	618.9
1975	387	15.8	41,979	57.5	108.5	395.8
1977	711	8.6	70,188	42.2	98.7	485.6
1978	793	8.6	73,736	40.4	93.0	438.3
1980	1,104	6.8	89,839	32.2	81.4	385.2
1981	1,216	4.7	88,921	31.1	73.1	485.5
1982	1,305	4.9	85,946	33.9	65.9	454.9
1983	1,351	5.8	94,631	31.3	70.1	379.9
1984	1,441	5.7	106,413	32.7	73.9	424.7
1985	1,284	7.7	81,995	41.1	63.9	340.7
1986	1,090	11.0	75,178	42.9	69.0	280.5
1987	1,180	10.5	78,562	48.2	66.6	305.3

Sources: As for Tables 6 and 7.

panies in Hong Kong, at least vis a vis their counterparts in the textile industry.

While it is clear that the bulk of foreign direct investment in manufacturing has been increasingly directed towards the electronics sector, to what extent is the electronics industry as a whole controlled by foreign interests? By comparing the data presented in Tables 6 and 7, it is possible to develop an estimate of the situation. Table 8 displays this estimate. It shows that in terms of factory ownership and the proportion of the work force which those factories employ, foreign control of the Hong Kong electronics industry declined significantly during the 15 years from the early 1970s to the late 1980s. This evidence of decline in foreign control must be tempered, however, with the recognition that in terms of investment, foreign control has probably remained fairly stable.[10] Equally significant about the data in Table 8, however, is that as noted elsewhere for South Korea and Taiwan (Henderson, 1989a: Chapter 4), it demonstrates the substantial growth in Hong Kong of a locally-owned electronics complex. The growth of this complex is emphasized, additionally, by the persistent decline in the average size of all factories relative to the much larger and relatively stable average size of the foreign-owned factories (Table 8; see Sit, et al., 1979, on the very small size of the majority of Hong Kong-owned electronics factories). The development of a locally-owned electronics production complex in Hong Kong has been significant for the territory's emergence as a core of the East Asian regional division of labor in semiconductor production. Consequently, this issue will be discussed later in the paper.

While the broad parameters of foreign control of the Hong Kong electronics industry have been noted, it is necessary to explore the national origin of that control. Relevant data for this purpose are assembled in Table 9. If foreign control can be gauged in terms of indices such as the number of factories owned, the proportion of investment, and the proportion of the work force employed, then the U.S. and Japan dominate the foreign-owned sector of manufacturing, particularly electronics. Between them, they supplied around 75 percent of foreign direct investment in the manufacturing sector in 1981 and 1984, though this had fallen to 63 percent by 1987. Additionally they provided 66, 56 and 60 percent of jobs in the foreign-owned sector in those years respectively (Table 9). The presence of U.S. and Japanese business interests in the electronics industry has been even more pronounced. In 1981, they provided 97.2 percent of foreign direct investment, and 91.1 percent of foreign sector jobs in the industry. The equivalent proportions for 1984 were 93.6 and 71.3 percent and for 1987, 94.1 and 64.0 respectively. Also of significance is that in 1987, while the U.S. and Japan owned only six percent of Hong Kong's electronics factories, together they employed nearly 31 percent of the industry's total

Table 9. Foreign Investment in the Electronics and Manufacturing Industries of Hong Kong Country Sources, 1981, 1984 and 1987

| | 1981 | | | | | | 1984 | | | | | | 1987 | | | | | |
| | A | | B | | C | | A | | B | | C | | A | | B | | C | |
	M	E	M	E	M	E	M	E	M	E	M	E	M	E	M	E	M	E
U.S.	111	30	43.7	63.6	41,227	19,176	124	43	53.7	83.3	39,708	21,397	163	58	44.0	73.7	38,276	18,661
Japan	111	43	31.6	33.6	23,066	3,793	117	14	21.0	10.3	18,574	3,891	134	26	19.0	10.4	22,635	5,559
U.K.	43	4	6.9	1.4	9,909	2,232	52	9	6.9	5.7	13,407	4,595	55	8	5.9	2.1	13,401	4,981
Netherlands	7	2	2.7	NA	2,872	NA	10	2	2.8	NA	4,462	NA	11	7	2.8	5.3	4,732	3,797
Switzerland	20	-	2.8	-	3,314	-	19	2	2.5	NA	3,547	NA	23	1	1.7	-	1,832	-
Denmark	4	-	2.3	-	564	-	2	-	NA	-	NA	-	4	-	0.7	-	644	-
Australia	21	-	2.2	-	2,672	-	25	1	1.6	NA	2,927	NA	18	2	1.2	-	3,188	-
Singapore	15	2	1.8	NA	1,818	NA	18	NA	2.1	NA	2,286	NA	22	1	1.2	-	3,332	-
Taiwan	23	2	1.4	NA	2,775	NA	17	NA	0.9	NA	1,416	NA	12	1	0.4	-	757	-
France	5	-	1.1	-	595	-	5	-	0.7	-	541	-	8	-	0.5	-	842	-
Philippines	4	-	0.7	-	1,230	-	7	-	2.6	-	1,146	-	7	2	1.7	-	1,310	-
W Germany	21	-	0.5	-	2,120	-	33	3	1.0	0.1	3,285	243	32	5	1.1	0.4	4,075	564
Thailand	11	-	0.5	-	780	-	12	-	0.4	-	772	-	15	-	0.6	-	1,439	-
Others	42	5	2.0	NA	4,554	NA	61	21	2.2	0.6	11,270	5,328	114	22	19.2	8.1	18,917	6,861
Totals	438	62	100	100	97,496	25,201*	502	95	98.4	100	103,341	35,454	618	133	100	100	115,380	40,463
	391†				90,059†						89,033†	34,824†	541†	124†			101,455†	37,853

Sources: *Reports on the Surveys of Overseas Investment in Hong Kong's Manufacturing Industry*, 1981, 1984 and 1987. Hong Kong Department of Trade, Industry and Customs.

A = Number of establishments; B = Proportion of total foreign investment (percent); C = Number of employees
M = All manufacturing; E = Electronics
* Denotes the actual number; † Underestimate due to unavailable data.
Discrepancy reflects double counting occurring when more than one overseas source invested in the same company.

Table 10. Market Share of Electronics Exports from Hong Kong 1976-87 (percent by value)

Market	1976	1977	1978	1979	1980	1981	1982	1983	1984	1985	1986	1987
U.S.	49.9	48.4	43.7	36.0	38.1	44.4	46.3	50.5	47.4	45.5	44.0	38.2
West Germany	14.5	12.8	13.9	14.2	11.7	8.6	7.2	6.8	5.8	5.3	6.9	6.9
U.K.	4.5	4.4	9.0	10.2	8.2	8.4	6.1	5.7	7.2	5.2	4.7	5.4
China					2.6	4.1	4.7	4.0	9.8	15.1	9.8	12.3
Netherlands	3.0	3.0	3.9	4.0	3.3	3.2	3.1	3.0	2.6	2.6	2.9	3.8
France	0.9	1.4	2.0	2.6	3.0	2.7	2.3	2.0	1.5		2.2	3.4
Singapore	2.0	2.1	2.4	3.0	3.1	1.5	1.6	1.7	2.1	2.1	2.6	3.3
Japan	1.6	1.3	1.4	2.2	1.7	1.5	1.7	2.2	2.3	2.1	2.7	2.8
Rest of the World	23.6	26.4	23.7	27.9	28.3	25.6	27.0	24.1	16.1	22.1	24.2	23.9
Totals	100.0	100.0	100.0	100.0	100.0	100.0	100.0	100.0	100.0	100.0	100.0	100.0

Sources: *Trade Statistics*, Hong Kong Department of Census and Statistics, various years. Adapted from Hong Kong Productivity Centre (1984, Table 1.5: 92). 1982-87: *Hong Kong Trade Review*, Hong Kong Trade Development Council.

work force. In fact, U.S. companies alone employed nearly 24 percent of the work force (see Tables 6 and 9).

Comparing the data for 1981, 1984 and 1987 (Table 9) it is clear that while the Japanese presence relative to other foreign interests has declined in manufacturing and particularly in electronics (in terms of investment, though not the work force, at least in electronics),[11] the U.S. presence generally has increased, or at least remained stable. For the manufacturing sector as a whole, U.S. investment, for instance, increased from about 44 to 54 percent of all foreign direct investment between 1981 and 1984, though by 1987 had dropped again to 44 percent. In the electronics sector U.S. investment increased from about 64 to 83 percent of the foreign direct totals between 1981 and 1984 and by 1987 amounted to about 74 percent. Of particular note for our later discussion, however, is that although U.S. investment in the electronics industry more than tripled between 1981 and 1987 (from U.S. S207.3 million to U.S. S707.1 million at current prices[12]), it did not result in an increase in employment (see Table 9). Although these data should be treated with caution, they would seem to imply that U.S. electronics firms in Hong Kong may be involved in a process of capital deepening, and hence, presumably, an upgrading of the technological sophistication of their labor processes. As with our earlier comment in this vein, this issue will be discussed in a subsequent section.

Before investigating the semiconductor branch of the Hong Kong electronics sector, the destination of electronics exports from the territory should be indicated. Table 10 provides data on the share of exports consumed by Hong Kong's principal electronics markets. While the U.S. was, and remains, the dominant market for Hong Kong's electronics products with an average annual share of 44.4 percent (1976-87), the principal EEC markets (U.K., West Germany, France and the Netherlands) are also particularly important, with an annual average of 21.3 percent over the 1976-87 period. Rather like the structure of the Hong Kong manufacturing sector generally, and the concentration of foreign control over its electronics industry, the territory's markets for its electronics products are narrowly based, with an average of nearly two-thirds of its exports being consumed by the U.S. and the EEC annually.[13]

Two items of subsidiary interest appear from the data in Table 10. The first is the very small export market for Hong Kong's electronics products constituted by Japan (an annual average of only two percent, 1976-87). These data suggest not only that local electronics manufacturers have difficulty penetrating the Japanese market, but also that Japanese companies who manufacture in the territory produce mainly for the world, not the Japanese market. Second, the emergence of China as the second largest national export market since the mid-1980s should be marked. While this development is consistent with China's re-emergence as, in effect, Hong Kong's domestic market, it should be remembered that it is unlikely that China can be anything other than a market for technologically low-grade electronic products for the foreseeable future. At this point, we turn directly to the development of the Hong Kong semiconductor industry.

Semiconductors

Fairchild Semiconductor, the "mother" of Silicon Valley, was the first semiconductor firm in the world to seek to reduce its production costs by internationalizing the most labor-intensive part of its production process, assembly. As mentioned earlier, Hong Kong became its first international location in 1961. While I shall deal with the determinants of semiconductor production in Hong Kong in the next section, it is necessary here to bear in mind that Fairchild moved offshore in the context of substantial Japanese price competition in transistor markets. Japanese manufacturers were able to undercut their U.S. competitors because of their access to cheap domestic labor. The response of U.S. manufacturers took one of two forms. Like Fairchild, they either moved assembly offshore in search of unskilled labor even cheaper than that to which Japanese companies had access, or they opted for automated assembly in the U.S. At that time (late 1950s to early 1960s) semiconductor technology was subject to rapid cycles of innovation and hence short production runs, and re-programmable assembly technology was not yet available. As a result, automated assembly proved uneconomic and firms who opted for that "solution," such as Philco, suffered disastrous consequences (Grunwald and Flamm, 1985: 69-70). The "Fairchild solution," however, proved highly successful, and as a result, U.S. merchant producers in rapid succession began to invest in assembly facilities in various parts of East Asia. At the high point of the U.S. semiconductor presence in Hong Kong (early- to mid-1970s), eight companies had assembly plants which probably employed around 15,000 workers.[14] Fairchild alone employed over 4,500 people at that time (UNCTC, 1986: 383-89).

By the late 1960s, Hong Kong had become the principal Asian assembler of semiconductors for the U.S. market. By 1972 however, it had begun to be overtaken by South Korea and Singapore. By 1983 its exports to the U.S. market had slipped to only 1.2 percent of the total for the developing countries of East Asia, falling behind even Indonesia, which, with only two plants had the least developed semiconductor industry in the region in 1983 (see Table 11).

This relative decline in exports to the U.S., however, is not evidence of a decline in the industry itself. On the contrary, the data collected in Table 12 imply the opposite. This may be circumstantial evidence of an

Table 11. Principal Sources of Assembled Semiconductor Devices
Imported into the United States
under Tariff Items 806.30 and 807.00

	Hong Kong %	Indonesia %	Korea %	Malaysia %	Philippines %	Singapore %	Taiwan %	Thailand %	All Asia ($000,000)*
1969	49.2		22.9			9.8	14.8		228
1970	44.6		23.2			17.9	8.9		254
1971	32.7		30.9			23.6	12.7		270
1972	25.4		26.9			37.3	10.4		452
1973	19.4		23.6	8.3	1.4	33.3	12.5		740
1974	17.1		22.9	21.4	2.9	22.9	12.9		977
1975	11.8		17.1	30.3	5.3	26.3	7.9		858
1976	13.1		20.7	25.6	7.3	28.0	7.3		1,240
1977	8.0	1.1	21.8	27.6	6.9	24.1	9.2	1.1	1,567
1978	6.8	1.1	17.0	34.1	9.1	22.7	5.7	3.4	1,948
1979	4.6	2.3	13.8	33.3	11.5	23.0	4.6	2.3	2,212
1980	4.5	2.3	10.2	34.1	15.9	25.0	4.5	3.4	2,518
1981	3.4	2.3	9.2	34.5	18.4	23.0	4.6	4.6	2,536
1982	3.4	2.2	8.9	36.0	20.2	19.1	4.5	3.4	2,800
1983	1.2	2.4	16.5	36.5	21.2	12.9	4.7	4.7	2,876

* All values in constant 1983 dollars
Source: Calculated by Scott (1987, Table 4: 146) from Table 3-7 in Grunwald and Flamm (1985).

Table 12. Hong Kong: Exports of Semiconductors,
1974-1987 (Thousands of U.S. Dollars)

	Domestic exports		Re-exports	
	ICs	Transistors and diodes	Mounted ICs	Transistors and diodes
1974	46,640	78,819	2,230	14,257
1975	32,373	51,440	2,582	13,307
1976	56,923	75,112	5,564	29,745
1977	54,388	82,774	11,235	30,119
1978	63,086	89,736	41,432	32,688
1979	89,329	87,106	82,458	59,216
1980	101,754	125,34	110,136	94,932
1981	113,840	98,635	132,359	189,084
1982	89,098	90,415	140,810	102,932
1983	82,771	62,698	273,615	92,534
1984	132,131	67,792	487,209	116,142
1985	106,918	71,493	403,414	103,581
1986	82,276	77,919	498,398	121,620
1987	99,513	103,360	811,105	168,633

Sources: *Hong Kong Review of Overseas Trade* (various editions).
Data for 1974-81 adapted from UNCTC (1986, Table VIII. 1: 385).

alteration in the types of labor processes that have emerged in the territory since the late 1970s, such that less *assembly* work is done there relative to other parts of the region.

It was earlier suggested that U.S. companies operating in the developing countries of East Asia in recent years, had been in effect diverting larger proportions of their investment in assembly processes to the "periphery" of the regional division of labor, while investment in more capital-intensive, technologically advanced labor processes (such as final testing) had tended to locate in the "gang of four," particularly in Singapore and Hong Kong. While some of the reasons for this phenomenon have been explored elsewhere (Henderson, 1989a: Chapter 4) and shall be examined specifically in relation to Hong Kong in the next section, it is necessary here to convey some sense of the nature of semiconductor manufacturing operations which currently exist in the territory.

First, Hong Kong is no longer a production site which specializes in the *assembly* of semiconductors. As the data collected in Table 12 show, the re-export of ICs and transistors/diodes imported into Hong Kong already assembled, now substantially exceeds the export of devices assembled in the territory. While a proportion of re-exports may be because Hong Kong is the regional marketing headquarters of a number of U.S. semiconductor firms (specifically Motorola, Sprague and Zilog), and hence could be used merely as a trans-shipment point, it is likely that the data in part reflect the emergence of the territory as a center for the final testing of a variety of ICs and transistors assembled elsewhere in the region.

Table 13 indicates the type of labor processes operated in 1986 by Hong Kong's semiconductor manufacturers. If one compares the situation in Hong Kong with the labor processes in other parts of the East Asian regional division of labor evident in Table 2, it is clear that Hong Kong probably has a higher concentration of testing functions than anywhere else in the area, with the exception of Singapore. All foreign-owned plants in the territory incorporate testing facilities, and three of them (Motorola, Fairchild and Sprague) possess no assembly function, opting to concentrate on testing alone.

In addition to the emergence of Hong Kong as a regional testing center, it is interesting to note that six foreign-owned companies (three U.S., two Japanese and one British) have set up customer-related design centers in the territory (in two cases, Zilog and Oki without also having manufacturing facilities), and as already mentioned, three U.S. companies now have their Asian regional headquarters there as well.

Finally, we simply need to call attention to the emergence of a locally-owned semiconductor industry currently consisting of seven firms. One is a fully-owned subsidiary of the Chinese Government's National Light

Table 13. Semiconductor Manufacturers in Hong Kong, 1986

Company	Country of Ownership	Labor Processes	Approximate Employment
Motorola	U.S.	d, t, r	750
National Semiconductor	U.S.	a, t	1,000
Fairchild	U.S.	t	100
Siliconix	U.S.	d*, a, t	550
Teledyne	U.S.	a, t	200
Sprague	U.S.	t, r	200
Commodore	U.S.	a, t	200
Microsemiconductor	U.S.	a, t	100
Zilog	U.S.	d, r	100
Hitachi	Japan	d, a, t	200
Sanyo	Japan	a, t	200
Oki	Japan	d	20
Philips	Netherlands	a, t	500
Ferranti*	U.K.	d, a, t	500
Hua Ko	PRC	d, w, a, t	300
Elcap	Hong Kong	w, a, t	300
RCL	Hong Kong	w, a, t	200
Micro Electronics	Hong Kong	w, a, t	400
Semiconductor Devices	Hong Kong	a, t	900
Swire Technologies	Hong Kong	a, t	500
Century Electronics	Hong Kong	a	N/A

Key: d - design center   w - wafer fabrication
      a - assembly   t - final testing
      r - regional headquarters
* Joint-venture with Hong Kong firm

Sources: Interviews; Company Reports, Hong Kong Productivity Centre, *Electronics Bulletin* (various issues); *Global Electronics* (formerly *Global Electronics Information Newsletter*) (various issues); UNCTC (1986).

Industries Corporation (*Asian Wall Street Journal Weekly*, August 2, 1982), and operates a design center as well as having wafer fabrication capability. Three others fabricate, assemble, and test semiconductors.

The significance of these locally-owned developments combined with the other changes described above will be addressed in the next section. It is to that section and hence our analysis of the reasons why Hong Kong has emerged as a "core" of the regional division of labor that we now turn.

The Making of a Regional Core

When seeking to understand the emergence and operation of an industrial branch at a given location (or, indeed, economic development generally), it was important to recognize that those processes that were significant determinants originally may, and often do, alter and develop a different relative significance over time. Conversely, processes that had little or no significance initially, sometimes emerge and become important determinants of the future development of the phenomenon. Here, then, we will be concerned not merely with those processes that led to the emergence of the branch in Hong Kong. We shall also be concerned with the way in which those processes have altered (or been formed) historically in the intervening 25 years, to give rise to a production system which plays a different role in the international division of labor than was initially the case.

Following one of the methodological leads which emerge from realist analysis (cf. Sayer, 1984) we begin our account of the emergence of Hong Kong as a regional core of semiconductor production by focusing on the processes that have been internally necessary to this development: those associated with both the production and realization of surplus value in the semiconductor branch.

Markets

We begin with the influence of markets on the development of Hong Kong as a regional core of semiconductor production, not because the "realization issue" is central with regard to the prospects for development. Indeed, I have explicitly argued against this idea insofar as it has held sway in the forms of dependency theory associated with Frank, Amin, etc. (Henderson, 1986b). Rather, the decision to begin with markets stems, in the Hong Kong case, more from convenience than from its significance in the theoretical system. By this I mean that the nature and structure of markets historically have been of much less significance for the origin and development of semiconductor production in Hong Kong, than they have been, for instance, in Scotland and other European locations (Henderson, 1987). As a result, in the case of Hong Kong, they can be briefly dealt with. As shown below, however, the question of markets may have greater import for the future development of semiconductor production in the territory, than it has had in the past.

The first point to be emphasized is that U.S. semiconductor manufacturers did not invest in production facilities in Hong Kong in order to penetrate the local or regional (including Japanese) markets. Those markets then (1960s) were either almost non-existent or, in the case of Japan, were closed off to foreign producers behind high tariff barriers (Okimoto, et al., 1984; Grunwald and Flamm, 1985; UNCTC, 1986). Though regional markets have become more significant in recent years, particularly for re-exports, the U.S. and the EEC were, and largely remain, the *raison d'etre*, in terms of markets, for both electronics (see Table 10) and semiconductor production in the territory. In the case of IC exports in 1981, for instance, the U.S. and the EEC together constituted 79.6 percent of Hong Kong's export market (UNCTC, 1986).

If the realization of the surplus value generated by the territory's semiconductor industry has been dependent historically on markets at some distance from the production site, what is likely to be the situation in the future? While regional markets have taken on a growing, if still limited significance for Hong Kong's semiconductor industry, of particular note is the increase in the proportion of sales to China (see Table 10 for electronics generally). At present the Chinese market is particularly important for the four locally/PRC-owned producers (Hua Ko, RCL, Elcap and Micro Electronics). Should the Chinese government's plans for economic expansion and industrialization be successful, then one would expect the Chinese market (which, after the transfer of power from the British colonial regime in 1997, will become formally Hong Kong's domestic market) to become increasingly significant for foreign as well as local producers in Hong Kong. The problem for the territory's semiconductor and electronics industries, however, particularly in light of certain structural changes in the world economy, might be whether the Chinese economy can develop quickly enough to absorb an increasing proportion of the output. For the foreseeable future, for a variety of economic and political reasons, Chinese development must remain an open question.

Labor Processes, Labor Power, and the State

If U.S. semiconductor investment in Hong Kong was and is driven more by concern with the production of surplus value than by its realization, we need to examine and assess the relative causal weights of the factors that brought semiconductor firms to the territory in the first place. We also need to assess the significance of changes in the original factors, as well as the emergence of new factors that have helped to maintain the presence, but alter the nature of the operation, of those firms that continue to produce in Hong Kong.

This section explores the inter-related determinants that have emerged historically, at both the level of the world system and internal to Hong Kong itself, such that the territory over the past quarter century has come to be seen by semiconductor firms as a "good place" to do business. Clearly many of the social, economic and political features of Hong Kong that have encouraged investment in semiconductor production are the same as those that have encouraged investment in manufacturing industry generally (and other industries as well), and thus have helped create Hong Kong as one of the world's most economically successful NICs. Although this is not the place to provide a complete account of the territory's economic development, it will be necessary to discuss a number of the elements of such an account.

At the time of initial semiconductor investment in the early 1960s, the legacy of Hong Kong's historical -- indeed traditional -- role in the world economy meant that the territory possessed many of the contingent factors which many theorists (i.e., Frobel, et al., 1980) regard as important for export-oriented industrialization based on foreign investment. Hong Kong's traditional role as a British colonial entrepôt helped ensure that the territory was a free port. As a result the import and export of the materials necessary for the production of manufactured commodities were not subject to customs duties and no constraints were placed on the repatriation of profits. This freedom from state levies on surplus value may have been an important inducement to prospective industrial investors at a time when other East Asian countries did not possess the export processing/ free trade zones (with their liberal fiscal arrangements) that they were subsequently to develop.[15]

Hong Kong's free port status not only meant that foreign investors could profit from the absence of fiscal and other state restrictions, but they could also take advantage of the relatively well developed transport and communications infrastructure which again was usually part of the historical legacy of performing an entrepôt function.

Some commentators (e.g. Reidel, 1972) have mentioned another historically contingent factor, an English-speaking population, which they believe may have initially attracted foreign manufacturers to Hong Kong rather than elsewhere in the region. Unfortunately, this factor cannot be given much weight in our explanation when one recognizes that less than 25 percent of Hong Kong's population speak any English at all (Bolton and

Luke, 1986). Other than the benefits which accrued to Hong Kong because of the legacy of its entrepôt function, there were few contingent factors which marked off the territory from its potential competitors in the region, as a location particularly suitable for foreign-owned, export-oriented, commodity production.

What then of the locational determinants which arise from the social relations internal to manufacturing, and essential to it, as part of the process of capitalist commodity production? Elsewhere these "internally necessary relations" have been identified as being sited within the valorization process, and hence associated with the nature and organization of the labor process and of the form and cost of labor power (Henderson, 1989a: Chapter 2). From our earlier discussion, and drawing on some of the more "orthodox" accounts of the internationalization process, we know that the concern to reduce costs in the face of Japanese competition was perhaps the single most important reason why U.S. semiconductor companies moved their assembly functions offshore. In the 1960s, however, there was little to distinguish Hong Kong as a source of cheap unskilled labor, from the other areas of the region that were potentially sites for U.S. investment. Indeed, wages in Hong Kong were possibly slightly higher than many other parts of the region.

What did set Hong Kong aside from its potential competitors, however, was not the cheapness of its labor per se, but a combination of relative cheapness with a particular *quality* of labor. By the early 1960s, Hong Kong, alone among its Asian counterparts, with the exception of Japan, had already produced a work force habituated to the social and personal demands of manufacturing labor processes for over ten years. As a result of the combination of world system factors discussed earlier in this paper, Hong Kong, via the development of its textile industry, had gained a head start in the (newly) industrializing stakes.[16] As such, it could provide prospective manufacturers with a labor force well on the way to being culturally proletarianized and hence already socially adjusted to the regimes and rigors of factory labor.[17] Though empirical evidence to support this contention is lacking, it seems likely that Hong Kong, unlike its competitors, was able to deliver a work force which could be quickly trained for electronics assembly work, and could be induced to operate effectively and productively (without high rates of absenteeism, for instance) within a relatively short period of time.[18]

If cost and quality of manual labor were the principal initial "draw-cards" which Hong Kong possessed vis-a-vis its neighbors, what were the factors which ensured the continuation of foreign and local investment, not only in semiconductors and electronics, but also across the territory's manufacturing base? There seem to have been four inter-related factors.

First, although labor costs rose consistently through the early 1980s, they were maintained at levels below what they might otherwise have been, in part by indirect subsidies from both the Hong Kong and Chinese governments. Second, the quality of the labor power in the electronics industry was associated with an historic aversion to militant action by the local trade union movement. The third factor which is particularly important for in explaining the recent technological upgrading of the semiconductor industry, was Hong Kong's ability to deliver highly skilled technical and engineering labor at a cost far below that which would be necessary in, say, the U.S., Western Europe or Japan. The final factor was the benefits, in terms of the local sourcing of components and materials and the availability of skilled workers, which accrued to foreign firms from the emergence of the local electronics and semiconductor production complex. The remainder of this paper will assess the role of these factors in the emergence of Hong Kong as a regional core of semiconductor production.

Subsidizing Labor Costs

The ideologues of neo-classical economics have argued that the NICs of East Asia, particularly Hong Kong, have been economically successful because they have been relatively free from state interference with the "normal" working of market processes (Friedman and Friedman, 1981; Rabushka, 1979). Hong Kong economists, from the first account of the territory's economic "miracle" (Szczepanik, 1958) to more recent expositions (Lin, et al., 1980; Cheng, 1985), have repeated these claims, as have the respective governments themselves (particularly the Hong Kong government with its persistent use of the oxymoron, "positive non-interventionism" in reference to its economic policies). Unfortunately for the economic orthodoxy, it is now becoming clear that far from the East Asian "gang of four" being shining examples of what free-market economics can do, they turn out, on closer inspection, to be examples of state-led economic development. This counter-argument is now reasonably well-accepted (except by the Chicago ideologues and their acolytes), at least as far as the development of South Korea, Taiwan (see Browett, 1986; Harris, 1987; Gold, 1986; Deyo, 1987) and Singapore (see Lim, 1983; Harris, 1987: 60-67) are concerned. The relationship between state policies and the economic development of Hong Kong, however, is less well known (see, for instance, Harris, 1987: 54-60).

While the Hong Kong government has not intervened directly in the capital market or in funding R & D, as the Taiwanese and South Korean governments have done (Hamilton, 1983; Schmitz, 1984; Browett, 1986; Harris, 1987; Cummings, 1987; Koo, 1987), it has intervened directly in the labor market and indirectly in both the capital and labor markets. Its intervention in the capital market has taken the form of very low corporate and personal taxation (both currently standing at 15.5 percent maximum). These low tax rates (which remain lower than other states in the region; see BBDO, 1987), given the government's substantial expenditure on education and welfare have been achieved only because of its historic ability to generate a high proportion of its revenues from non-taxation sources. In fact, from 1949-50 to 1975-76, non-taxation revenues averaged over 34 percent of total government revenues (Schiffer, 1983: 23). By far the largest source of non-taxation revenues has been the sale of leases on government-owned land, and in Hong Kong, the government owns over 95 percent of *all* land. Its subsidies to private capital, by means of low taxation, have come about, in large measure, because, perhaps unique among capitalist societies, land in Hong Kong is nationalized.

The Hong Kong government has intervened in the labor market directly, by means of its extensive educational provision at secondary and tertiary levels (and hence the "extended" reproduction of labor power), but indirectly and particularly by its contributions to the "social wage." These contributions have largely taken the form of welfare provision, and especially of low-cost housing. Since 1954 the Hong Kong government has developed the second-largest public housing system in the world (in terms of the proportion of the population housed), housing about 45 percent of the total population, and over 80 percent of the territory's working class (Castells, 1986; S.Y. Ho, 1986). In addition, the government organizes what is in effect a cartel to control the prices of basic foodstuffs such as rice and vegetables.

Paradoxically, the Chinese government from the beginning (1949) has helped subsidize the wages of Hong Kong workers. It has done this by supplying the bulk of the territory's food requirements (rice, poultry, meat, vegetables) at "administered" prices, that is, at prices significantly below those on the open market. In addition, it has provided cheap clothing (far below the cost of imported or domestically produced items) for the territory's working class via its numerous retail outlets in the territory. In an important, as yet unpublished paper, Jonathan Schiffer has calculated that "non-market" forces (i.e., the combined efforts of the Hong Kong and Chinese governments) subsidize the household expenditure of Hong Kong's working class population to the tune of 50.2 percent! (Schiffer, 1983, Table 4: 19). Without such subsidies, manual wages would undoubtedly have risen faster in the territory than has been the case.

Intervention in both capital and labor markets has had the effect of reducing production costs and thus acting as a significant inducement to investment by both foreign and local manufacturers. While it is in one sense difficult to distinguish the determinants of the cost of labor power from the determinants of its features when it is converted, via the labor process, into concrete labor, this distinction must be made. Consequently we now move to the question of how the quality of the labor force (that is, of concrete labor), has been reproduced over the years subsequent to initial semiconductor investment.

Reproducing the Quality of Labor

It was argued previously that the early social adaptation of Hong Kong workers to factory labor was probably a key factor in the initial attraction of U.S. semiconductor manufacturers to the territory. The quality of Hong Kong labor was based not merely on the fact that workers could perform the routines of assembly work efficiently and quickly, but also because they tended to do so with seemingly few expressions of resistance, either organized or individualistic.[19]   That this situation has remained substantially true to the present (with the exception of the anti-colonial riots of 1966-67) requires explanation.

While a comprehensive explanation of this phenomenon would have to take into account the processes of legitimation and control within the colonial state and the mechanisms of ideological transmission, as well as the production of workers' consent within the work place (cf. Burawoy, 1979),[20] this is not the place to address those questions (but see Henderson, 1989b). For the purposes of the current discussion, however, we focus on the role of trade unions and the composition of the labor force.

Though Hong Kong has had a trade union movement which has organized between 13.5 (in 1968) and 25.2 (in 1976) percent of the employed labor force and in 1984 organized 16.1 percent (Ng, 1986a, Table 10.2: 276-277), it has not mobilized its members around the standard (for Western trade unions) issues of wages and working conditions. Neither has it adopted a militant stance to the work place problems of its membership. Indeed, as can be seen from Table 14, labor militancy gauged in terms of strike activity, though never high by European or American standards (or indeed by the standards of other East Asian countries, such as the Philippines), has declined substantially, in terms of working days lost, in recent years.

This situation of a lack of interest in work place issues together with an absence of militant struggle is explained in the literature as being the result of the convergence of many factors. Authoritative commentators (principally Turner et al., 1980; England and Rear, 1981) agree, for instance, that trade unions in the territory traditionally have been concerned predominantly with their role as welfare and "political" agencies. In periods

Table 14. Work Stoppages in Hong Kong

Year	Number of Lock-outs and Strikes	Working Days Lost
1951-2	12	53,436
1956-7	12	78,852
1961	10	38,558
1966	12	24,355
1971	42	25,600
1972	46	41,834
1973	54	56,691
1974	19	10,708
1975	17	17,600
1976	15	4,751
1977	38	10,814
1978	51	30,927
1979	46	39,743
1980	37	21,069
1981	49	15,319
1982	34	17,960
1983	11	2,530
1984	11	3,122
1985	3	1,160
1986	9	4,908
1987	14	2,774

Sources: Commissioner for Labor, *Departmental Annual Reports* and Census and Statistics Department, *Monthly Digest of Statistics*.

Data for 1951-1984 compiled by Ng (1986a: 272)

when the social wage was very limited, their welfare function clearly must have been of some significance for workers. Similarly, many Hong Kong unions, at least those organized by the Federation of Trade Unions and the Trade Union Council, were forged during the political and military battles between the Communist Party and the Kuomintang. As a result they continue to put much of their energy and money into political propaganda and mobilization on behalf of China and Taiwan respectively.

Since the early 1970s, new labor organizations have emerged. While many of these have been formally constituted as unions, they have been independent of the two federations, and hence of their "external" political concerns. These new unions, however, have developed primarily among public sector employees. As well as being relatively combative over wage issues, they have been involved in mobilizing around non-work place concerns such as utilities and public transport costs (Tso, 1984; Ng, 1986b).

Of greater interest for the current discussion, however, has been the emergence of a number of non-trade union labor organizations. Born out of a combination of religious and student radicalism, the largest and most militant of these organizations has been the Hong Kong Christian Industrial Committee. While the CIC has been much more involved with work place issues than most industrial unions, and has close contacts with new "independent" unions such as the small (fewer than 1,000 members) Electronics Workers' Union, it has tended to concentrate the bulk of its energies on fighting for redundancy and maternity payments (often illegally denied by local employers) and educating workers about their legal rights, health and safety issues etc. (Chiu, 1986).

Though not as directly repressive as in some parts of East and Southeast Asia (i.e., South Korea, Taiwan, Indonesia, the Philippines under Marcos), labor legislation has operated to discourage work place solidarity and mobilization. Trade union ordinances on the one hand allow minute sectional interests to gain formal expression (as few as seven workers are legally entitled to form a union) and on the other, ban general unions. What is more, since as early as 1927 (in the immediate aftermath of the 1925-26 general strike), sympathy and "political" strikes have been illegal (England and Rear, 1981: 124-130).

In addition to the "peculiar" features of the territory's trade union movement, commentators such as England and Rear (1981) have pointed out that since the late 1940s, the "simple" reproduction of labor power in Hong Kong in part has taken the form of immigration from China. The argument has been that because new arrivals have been escaping from political repression and poverty in China, their overriding concern in Hong Kong has been to provide materially for their families. To do that, they have been willing to tolerate hard work, bad working conditions, long work weeks, and general exploitation. Unfortunately, when viewed from a comparative per- spective, arguments about the supposed relation between immigrants and high levels of work discipline and docility do not carry much weight. The labor history of the U.S., for instance, a country whose industrial dynamism was built in part on wave after wave of immigrant labor, was also, prior to World War II, that of one of the most combative working classes industrial capitalism has yet known (of the enormous literature see, for instance, Brecher, 1973; Aronowitz, 1974; Gutman, 1977; Montgomery, 1979; and in a more general context, Henderson and Cohen, 1982).

If immigration per se does not help us to account for the "quality" of the Hong Kong work force, is there something about the historical con- struction of Chinese culture which *in articulation with* the relations of power within the factory, and within the colonial state generally, helps to produce this effect? While we are unable to explore this hypothesis in any depth here, at least one (Hong Kong) Chinese scholar has argued that the "deep structures" of Chinese culture tend to help reproduce, over time, a ready acceptance of authority and an abhorrence of face-to-face conflict (Sun, 1983). If this is indeed the case, then it might take us some way to explaining the seemingly low levels of worker resistance to factory labor processes.[21]

A significant feature of the electronics and semiconductor industries in Hong Kong, as in other parts of the world (cf. Lim, 1982; Lin, 1987, on Southeast Asia), is that an overwhelming majority of the work force are women (see Table 6). Work place ethnographies which have focused on women in wage labor in Western societies have tended to argue that the patriarchal relations of domination into which women are socialized within the family are transferred to the work place where they are used creatively by managers and supervisors as a major component of the social basis of control (see, for instance, Downing, 1981; Pollert, 1981; West, 1982). In the Hong Kong semiconductor industry, companies seem to recruit women for assembly work because they are "dexterous and more willing to tolerate monotonous work" than are men.[22] Although there is no empirical work that deals specifically with the issue, it seems likely that systems of patriarchal control operate in Hong Kong factories as much as they do elsewhere. In addition, Janet Salaff's (1981) and Claire Chiang's (1984) work shows that the principal life interests of female manual workers in the territory lie not within the experience of labor, but rather are heavily determined by familial obligations. They work because they are obliged to contribute to the household income.

The above comments are not meant to constitute an argument that women electronics workers in Hong Kong do not resist assembly labor pro- cesses. On the contrary, there is evidence that individualistic forms of resistance do occur (Djao, 1976; Chiang, 1984), and high worker mobility ("labor turnover") rates are endemic in the Hong Kong electronics and textile industries. As Cohen and I have argued (Henderson and Cohen, 1979), in the context of factory-based production systems, worker mobility, under certain conditions, can become an important form of resistance. The point, however, is that in the absence of research that specifically sets out to chart workplace resistance among Hong Kong women, we are left with the conclusion that resistance is less evident in both quantity and significance than it is, say, among their British counterparts (cf. Pollert, 1981).

The Semiconductor Production Complex

The previous discussion was an attempt to identify some of the principal reasons why U.S. semiconductor manufacturers came to Hong Kong and remained there. Much of the weight of our argument was placed on the cost and quality of labor power and on the processes by which these were reproduced. In this section, we engage directly with the question of why U.S. semiconductor firms have upgraded their operations, such that Hong Kong is now one of the technological cores of the East Asian regional division of labor. We begin, however, by recuperating some of the earlier discussion.

It was suggested earlier that until the late 1970s, U.S. semiconductor production in Hong Kong was much the same as it was in other parts of the East Asian region. It was involved overwhelmingly in the manual assembly of transistors, diodes, and integrated circuits. The data presented in Table 1 confirmed this situation. It was then suggested that by the mid-1980s, the situation had changed drastically. In Hong Kong, as in Singapore (and, to a lesser extent, South Korea and Taiwan) U.S. companies had restructured their operations by engaging in a process of capital deepening and begun to specialize in more technologically advanced labor processes such as final testing and circuit design. In addition, a number of companies established their regional headquarters in one or another of these locations. What assembly functions remained tended to be automated. The data presented in Table 2 confirmed the emergence of Hong Kong and Singapore as the technological and managerial cores of the regional division of labor, and Table 13 presented the Hong Kong situation in more detail.

As of late 1986 there were 21 companies in Hong Kong engaged, in some way, in the manufacture of semiconductors. Of these, eight were American, three Japanese, one Dutch, one British, one Chinese and six Hong Kong-owned. All the U.S. companies in the territory have testing facilities. In earlier periods, when discretes and ICs were less technologically sophisticated than now, testing was a relatively simple process. More recently, however, it has become an automated, technologically complex labor process (using lasers and computers to identify faults), requiring a high degree of engineering and technical labor, as well as significant amounts of unskilled labor. This latter group of workers manually load the semiconductors into the channels which feed them into the testing equipment. Thus, Motorola's Hong Kong plant, probably the most advanced testing center in the developing world, employs 750 workers, of whom only 300 are unskilled (and all of whom are women). Five of the U.S. companies in the territory (National Semiconductor, Siliconix, Teledyne, Commodore and Microsemiconductor) still engage in semiconductor assembly (Motorola has never assembled in Hong Kong). In all these cases, however, assembly is automated, to a greater or lesser extent, depending on the technological sophistication of the device itself. Typically, microprocessors and the more advanced-memory ICs (which require more "bonding" operations) will be assembled automatically. This ensures not only greater productivity, but higher yields, and hence higher-quality products. Less advanced devices tend to be assembled semi-automatically.

Three of the U.S. companies (Motorola, Siliconix and Zilog) have design centers in Hong Kong. Motorola's design center is one of its three largest outside of the U.S., Siliconix's is a joint venture operation with an independent Hong Kong-owned design house (Central Systems Design), and Zilog's design center is its only productive operation in the territory, and complements its Asian regional headquarters which is also located in Hong Kong.

The other foreign companies producing in the territory, with the exception of the Japanese firm, Oki, have invested in assembly and test facilities. In addition, two of the Japanese companies (Oki and Hitachi) have set up design centers, as has the single British producer in the territory, Ferranti. In the latter case, production has been developed on a joint-venture basis with the territory's largest subcontract assembler, Semiconductor Devices. Ferranti custom-design the circuitry in Hong Kong (but with a satellite link to the company's R & D center in Britain), the masks are produced and the wafers fabricated in Britain and the ICs are assembled and tested in Hong Kong from whence they are distributed directly to the markets (Hong Kong Productivity Center, *Electronics Bulletin,* 3(1), 1983: 30-31).

Before discussing the determinants of upgrading semiconductor production in Hong Kong, let us comment on the emergence of a locally-owned presence in the industry.

There are now seven locally-owned firms manufacturing semiconductors in Hong Kong. Of these, three are subcontract assembly houses. The largest of them, Semiconductor Devices, has advanced testing facilities and semi-automated assembly processes. As a result, it is able to assemble and test some of the most technologically sophisticated devices, including microprocessors. A fourth firm, Microelectronics, was and remains a sub-contract assembler, but has recently moved into wafer fabrication.

After 1982 the other three firms emerged with wafer fabrication capabilities from the very beginning. One of them (Hua Ko) is wholly owned by the Chinese government, and the others (Elcap and RCL) are re-puted to have some Chinese (PRC) equity participation. All have acquired equity participation in Californian design houses, though one (Hua Ko) has its own additional design capability. Both Hua Ko and RCL have had a number of their engineers trained in California (in the former case, engineers from the PRC, not Hong Kong).

These companies have a similar operation. They design and have their masks produced in California, and they fabricate the wafers, assemble and test in Hong Kong. So far, they have been able to produce only the less sophisticated devices, up to and including 64K memory ICs, and re-putedly suffer from low yields, suggesting that they have quality control problems. While RCL is trying to move into the more advanced (256K) memory production, and two of them (Hua Ko and RCL) are attempting to develop microprocessor capabilities, they remain, for the moment, technologically confined to the lower end of the market. Indeed, their principal customers are the Chinese consumer electronics industries and Hong Kong's watch industry (Hong Kong Productivity Center; *Electronics Bulletin*, various issues).

Determinants of Restructuring

We can now direct our attention to the question of why semi-conductor production in Hong Kong should have been restructured along the lines indicated above.

The first point is that unlike its counterparts in South Korea, Taiwan and Singapore, the Hong Kong government has not been involved in an attempt to shift the industry from a regime of absolute to a regime of relative surplus value creation.[23] There are no incentives or pressures for manufacturers to technologically upgrade their operation. While the Hong Kong government supports a semiconductor design facility (as part of the Hong Kong Productivity Center's Electronics Division), the amount of investment the facility receives is infinitesimal, compared with current investment (equivalent to three percent of sales) by the South Korean and Taiwanese governments, for instance.

If the restructuring of semiconductor production has not been a result of state development strategy, what else has it resulted from? While comments on the determinants are scattered throughout the previous discussion, they are combined and highlighted here.

First, Hong Kong, along with the other members of the "gang of four," were successively "priced-out" of the cheap labor market beginning in the late 1960s. In the case of Hong Kong, this was not the result of deliberate state intervention (as it was in Singapore, see Lim, 1983; Harris, 1987: 60-67), nor does it seem to have been associated with actual, or anticipated, labor militancy. We must, however, immediately qualify this last statement. Although official data are not available, employers (particularly in the electronics, textiles and plastics industries) and authoritative commentators (Turner, et al., 1980: Chapter 5; England and Rear, 1981) consider the Hong Kong work force to be highly mobile. Interviews with semiconductor industry executives confirm this picture, with some of them (Fairchild and National Semiconductor, for instance) reporting worker mobility rates in excess of 20 percent per annum by the late 1970s. In the context of persistent labor shortages since the late 1950s, only partially remedied by waves of legal and illegal immigration, labor mobility by individual workers in search of a slightly better wage and a slightly more congenial labor process made sense.

Under circumstances of rising labor costs, semiconductor and other manufacturers could presumably have relocated their entire production operations to other parts of the region where wages remained lower than in Hong Kong. As already suggested, new investment in labor-intensive assembly processes was directed to Malaysia, the Philippines and the like. But U.S. producers largely remained in Hong Kong, though on the basis of a technologically upgraded operation. A major reason for the retention of restructured production units in Hong Kong (and Singapore, etc.), was that by the mid- to late 1970s, the Hong Kong education system could provide the qualified engineers and technicians who are the *sine qua non* of advanced testing facilities, design centers, and wafer fabrication plants, and in reliable quantities.

This is not to say that the Hong Kong tertiary education system can produce electronics engineers with innovative R & D capabilities. As with its equivalents elsewhere in the region, it probably cannot. But the most advanced semiconductor labor process currently implanted in the territory, circuit design, does not require fundamental innovative research capabilities. Like other labor processes, circuit design has been taylorised in recent years, such that much of the work involves the fairly routine adaptation of innovative work to specific customer requirements. While this absence of an innovative R & D capacity may not pose a problem for the Hong Kong and other semiconductor industries in the region, it may have serious consequences for future development.

The retention of upgraded production facilities in Hong Kong by U.S. semiconductor companies does not merely result, of course, from the territory's reliability as a source of engineering and technical labor. This is clearly true to a far greater extent for the U.S., Western Europe, and some other developing societies, such as India. What distinguishes Hong Kong, Singapore, South Korea, and Taiwan from the former, though not from the latter territorial units is that electronics engineering and technical labor can be provided there, not only reliably, but also far more cheaply than it can, in, for instance, the U.S. and Scotland. Thus, in 1981, annual wages for electronics engineers in Hong Kong were 60 percent lower than they were for their equivalents in the U.S., *three years earlier*, in 1978. Similarly, the wages for electronics technicians were 76 percent lower than their U.S. counterparts in the same time periods (see Table 15). It is partly for this reason that U.S., Japanese and British companies have developed design centers in the territory, in addition to restructuring their productive operations to concentrate, to a significant extent, on testing functions.

The third reason that U.S. companies have remained in Hong Kong on a restructured basis stems from the emergence of the semiconductor (and the more general electronics) production complex itself. As argued elsewhere (Henderson, 1986a; Henderson and Scott, 1987; Scott, 1987), the emergence of a production complex on the basis of both the horizontal and vertical disintegration of production units tends to result in those units becoming insistently locked into a particular spatial location. This is because important sets of technical and other specialized services and supplies develop around the principal producers, resulting in a reduction of transaction costs. Also, in an industry as based on knowledge as semiconductor production is, regular interaction between executives and engineers becomes an important mechanism whereby new ideas and market information are acquired. Insofar as it is important to one's operation to know what developments are taking place within Asian semiconductor production, there is no point in having one's most advanced functions (i.e., design) in the Philippines or Thailand. There is every point, however, in locating them in Singapore, Taiwan, South Korea or Hong Kong.

Once a company has implanted production facilities in a particular territorial unit, and once a production complex begins to develop and deepen in that location, then for the reasons indicated above and assuming continuing access to major markets, there may well be compelling economic, social and technical reasons for continuing to invest and upgrade production there, rather than at other potentially competitive locations.

Table 15. Comparative Annual Wage Rates:
Electronics Engineers and Technicians
(in U.S. dollars*)

	U.S.†	Scotland‡	Hong Kong§
Electronics Engineer	19,188	11,876	7,562
Electronics Tech.	15,288	9,189	3,676

* The exchange rate for Pound Sterling and Hong Kong Dollars against U.S. dollars as at mid-1982 prices.

† Figure for June 1978
‡ Figure for Spring 1982
§ Figure for April 1981

Figures adapted from: Troutman (1980), Locate in Scotland (1983), Hong Kong Productivity Centre, *Salary Trends and Fringe Benefits in the Electronics Industry*, 1981.

___

Conclusion

This paper has examined the role of the external and internal political economies of Hong Kong in the technological transformation of its electronics and particularly semiconductor industries. It has suggested that this transformation has largely been a consequence of the articulation of economic and geo-political factors associated with the changing world system with internal processes such as labor force formation, state policy and most recently the emergence of a local complex of electronics production activity. Additionally, it has examined the significance of foreign and local capital to these developments. Rather than summarize my argument in any greater detail, however, this concluding section will briefly indicate the likely trajectory for the continuing restructuring of electronics production in Hong Kong.

The processes beginning to impact on electronics production in the territory emerge, in part, from the current restructuring of the world economy, particularly from shifts in market demand. Two tendencies seem to be particularly important here. First, with regard to semiconductors, world demand is beginning to shift away from standardized, volume products and toward an emphasis on customized ICs, designed or rather adapted for specific consumers (Ernst, 1987). Second, price competition in consumer electronics markets is beginning to be replaced by product competition (Ohmae, 1985). Both developments imply that the competitive edge is now increasingly dependent on technological innovation. Whereas these tendencies affect all competitors, it is obvious that they are potentially more problematic for those semiconductor and electronics industries that lack the necessary capital and expertise essential for technological innovation, namely, electronics industries in developing countries.

While state agencies in South Korea, Taiwan and Singapore have acted to improve the technological capacities of their electronics industries (by substantial investment in R and D, for instance) the Hong Kong government, hiding behind its "non-interventionist" ideology, has not. Given the relatively small size (fewer than 100 employees on average) of the indigenous firms in the Hong Kong electronics industry, and the potentially destabilizing geo-political context in which they currently find themselves (which is addressed below), it is clear that they have neither the capacity nor the inclination to undertake the necessary investment themselves. The consequence, then, of the situation seems to be that Hong Kong producers are likely to become increasingly uncompetitive in relation to their counterparts in the region.

The changing geo-political context likely to impact on the industry's future development, similarly has two components. First, cut-throat competition among "national" electronics producers in the context of deepening economic crisis is leading to protectionist demands in the principal markets for electronic products: the U.S. and EEC (Japan has always had a protected market). While these developments are unlikely to affect prospects for Hong Kong producers any more than those for their regional competitors, when the second geo-political component is taken into account, their implications could be especially problematic.

The second component is the absorption, already underway, of Hong Kong into the Chinese economy and state. In spite of guarantees by the Chinese government and the promulgation of a "basic law" for what will become in 1997 the "Special Administrative Region" of Hong Kong, there remains serious doubt that "business confidence" among Hong Kong capitalists will survive the decolonization period. Clearly, though such a situation is still conducive to making profits, at least in the short term, it is hardly conducive to making the expensive investments in R and D that are becoming increasingly important for medium- and longer-term competitiveness.

In the meantime, Hong Kong manufacturers, including those in electronics, in search of yet more opportunities for absolute surplus value creation, have begun to relocate in China those labor processes that still rely on cheap unskilled labor.   Already some 10,000 Hong Kong-owned factories, reputedly employing over one million people, have been set up in Guandong Province (immediately adjacent to the Colony), producing mostly cheap clothing and electronics.[24]   Of the foreign semiconductor firms in the territory, National Semiconductor plans to assemble in China in the near future, while Sanyo recently (1987) fled Hong Kong completely, transferring production to a new plant in the Shenzhen Special Economic Zone just north of the border.

While locally-owned electronics firms could continue to shift production to China, at least for their lower grade products, it is unlikely that foreign or local semiconductor producers are likely to follow Sanyo's example.   It is more likely that Hong Kong will become the technological core and managerial control center of a domestic Chinese division of labor in semiconductor production.   Design work, wafer fabrication (by Hong Kong and foreign firms) and testing will probably remain in Hong Kong while labor-intensive assembly processes will be increasingly relocated in China.   Such developments, however, will compound the declining contribution manufacturing industry makes to employment in the territory, which in the context of the deepening world economic crisis and Hong Kong's extreme exposure to the vagaries of the world economy (by virtue of the absence of a domestic market) could have serious social and political consequences *prior* to the territory's formal absorption by China.

Notes

1. I am grateful to the Urban Studies and Urban Planning Trust Fund of the University of Hong Kong for providing the grant for the research on which this paper draws. In addition I am indebted to the University of New England, and particularly the members of its Department of Sociology, for inviting me to join them as a Visiting Professor during September 1988. It was while I was at the University that this paper was drafted in its final form.

2. South Korea, Taiwan, Singapore, and Hong Kong.

3. In spite of recent investment by Japanese, European and domestic producers, U.S. semiconductor companies remain the dominant presence in the semiconductor industries of developing East Asia.

4. Table 2 does not take account of the strong, indigenously-owned semiconductor industries of South Korea and Taiwan. If it did, it would indicate that these countries had also become "cores" of the East Asian Regional Division of Labor. Additionally, of the "peripheries," the emergence of wafer fabrication in Malaysia is of some significance. The nature and extent of fabrication *thus far* in Malaysia however, is so limited as to not fundamentally disturb the current regional division of labor. For the details behind this contention, see Henderson (1989a: Chapter 4).

5. No reliable data on the Hong Kong economy prior to World War II are available, but all the standard accounts of Hong Kong's development (e.g. Szczepanik, 1958; Chou, 1966; Riedel, 1972; Lin and Ho, 1980; Cheng, 1985) are in accord with this statement.

6. By 1975 Hong Kong had overtaken Italy as the world's largest exporter of clothing (Lin and Ho, 1980: 34).

7. As a consequence of crisis and overproduction in the international semiconductor industry in the 1980s (cf. Ernst, 1987), Fairchild substantially reduced its Hong Kong operation in 1983 and finally closed its factory in 1986, shipping production equipment to its South Korean facility.

8.   Some indicative figures for the proportion of employment provided by manufacturing industry (1986) are: Hong Kong, 34 percent; Taiwan, 32.5 percent; Japan, 25 percent; Singapore, 25 percent; South Korea, 22.5 percent; Malaysia, 14.6 percent; Indonesia, 10.4 percent; Philippines, 9.5 percent; and Thailand, 8.3 percent. Apparently, of all East Asian countries, only North Korea has a higher proportion of its work force (53.2 percent) employed in manufacturing industry (BBDO, 1987: 3).

9.   Readers who have never been to Hong Kong and have an image of factories as buildings which occupy space horizontally may wonder where the land for 1,200 electronics factories, in a territory of 1,000 square kilometers and 5.6 million people, comes from. The answer, of course, is that like the population itself, factories in Hong Kong occupy space vertically!

10.   Unfortunately, because of the absence of a disclosure law in Hong Kong, and the unwillingness of local industrialists to respond to questions about investment, it is almost impossible to generate reliable date on investment in the locally-owned electronics sector. Consequently, data that could corroborate this point cannot be presented.

11.   This decline has probably been associated with the crisis in the worldwide consumer electronics industry, associated particularly with the saturation of the VCR (dominated by Japanese producers) and micro-computer markets by the early to mid-1980s. On the general significance of this crisis for both Japanese and U.S. producers, see Ernst (1987).

12.   Based on unpublished data drawn from the *Reports on the Surveys of Overseas Investment in Hong Kong's Manufacturing Industry, 1981 and 1987.* Available from the Hong Kong Department of Trade, Industry and Customs.

13.   Given that Table 10 does not include data on the minor EEC markets (for Hong Kong produced electronics goods), this figure must underestimate the market dominance of the U.S. and the EEC.

14.   In addition to the U.S. companies listed in Table 13, NCR and Silicon Systems had semiconductor assembly plants in Hong Kong until the early 1980s (Grunwald and Flamm, 1985; UNCTC, 1986).

15.   The first EPZ/FTZs in the region were not set up until 1966 (in Taiwan and South Korea). Those in Malaysia and the Philippines did not begin operations until 1972 and 1973 respectively (Grunwald and Flamm, 1985: 78). The penetration of U.S. semiconductor investment into the latter three countries was directly associated with the emergence of their EPZs. The only other territorial unit in the region which offered the same free port advantages as Hong Kong was Singapore. Like Hong Kong, its free port status stemmed historically from its role in the world economy as a British colonial entrepôt.

16.   Significant industrialization in Taiwan and South Korea, for instance, did not begin much before the early 1960s (see Gold, 1986; Deyo, 1987).

17.   General accounts of the processes and significance of habituation to factory labor have been provided by Henderson and Cohen (1979, 1982), among others.

18.   Accounts of the cultural problems (resistance) associated with attempts to convert peasants or agricultural laborers into factory workers are legion, and refer to a variety of racial and ethnic groups and to both sexes. For instance, see Cohen (1980) on Africa and Heyzer (1986) on Southeast Asia. The classic historical accounts, however, remain those by Thompson (1967) and Braverman (1974).

19.   This has not always been the case. There were apparently a number of strikes during the 19th century, and in the 1920s, a series of seamen and dockworker strikes culminated in the 15-month general strike of 1925-26 (Turner, et al., 1980: 19-20; England and Rear, 1981: 124-33).

20.   Probing the formation of work force consent could only be achieved by the use of ethnographic techniques, which would need to include extensive periods of participant observation within the work force. For obvious reasons, I am incapable of doing this type of research. While three ethnographies of work places in Hong Kong have been completed (Djao, 1976, 1978; Salaff, 1981; Chiang, 1984), none used the formation of work place consent as part of their theoretical problematic.

21. Sun's book is currently available only in Chinese. I am grateful to Ho Shuet Ying for providing me with a detailed exposition of Sun's arguments. For a brief English language summary, see Jaivin (1987).

I am of course aware that in other historical and structural contexts, Chinese workers have been as militant as any others. I have already referred to the labor militancy in Hong Kong during the inter-war period, for instance, and thanks to the work of Jean Chesneaux (1968) among others, we now know a great deal about working class militancy in China itself. In no sense, then, should my comment be seen as a culturalist explanation for the present lack of militancy among the Hong Kong work force. Rather my position is that culture (as a changing, not invariant form) may be one element of the explanation. We cannot even begin to understand its significance, however, unless a) we approach the question by means of a theoretical framework which recognizes that culture is articulated with other structural elements and that *the articulation changes over time*, and b) that empirical work is required to identify its significance in particular institutional contexts at particular historical moments.

22. In my interviews with the managers of U.S. semiconductor plants in Hong Kong, this comment was invariably given in response to the question of why assembly workers in the factory were women.

23. Marx's concept of "absolute surplus value" refers to the situation were a capitalist seeks to increase surplus value (and hence capital accumulation) by increasing the ratio of surplus labor time (that part of the work period when surplus value is created) to necessary labor time (that part of the work period when the worker produces the value necessary for his or her own and the family's subsistence needs). Under conditions of absolute surplus value creation, the ratio of surplus to necessary labor time is increased by forcing down wages, forcing people to work harder for the same wage and/or lengthening the working day. The creation of absolute surplus value is associated, therefore, with the "super-exploitation" of the labor force, or more recently to what Lipietz (1987) refers to as "bloody taylorisation."

The concept of relative surplus value, on the other hand, refers to a situation where surplus value is expanded without necessarily having recourse to "super-exploitation." This is done by increasing productivity by the application of (new) technology. Under a regime of relative surplus value creation, it is quite possible for wages to increase at the same time as increases in surplus value occur. The classic discussions of absolute and relative surplus value are contained, of course, in the first volume of *Capital* (Marx, 1967: Parts III and IV). However, also see Harvey's (1982: Chapter 1) useful account.

24.   For an "early" account of the absorption of the Hong Kong by the Chinese economy, see Youngson (1983).

References

Aronowitz, S. (1974) *False Promises: The Shaping of American Working Class Consciousness*. New York: McGraw-Hill.

Baran, P. and P. Sweezy (1966) *Monopoly Capital*. Harmondsworth: Penguin.

BBDO (1987) *A Regional Focus: Hong Kong and S.E. Asia*. Hong Kong: BBDO Ltd.

Berger, P. (1986) *The Capitalist Revolution*. New York: Basic Books.

Bolton, K.R. and K.K. Luke (1986) The socio-linguistic survey of language in Hong Kong. Mimeo, Department of English Studies and Comparative Literature, University of Hong Kong.

Braverman, H. (1974) *Labor and Monopoly Capital*. New York: Monthly Review Press.

Brecher, J. (1973) *Strike!* San Francisco: Straight Arrow Books.

Browett, J. (1986) Industrialisation in the global periphery: The significance of the newly industrialising countries of East and Southeast Asia, *Environment and Planning D: Society and Space*, 4(4): 401-418.

Burawoy, M. (1979) *Manufacturing Consent*. Chicago: University of Chicago Press.

Castells, M. (1986) The Shek Kip Mei syndrome: Public housing and economic development in Hong Kong, *Working Paper 15*, Centre of Urban Studies and Urban Planning, University of Hong Kong.

Chen, E.K.Y. (1971) *The Electronics Industry of Hong Kong: An Analysis of its Growth*. M. Soc. Sc. thesis, University of Hong Kong.

Cheng, T.Y. (1985) *The Economy of Hong Kong*. Hong Kong: Far East Publications.

Chesneaux, J. (1968) *The Chinese Labor Movement, 1919-1927*. Stanford: Stanford University Press.

Chiang, S.N.C. (1984) *Women and Work: Case Studies of Two Hong Kong Factories*. M.Phil. thesis, University of Hong Kong.

Chiu, P.K.Y. (1986) *Labour Organisations and Political Change in Hong Kong*. M. Soc. Sc. dissertation, University of Hong Kong.

Chou, K.R. (1966) *The Hong Kong Economy: A Miracle of Growth*. Hong Kong: Academic Publications.

Cohen, R. (1980) Resistance and hidden forms of consciousness among African workers, *Review of African Political Economy, 19*: 8-22.

Cooper, E. (1981) *Woodcarvers of Hong Kong*. Cambridge, Cambridge University Press.

Cummings, B. (1987) The origins and development of the Northeast Asian political economy: Industrial sectors, product cycles and political consequences. In F. Deyo (Ed.), *The Political Economy of the New Asian Industrialism*. Ithaca: Cornell University Press: 44-83.

Deyo, F. (Ed.) (1987) *The Political Economy of the New Asian Industrialism.* Ithaca: Cornell University Press.

Djao, A.W. (1976) *Social Control in a Colonial Society: A Case Study of Working Class Consciousness in Hong Kong.* Ph.D. dissertation, University of Toronto.

Djao, A.W. (1978) Dependent development and social control: Labour-intensive industrialization in Hong Kong, *Social Praxis,* 5(3-4): 275-293.

Downing, H. (1981) *Developments in Secretarial Labour: Resistance, Office Automation and the Transformation of Patriarchal Relations of Control.* Ph.D. thesis, University of Birmingham.

Ehrlich, P. (1988) Malaysia: Fabrication hot spot? *Electronic News,* 6(18), June.

England, J. and J. Rear (1981) *Industrial Relations and the Law in Hong Kong.* Hong Kong: Oxford University Press.

Ernst, D. (1987) U.S.-Japanese competition and the worldwide restructuring of the electronics industry: A European view. In J. Henderson and M. Castells (Eds.), *Global Restructuring and Territorial Development.* London: Sage Publications: 38-59.

Friedman, M. and R. Friedman (1981) *Free to Choose.* Harmondsworth: Penguin.

Frobel, F., J. Heinrichs and O. Kreye (1980) *The New International Division of Labour.* Cambridge: Cambridge University Press.

Gold, T. (1986) *State and Society in the Taiwan Miracle.* Armonk: M.E. Sharpe.

Gregory, C. (1985) *British Labor in Britain's Decline.* Ph.D. dissertation, Harvard University.

Grunwald, J. and K. Flamm (1985) *The Global Factory.* Washington D.C.: The Brookings Institution.

Gutman, H.G. (1977) *Work, Culture and Society in Industrialising America.* Oxford: Basil Blackwell.

Hamilton, C. (1983) Capitalist industrialisation in East Asia's Four Little Tigers, *Journal of Contemporary Asia,* 13(1): 35-73.

Harris, N. (1987) *The End of the Third World.* Harmondsworth: Penguin.

Harvey, D. (1982) *The Limits to Capital.* Oxford: Basil Blackwell.

Henderson, J. (1986a) The new international division of labour and American semiconductor production in Southeast Asia. In C. Dixon, D. Drakakis-Smith and H.D. Watts (Eds.), *Multinational Corporations and the Third World.* London: Croom Helm, 91-117.

Henderson, J. (1986b) The new international division of labour and urban development in the contemporary world system. In D. Drakakis-Smith (Ed.), *Urbanisation in the Developing World.* London:

Croom Helm, 63-82.

Henderson, J. (1987) Semiconductors, Scotland and the international division of labour, *Urban Studies, 24*(5): 389-408.

Henderson, J. (1989a) *The Globalisation of High Technology Production: Society, Space and Semiconductors in the Restructuring of the Modern World.* London: Routledge.

Henderson, J. (1989b) *The Political Economy of Hong Kong.* London: Routledge (forthcoming).

Henderson, J. and R. Cohen (1979) Capital and the work ethic, *Monthly Review, 31*(6): 11-26.

Henderson, J. and R. Cohen (1982) On the reproduction of the relations of production. In R. Forrest, J. Henderson and P. Williams (Eds.), *Urban Political Economy and Social Theory.* Aldershot: Gower, 112-143.

Henderson, J. and A.J. Scott (1987) The growth and internationalisation of the American semiconductor industry: Labour processes and the changing spatial organisation of production. In M. Breheny and R. McQuaid (Eds.), *The Development of High Technology Industries: An International Survey.* London: Croom Helm, 37-79.

Heyzer, N. (1986) *Working Women in Southeast Asia.* Milton Keynes: Open University Press.

Ho, S.Y. (1986) Public housing. In J.Y.S. Cheng (Ed.), *Hong Kong in Transition.* Hong Kong: Oxford University Press, 331-335.

Ho, Y.P. (1986) Hong Kong's trade and industry, changing patterns and prospects. In J.Y.S. Cheng (Ed.), *Hong Kong in Transition.* Hong Kong: Oxford University Press, 165-207.

Jaivin, L. (1987) The raw or cooked versions of being Chinese, *Far Eastern Economic Review*, 23 April: 43-45.

Koo, H. (1987) The interplay of state, social class and world system in East Asian development: The cases of South Korea and Taiwan. In F. Deyo (Ed.), *The Political Economy of the New Asian Industrialism.* Ithaca: Cornell University Press, 165-181.

Lim, L.Y.C. (1982) Capitalism, imperialism and patriarchy: The dilemma of Third World women workers in multinational factories. In J. Nash and M.P. Fernandez-Kelly (Eds.), *Women, Men and the International Division of Labor.* Albany: State University of New York Press, 70-91.

Lim, L.Y.C. (1983) Singapore's success: The myth of the free market economy, *Asian Survey, 23*(6): 752-764.

Lin, T.B. and Y.P. Ho (1980) *Export-Oriented Growth and Industrial Diversification in Hong Kong.* Hong Kong: Economic Research Centre, Chinese University of Hong Kong.

Lin, T.B., V. Mok and Y.P. Ho (1980) *Manufactured Exports and*

Employment in Hong Kong. Hong Kong: Chinese University Press.

Lin, V. (1987) Women electronics workers in Southeast Asia: Emergence of a working class. In J. Henderson and M. Castells (Eds.), *Global Restructuring and Territorial Development.* London: Sage, 112-135.

Lipietz, A. (1987) *Mirages and Miracles: The Crises of Global Fordism.* London: Verso.

Locate in Scotland (1983) *The Semiconductor Industry in Scotland.* Glasgow: Scottish Development Agency.

Marx, K. (1967) *Capital*, Vol. I. New York: International Publishers.

Mok, C.H. (1969) *The development of the cotton spinning and weaving industries in Hong Kong, 1946-1966.* M.A. thesis, University of Hong Kong.

Montgomery, D. (1979) *Workers' Control in America.* New York: Cambridge University Press.

Ng, S.H. (1986a) Labour. In J.Y.S. Cheng (Ed.), *Hong Kong in Transition.* Hong Kong: Oxford University Press, 286-299.

Ng, S.H. (1986b) Electronics technicians in an industrialising economy: Some glimpses on the "New Working Class," *Sociological Review, 34*(3): 611-640.

Ohmae, K. (1985) *Triad Power: The Coming Shape of Global Competition.* New York: The Free Press.

Okimoto, D.I., T. Sugano and F.B. Weinstein (Eds.) (1984) *Competitive Edge: The Semiconductor Industry in the U.S. and Japan.* Stanford: Stanford University Press.

Phelps Brown, E.H. (1971) The Hong Kong economy: Achievements and prospects. In K. Hopkins (Ed.), *Hong Kong: The Industrial Colony.* Hong Kong: Oxford University Press, 1-20.

Pollert, A. (1981) *Girls, Wives, Factory Lives.* London: Macmillan.

Rabushka, A. (1979) *Hong Kong: A Study in Economic Freedom.* Chicago: University of Chicago Press.

Riedel, J.C. (1972) *The Industrialization of Hong Kong.* Ph.D. dissertation, University of California, Davis.

Salaff, J. (1981) *Working Daughters of Hong Kong.* Cambridge: Cambridge University Press.

Sayer, A. (1984) *Method in Social Science.* London: Hutchinson.

Schiffer, J. (1983) Anatomy of a "laissez faire" government: The Hong Kong growth model reconsidered. Mimeo, Centre of Urban Studies and Urban Planning, University of Hong Kong.

Schmitz, H. (1984) Industrialisation strategies in less developed countries: Some lessons of historical experience, *Journal of Development Studies, 21*(1): 1-21.

Scott, A.J. (1987) The semiconductor industry in Southeast Asia: Organisation, location and the international division of labour, *Regional Studies, 21*(2): 143-160.

Scottish Education and Action for Development (1984) *Electronics and Development: Scotland and Malaysia in the International Electronics Industry.* Edinburgh: Scottish Education and Action for Development.

Siegel, L. (1980) Delicate bonds: The global semiconductor industry, *Pacific Research, XI*(1).

Siegel, L. and J. Markoff (1985) *The High Cost of High Tech: The Dark Side of the Chip.* New York: Harper and Row.

Sit, V.F.S. (1983) *Made in Hong Kong.* Hong Kong: Summerson.

Sit, V.F.S., et al. (1979) *Small Scale Industry in a Laissez Faire Economy: A Hong Kong Case Study.* Hong Kong: Centre of Asian Studies, University of Hong Kong.

So, A.Y. (1986) The economic success of Hong Kong: Insights from a world-system perspective, *Sociological Perspectives, 29*(2): 241-258.

Sun, L.J. (1983) *The Deep Structure of Chinese Culture.* Hong Kong: Yat Shan Publications (in Chinese).

Szczepanik, E. (1958) *The Economic Growth of Hong Kong.* Oxford: Oxford University Press.

Thompson, E.P. (1967) Time, work-discipline and industrial capitalism, *Past and Present, 38*: 56-97.

Troutman, M. (1980) The semiconductor labor market in Silicon Valley: Production wages and related issues. Mimeo. Mountain View, CA: Pacific Studies Center.

Tso, T.M.T. (1984) *Civil Service Unions as a Social Force in Hong Kong.* M. Soc. Sc. dissertation, University of Hong Kong.

Turner, H.A., et al. (1980) *The Last Colony: But Whose?* Cambridge: Cambridge University Press.

UNCTC (1986) *Transnational Corporations in the International Semiconductor Industry.* New York: United Nations Center on Transnational Corporations.

West, J. (Ed.) (1982) *Women, Work and the Labour Market.* London: Routledge and Kegan Paul.

Wong, S.L. (1979) *Industrial Entrepreneurship and Ethnicity: A Study of the Shanghainese Cotton Spinners in Hong Kong.* D. Phil thesis, University of Oxford.

Youngson, A.J. (Ed.) (1983) *China and Hong Kong: The Economic Nexus.* Hong Kong: Oxford University Press.

URBAN CHANGE AND THE INTERNATIONAL ECONOMY: JAPANESE CONSTRUCTION CONTRACTORS AND DEVELOPERS UNDER THREE ADMINISTRATIONS

Peter J. Rimmer
Australian National University

Japanese construction contractors (and property developers) operating above national boundaries, have been key agents in translating international capital into the built environment of overseas cities. They have been active in remodelling the structures of urban areas in Australia, Southeast Asia and the U.S. This raises the question of the effect of the internationalization of capital on cities within Japan and the part played by Japanese construction contractors and developers in remodelling them under three administrations -- Tanaka, Fukuda and Nakasone.

Planners, geographers, urban economists and others concerned with "urban questions" have produced a considerable and valuable body of literature over the last decades. They have, however, ignored or neglected the agents who produce and control the built environment. This is a serious shortcoming and therefore the object of this study is to address this issue by focusing on...construction contractors [and property developers] (Smyth, 1985: 1).

Captive Japanese Cities

Traditionally, urbanization in Japan has been conceptualized as the outcome of complex interacting internal forces. Japanese cities have been interpreted as a social ecology subject to individual forces inherent in the dynamics of population and space. Influenced by Castells (1972) and Harvey (1973), some scholars have abandoned factorial ecologies and social area analysis and viewed Japanese cities as the outcome of social forces triggered by the capitalist relations of production. In some quarters, there has been an attendant emphasis on the production of the built environment.

The connection between the status of cities and the world economy, however, was not made until the 1980s (Friedmann, 1986). This new focus not only sharpened insights into the processes of urban change but also offered a spatial perspective on the role of Japanese cities in an economy that transcended national boundaries. The nature of the link between urbanization in Japan and global economic forces was forged by using as a framework for analysis Friedmann and Wolff's (1982) world city hypothesis that *the mode of world system integration (form and strength of integration; spatial dominance) will affect in determinate ways the economic, social, spatial and political structure of world cities and the urbanizing processes to which they are subject.*

An attempt to apply Friedmann and Wolff's (1982) world city hypothesis in a Japanese context raised a host of definitional problems (Rimmer, 1986). Their perspective gave too much emphasis to external pressures which downplayed the importance of internal forces. Although Japan's economic life has been caught up in the world economy, its society and polity have remained insulated. This criticism does not mean, however, that researchers should retreat into examining only domestic modes of production or national class interests. A deeper understanding of Japan's cities must hinge on an integrated treatment of external pressures and the internal forces of production and class interests. When the paper on Japanese world cities was reviewed by Mei-Po Kwan (1987), however, she argued that the role of mediating processes and agents remained implicit.

In a bid to answer this criticism and make the role of mediating processes and agents explicit we begin with the premise that Japanese cities are captive; they depend on forces of production and investment. With the transnationalization of business organizations, production and investment are increasingly global in scope. Sustained crises in the world economy, therefore, are reflected in the built environment. Property developers and construction contractors are sensitive to these crises because they are engaged in producing and controlling the built environment by transforming capital investment into urban forms. As borne out by an examination of their activities in Japanese cities, property developers and construction contractors are different from manufacturers in terms of their relationship to the market and reaction to economic crises. It is not possible here, however, to discuss both property developers and construction contractors. Hence, attention is focused on construction contractors because their activities faithfully reflect how production and control of the built environment relates to the performance of the national economy. The narrower focus also provides the opportunity for exploring the argument that the economic variable is decisive in explanation (Friedmann, 1986).

Ideally, this examination of construction contractors, the economy, urban development, and changing political administrations should begin from the beginning of the Pacific War because three important phases need to be discussed: 1) the role of construction contractors and the state in facilitating shifts in economic activities from designated controlled urban areas during the wartime economy (1939-45); 2) the restructuring of the construction industry (i.e., mergers and expansion) during the reconstruction of the country's economy and cities (1946-1960), whereby major construction contractors concentrated on large-scale works and subcontractors performed the specialty trade functions; and 3) the high workloads among construction contractors during the period of high-speed growth (*kodo seicho*) which created the urban-industrial corridor along the Pacific coast (1960-72). As these matters are beyond the range of the present enquiry, attention is concentrated on the history of the construction sector since 1972, the period marking the end of the post-war boom and the first signs of the onset of an economic crisis. Before we are in a position to undertake this task we need to examine trends in the economy, the construction industry, urban areas and political administrations (Section 2). This strategy will enable us to consider, albeit briefly, the theoretical arguments underlying Smyth's (1985) study of Britain's construction industry (and property development) in a Japanese context. It will also raise the key questions that are addressed in subsequent sections.

Juggling the Economy, Construction and the Built Environment

Accounts of the Japanese construction industry invariably concentrate on its large size and complex structure (Hippoh, 1983; Nakamura, 1982, 1985). They highlight that the construction industry: 1) accounts for 16 percent of investment in gross national product compared with an average of 10 percent in North America and European countries; 2) comprises over 510,000 companies (over 15 percent of the nation's businesses) and over 3.5 million employees (five percent of the national total); and 3) exhibits a sharp dichotomy in terms of size between a small number of large general construction companies acting as prime contractors (*motouke*) and a host of small and medium contractors, (over 99 percent have under Y100 million in capital and employ less than 300 workers), most of them being subcontractors (*shitauke*). Accounts of the industry then distinguish two market sectors (Figure 1). First is the housing market in which those engaged in constructing traditional wooden buildings (*machiba*), and employing many unlicensed carpenters are being challenged by industrialized housing corporations (e.g. Sekisui House Ltd, Misawa Homes Co., Ltd and Daiwa House Industry Co., Ltd) offering "houses-for-sale" (*nakachoba*). Second is the heavy construction market (*nochoba*), with an industrialized mode of production and imported technologies developed by the government's public works initiatives in which 500 large national construction contractors, buttressed by a multi-storied sub-contracting system, have grown up, though many of them are still family partnerships (Figure 1). The descriptions go on to stress the construction industry's atypical character

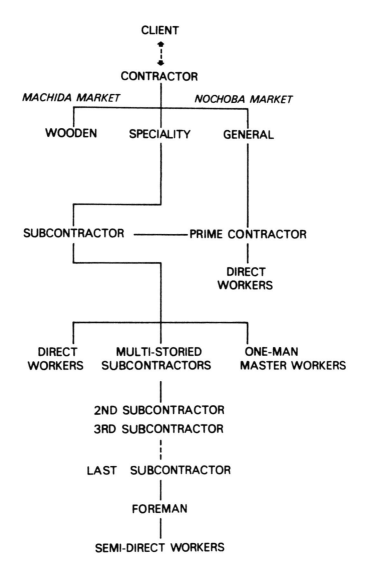

Figure 1: Structure of Japan's prime contractor (*motouke*) and multi-storied subcontractor system -- first level (lit. child contractor or *shitauke*) and second level (lit. grandchild contractor or *magouke*) (Hippoh, 1983: 18, 120). This system stretches to the labor supplier (*nimpu-dashi*).

compared with other industries -- high levels of capital turnover, mobile site location and insecurity in employment (Neo, 1976: 74).   No reasons are given for this difference.   Commentators merely point to the industry's low labor intensiveness, and low levels of capital investment and productivity. The inference is that the Japanese construction industry is backward in technology and outmoded in organization (i.e., the substitution of capital for labor has been low).

These descriptions of the Japanese construction industry are, in some respects, misleading.   Patently, as Smyth (1985) has stressed, the industry benefits from an inherent flexibility because it works to contracts rather than production for sale (except in the private housing market and where the construction contractor acts as a developer).   Coupled with plant hiring and subcontracting, contracts permit flexibility, allowing a run-down in activity when there is a lack of continuous work or a low demand and overcapacity during an economic crisis, and a rapid pick-up in activity when a period of reconstruction presages an economic recovery.   This adaptability is a sign of forwardness rather than backwardness!

A simple way of relating the Japanese construction industry to the economy is to plot annual percentage changes between 1970 and 1988 in gross national product, the value of contracts completed and, given our interest in cities, the land prices in built-up areas (Table 1).   When they are graphed in Figure 2 the resultant patterns raise a host of questions: why was there a precipitous decline in the annual growth rates in the Japanese economy, construction activity and land prices in built-up areas during the early 1970s; why was there a recovery in construction and land prices in built-up areas until the late 1970s when the growth in gross national product continued to fall; and why was there a marked drop in construction and land prices in the early 1980s and a subsequent recovery when the annual rate of change in gross national product had stabilized?

These questions are considered by drawing on Smyth's (1985) theoretical framework developed for studying the British construction industry (Table 2).   It allows us to demonstrate how trends in gross national product, contracts completed and land prices are related to phases in the international economy since the rate of profit began to fall in the late 1960s -- a means of highlighting how the construction industry differs from manufacturing in each phase.   Three phases are pertinent:

1.   *Late prosperity* during which tax and inflation had a detrimental effect on manufacturing returns though there was still considerable expenditure by the state that led to a marked increase in fixed capital nationally.

2.   *First phase of crisis* during which over-production occurred in the

Table 1. Gross National Product,
Construction Investments and Land Prices
in Built-up Areas, 1970-1988

Fiscal year	Gross National Product Ybillion	%	Construction investments Ybillion	%	Construction share of GNP percent	Land price in built-up areas percent[1]
1970	75,524	17.0	14,634		19.4	19.2
1971	83,166	10.1	16,677	13.9	20.0	17.6
1972	96,883	16.5	21,462	28.7	22.2	13.0
1973	117,257	21.0	28,667	33.6	24.2	14.0
1974	138,044	18.4	29,394	2.5	21.3	30.6
1975	151,797	10.0	31,624	7.6	20.8	18.0
1976	170,290	12.2	34,196	8.1	20.1	-5.0
1977	188,804	10.9	38,798	13.5	20.5	1.5
1978	206,762	9.5	42,686	10.0	20.6	2.0
1979	221,965	7.4	47,921	12.3	21.6	2.5
1980	238,893	7.7	49,772	3.7	20.8	7.2
1981	251,536	5.2	50,222	4.8	20.2	9.6
1982	269,721	5.8	50,069	-0.3	20.2	7.2
1983	277,975	3.0	47,557	-5.0	17.1	4.6
1984	293,628	5.6	47,951	0.9	16.3	3.0
1985	321,185	5.0	49,630	3.6	16.1	
1986	334,651	4.2	52,920	6.4	15.8	
1987	348,400	4.1	58,600	10.7	16.8	
1988	365,400	4.8				

1. Refers to calendar year

Source: Nomura sogo kenkyusho, 1983; Kensetsusho, 1987; National Land Agency, 1985.

Table 2. Smyth's (1985) Three Phases in the
Production of the Built Environment
After the Fall in the Profit Rate

Phase	Economy	Construction industry	Property development
Late prosperity	Rate of profit falls	Boom; most work internal but exports increase	Responded to demand for office and retail space
First phase of crisis	Overproduction and need for external markets	Favorable returns from property sector and overseas construction	Stimulus from need to speed capital accumulation
Second phase of crisis	Overproduction	Reaches limit of flexibility as underproducer in phase of overproduction	More selectivity about development activity and definition of prime investment and concentration through shakeouts, mergers & takeovers

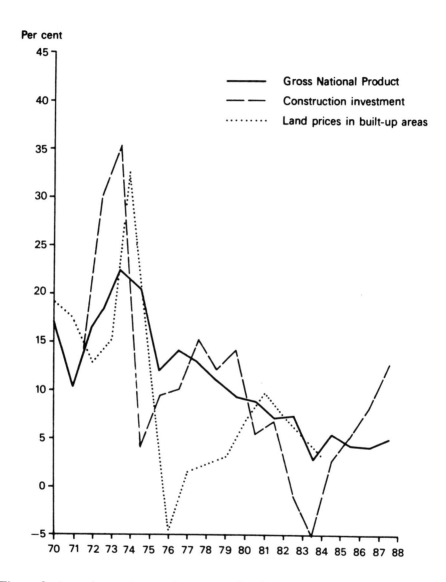

Figure 2: Annual growth rates in gross national product (nominal), construction investment and land prices in built-up areas (Sources: see Table 1).

economy as a whole though it was more favorable to the construction industry as it benefitted from spin-offs from property development, stimulated by the need to speed capital accumulation and overseas construction.

3.   *Second phase of crisis* during which the construction industry reaches the limits of its flexibility and becomes an underproducer in a phase of overproduction, a period marked by international and social tension.

In looking at the construction industry in Japan it needs to be stressed that "the picture is incomplete because individual...sectors and nations do not exhibit the outline presented here in microcosm but contribute to and experience the effects of the whole process" (Smyth, 1985: 30). This observation has to be borne in mind in gauging the extent to which the Japanese construction industry has followed British experience.

Table 3. Profile of the "Big Five" Construction Companies
1944 and 1965

Construction company	Established	Incorporated	Completed contracts 1944 Ymill.	1965 Ymill.
Kajima	1839	1930	229	147,549
Ohbayashi Gumi	1892	1956	512	121,423
Shimizu	1804	1937	727	124,552
Taisei	1873	1917	240	134,013
Takenaka Komuten	1610	---	346	130,053

Source: Nakamura, 1982, 1985.

In pursuing this question attention is centered on changes in domestic and overseas markets and concentration among the major construction companies. It is not possible, however, to cover all of the over 500 companies. Even following the industry's practice of dividing the population into the "Big 50 constructors" and "465 constructors" and concentrating on the former, would bring little relief. Attention, therefore, is centered on the "Big Five" -- Kajima Corporation, Ohbayashi Corporation (known as Ohbayashi Gumi Co., Ltd until 1984), Shimizu Construction Co., Ltd, Taisei Corporation Co., Ltd and Takenaka Komuten Co., Ltd -- a series of family-oriented firms with feudal roots that have dominated the post-war construction industry (Table 3). Only Taisei has followed the lead of large non-construction companies by abandoning the system of family succession to the presidency (Yanaga, 1968: 41). In a bid to strengthen their ties with government all of the Big Five have hired retired senior officials from central and local government and public corporations (i.e., the practice of *amakudari* or "descent from heaven"). As the activities of the Big Five epitomize developments within the construction industry, they provide a faithful barometer to the industry's reaction to changes in the economy, opportunities in Japan's urban areas and political connections.

Without denying the overriding significance of economic factors, an important political dimension can be added to the analysis by concentrating on construction and urban developments during three premierships that coincide with major changes in the economy since 1970. A study of construction contracting under Kakuei Tanaka (1972-74) provides an insight into urban change during the period of late prosperity that was brought to an end by the "first oil crisis" in 1973 (Section 3). This is followed by an examination of the heavy construction industry under Takeo Fukuda (1976-78) which reflects the period of "stable growth" and the resilience of the construction sector during the first phase of the economic crisis (Section 4). Then an examination is made of the construction industry under Yasuhiro Nakasone (1982-87) which, until 1985, saw a reduction in public works that stimulated an expanding overseas market; this was followed by an upsurge in domestic demand (Section 5). Most attention will be focused on the Nakasone era to determine whether the shift of construction activity has been part of an alleged "hollowing-out" (*kudoka*) of Japanese cities. Then, we are in a position to discuss likely developments in the construction industry under Noboru Takeshita (1987-) and his successors (Section 6). Finally, it is shown how this history of construction contracting in the Japanese economy informs urban theories.

The exploration has been prompted by arguments that the power of the bureaucratic elite over sensitive issues has waned since the "first oil shock" (cf. Johnson, 1982, 1987). As issues have become less clear-cut the locus of power has shifted to the politicians, notably those in the ruling Liberal Democratic Party (*Jiyuminshuto*), who have been able to orchestrate parliamentary business on construction through their intra-party divisional committee (*Kensetsu bukai*) which attracts the highest membership of any ministry (Inoguchi and Iwai, 1984). The group is orchestrated by an inner sanctum of influential members, the Construction Group Committee (*Kensetsu zoku giin*) which is deeply involved in the Ministry of Construction's policy-making, ranking of projects, drafting of legislation and revision of regulations that cover both the operation of the construction industry and city planning in Japan.   Indeed, the position of Minister of Construction (like that of Posts and Telegraph) is highly prized among the five factions (*habatsu*) of the Liberal Democratic Party as a source of political patronage (Table 4).   The present Minister (Iehi Ochi) is a member of the Nakasone faction.   Apart from a transitional spell under the Suzuki faction it has been held by Nakasone's followers since 1982.   Previously, however, the position was filled by a member of the mainstream Tanaka group.   Indeed, there is still much sympathy among older bureaucrats in the Ministry of Construction for the former prime minister, Kakuei Tanaka.

Table 4. Factions in the Ruling Liberal Democratic Party

	Mainstream			Substream	
Original Parties	Liberal Constitutionalists		Democratic Revisionists	Progressive Party	
	Group	Group ("Bureaucratic")	Group	Group	Group
Past Prime Ministers	Sato Tanaka	Ikeda Ohira Suzuki	Kishi Fukuda	Nakasone	Miki
Faction Leaders	Takeshita Nikaido	Miyazawa	Abe	Nakasone	Komoto

Source: Various

Faltering Late Prosperity under Tanaka (1972-74)

The Tanaka prime ministership provides an ideal opportunity for investigating the validity of Smyth's (1985) contentions about the end of the general period of prosperity in a Japanese context. Although there is a need to show that tax and inflation had a detrimental effect on manufacturing, the key issue is whether the considerable expenditure by the state in construction led to a marked increase in fixed capital nationally. Focusing on the Tanaka administration also allows consideration of both economic and political factors in providing a full explanation of urban change in Japan and the international economy during a period when general prosperity had shown initial signs of faltering.

Kakuei Tanaka became prime minister at a critical juncture in the trajectory of the world economy. Since the late 1950s, Japan had enjoyed a general period of prosperity during which the construction industry had outstripped gross national product and a strong urban-industrial base had been created for large, export-oriented corporations processing imported raw materials, such as iron, steel and petro-chemicals. The construction industry's rise to prominence was underpinned by state and private investments in economic overhead capital, and the built environment focused on the Pacific Belt and the Tokyo-Nagaoya-Osaka nexus in particular. Much of the industry's work came from government investments in urban infrastructure (e.g. power generation facilities, expressways and port development) within Tokyo, Ise and Osaka Bays and in inter-urban transport networks (notably highways and the super-express railway trunk line within the Pacific Belt); there was also a steady growth in housing and factory construction. This concentration of urban-industrial activity on the Pacific Belt was not without its social costs: long commuting times, traffic congestion, atmospheric and water pollution, rising land prices in urban areas and the accelerated abandonment of rural areas.

In 1969, the "New Comprehensive National Development Plan" (*Shinzenso*) superseded the original multinodal plan, concentrating development of a number of non-metropolitan growth poles brought down seven years earlier in a renewed bid to prevent the excessive expansion of urban areas and regional imbalance. As shown in Figure 3, the basic strategy was to construct a nationwide transport network of expressways and high-speed railways to make all areas equally accessible to urban life-styles and to provide the grid on which to graft a new set of growth poles -- the giant territorial production complexes (*kombinato*) (Yamaguchi, 1986). The aim was to bring about the functional integration of the Japanese economy under the high economic growth conditions prevailing during the late 1960s, a distinctive period termed the *Showa genroku* (equivalent to the buoyant

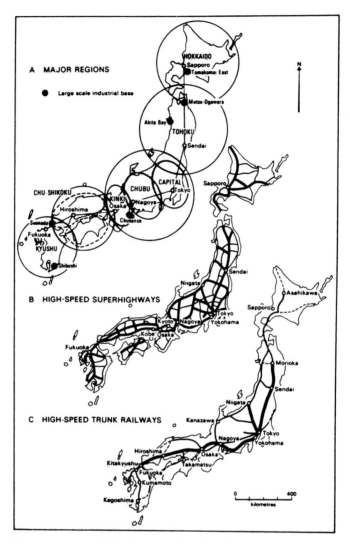

Figure 3: Japan as a spatially integrated national economy envisaged under the New Comprehensive National Development Plan (Shinzenso), 1969. Note Japan is subdivided into seven major regions in a way that recognizes the central management functions of Tokyo, the two supra-regions (east and west); and a range of nominated centers for decentralized management functions designed to overcome the vertical allocation of activities.

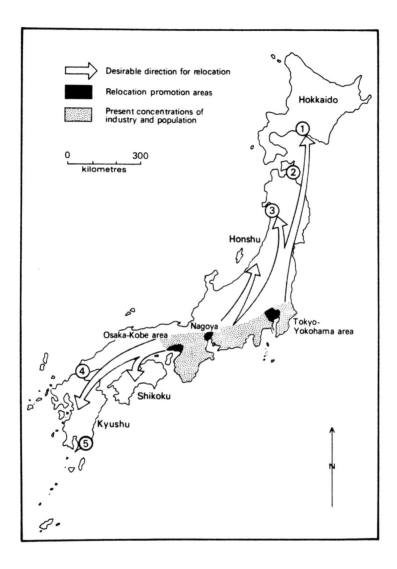

Figure 4:   Tanaka's new industrial pattern: 1. Tomakomai; 2. Mutsu-Ogawara; 3. Akita; 4. Suo-Nada; and 5. Shibushi (Source: Based on Tanaka, 1973: 85).

economic conditions during the Tokugawa's *Genroku* period between 1688 and 1704). The plan also allowed large national business corporations an opportunity to take a bird's eye view of the Japanese archipelago in making their export-oriented investment decisions.

The fall in the economy's and construction industry's growth rate during the late 1960s, however, suggests that the period of prosperity was almost at an end. In a bid to reverse these trends, Tanaka (1973), then aspiring to the prime ministership, put forward an even more ambitious, though unofficial, plan for "Remodelling the Japanese Archipelago" (*Nihon Retto Kaizo Ron*). As shown in Figure 4 it aimed at relocating industry from "overcongested areas" through tax exemptions on land and the creation of super-express, land-based transport and the accelerated development of all towns over 250,000. This ambitious plan buttressed Tanaka's successful bid for the prime ministership as it was well-received by the Liberal Democratic Party's predominantly rural base. Initially, however, Tanaka's plan set off a fever of pre-emptive land buying. Land prices soared, first in rural areas and then in urban areas. This was matched by a rapid recovery in both the economy and the construction industry; the latter being able to draw on reserves of labor through their multi-storied subcontracting systems.

The immediate beneficiaries were the major construction contractors, particularly the Big Five. Their overall domination of the post-war industry had been threatened by declining market shares since the late 1960s despite charges of favoritism in contracting for infrastructure projects (Hippoh, 1983: 274; Pepper, Janow and Wheeler, 1985: 80). Nevertheless, the Big Five still accounted for over half of the orders won by the "top 20" construction contractors in 1971 and 1972 (pers. comm., Japan Federation of Construction Contractors Inc. [*Nikkenren*]; no comparable figures are available for 1973 and 1974). As shown in Table 5, they were able to draw on business with the "Big Six" bank-centered conglomerate groups (*keiretsu*) -- Mitsubishi, Mitsui, Sumitomo, Daiichi Kangyo and Sanwa -- comprising financial, industrial, trading (*sogo shosha*) and real estate activities (e.g. Ohbayashi Gumi belongs to the Sanwa Bank Group); the major construction companies were linked to them through interlocking directorships and share ownership (Keizai chosa kyokai, 1982). Although some of the oligopolistic construction companies had established overseas offices in the U.S. (e.g. Takenaka Komuten in 1960; Kajima, 1964 and Ohbayashi Gumi, 1964), they were still dependent upon the sales-support systems of trading companies to seek out work for them overseas as they were reputedly weak in both finance and legal matters.

Between 1955 and 1972, they had undertaken only 783 overseas projects worth Y337,512 million; more than 70 percent of the value was in Southeast and Southwest Asia where reparations and resource undertakings were important (Kaigai kensetsu kyokai, 1980, 1985). There was an upsurge under Tanaka, however, as he adopted an Eastern Pacific Rim strategy focused on fomenting trade in a broad arc from Indonesia, through Australasia, South and Central America to North America with an accompanying emphasis on China, the Middle East and the Soviet Union (Rimmer, 1988). Spurred by an abiding concern to maintain access to fossil fuels and other mineral resources, this foreign policy initiative coincided with 488 projects worth Y346,445 million being undertaken between 1973 and 1974, not only in Southeast and Southwest Asia, but also in the Middle East and Central and South America (Kaigai kensetsu kyokai, 1985).

Table 5. The "Big Five" Japanese Construction Companies
1973-1974

Construction company	Head office	Bank group	Trading co.	Real estate	Completed contracts 1973 Ybill.	1974 Ybill.
Kajima	Tokyo	Sumitomo			377	498
Ohbayashi Gumi	Osaka	Sanwa	Nissho-Iwai		306	389
Shimizu	Tokyo	Dai-ichi Kangyo	C. Itoh	Daiichi Kaihatsu	347	449
Taisei	Tokyo	Fuyo			363	465
Takenaka Komuten	Osaka	Mitsubishi			313	403

Source: Keizai chosa kyokai, 1982; Nikkenren (pers.comm); Kyoikusha, 1980.

Before Tanaka's overseas initiatives and grand design for remodelling the Japanese archipelago could be pursued more fully Japan was confronted by an oil crisis in 1973, then by what threatened to be runaway inflation. Tanaka and his Cabinet were partially successful in dealing with both. Nevertheless, another precipitous decline in construction investments ensued and land prices in built-up areas collapsed. The overall decline in the economy's growth rate resulted in Tanaka's design for remodelling the

Japanese archipelago fizzling after his tenure ended ignominiously in the Lockheed scandal. By then the first phase of crisis was underway.

First Phase of Crisis under Fukuda (1976-78)

A convenient marker of the end of the first phase of the economic crisis and subsequent restructuring is provided by the Fukuda government. It gives an opportunity, in the light of Smyth's (1985) arguments, to consider two issues: had overproduction increased in manufacturing within Japan; and had the period of austerity been favorable to the construction industry through diversification into overseas markets and also spin-offs from property developments spurred by the need to speed capital accumulation?   Again, whether the economic variable was decisive or political factors were involved is explored.

By the time Takeo Fukuda had become prime minister the fundamental nature of the Japanese economy had shifted to a "stable growth" pattern. The economy's growth rate continued to decline as labor-intensive and energy-dependent industries moved offshore. As the collective attraction of the three major metropolitan areas waned with the "U-turn" phenomenon (i.e., people returning to their home prefectures) and decentralization of the electrical machinery and steel industries, the increase in land prices within built-up areas was negative after the hasty creation of the National Land Agency in 1972 before making a small gain. Paradoxically, the construction industry exhibited remarkable resilience, profiting from the increasing concentration of corporate headquarters in Tokyo and outer-suburban development. It was able to extricate itself from the prolonged "post-oil crisis" recession through an acceleration of the Fukuda government's spending on national and local public works, a housing program, and encouragement of investment in plant and equipment, a move prompted in 1976 by pressure from the U.S. and Japan's other trading partners to stimulate the domestic economy so it could absorb more imports. Consequently, the construction industry was able to maintain a growth rate of between 11 and 13 percent (though this represented a decline on the period between 1960 and 1973 when construction investments were over 20 percent).

Japanese planners responded to the changed circumstances within which the Fukuda government had to operate by dramatically shifting from the doctrine of functional integration of the national space economy (espoused under Tanaka) to the inward-looking concept of territorial integration in the "Third Comprehensive National Development Plan" (*Sanzenso*). Given that Tokyo and Osaka had 38 percent of the national population on less than eight percent of the land area the plan's target was to capitalize on the slower influx of population into these areas and to

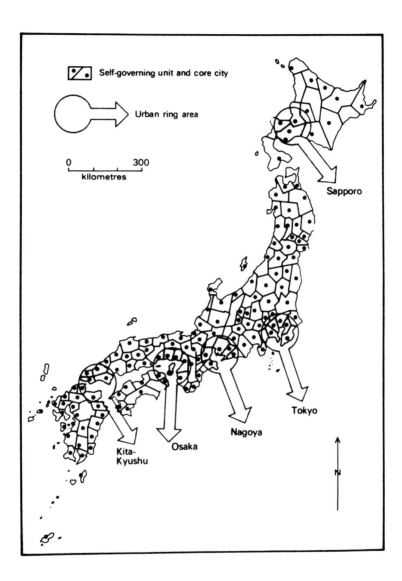

Figure 5: Self-governing units and main core regions (*teijuken*) established under the Third Comprehensive National Development Plan (*Sanzenso*) (Source: Yamaguchi, 1986)

encourage its stabilization by assisting people to remain in their home areas. As shown in Figure 5, the strategy was to co-ordinate environmental protection and industrial production within a framework based on over 200 integrated residential areas (*teijuken*), the fundamental sphere for daily activities. The cellular pattern was reinforced through its association with the "era of local initiative" (*chiho no jidai*). Both placed much emphasis on increased self-reliance and meeting human and social needs through an integration of rural and urban areas, a concept of decentralization with close affinities to Friedmann and Weaver's (1979) ideas on selective regional closure and agropolitan development.

In the long term the new planning structure boded ill for the large national construction contractors because it was the Fukuda government's intention to provide greater opportunities for both local, medium and small firms, reduce the scale of projects, disperse projects throughout Japan, and promote an improvement in the technical standards of small firms by encouraging technological transfer and leasing. These developments threatened the market share of the major construction companies that had been in continuous decline since the late 1960s. Between 1973 and 1978 the profit rate of the "Big 46" construction corporations had begun to fall, whereas wage increases matched those of factory workers; labor's share thus rising in the decreasing value added per capita. More pointedly, the Big Five's share of orders among the top 20 Japanese construction contractors had declined to 45 percent in 1978 and 1979 compared with 54 percent in 1973 (pers. comm., Japan Federation of Construction Contractors Inc. [*Nikkenren*]).

The Big Five firms could have insulated themselves from domestic competition by following the example of the large industrial corporations. The latter had switched from taking "a bird's-eye view" of the Japanese archipelago to adopting a worldwide perspective since they had been caught in the downswing of the economy after the oil crisis in 1973. Within their multinational organizations they were making investments to capitalize on the shifting patterns of comparative advantage to be found in the international economy. Indeed, the Third National Comprehensive Plan for Japan had not killed functional integration. It was alive and well, albeit in an international guise, based on the opening of new fields of surplus production using improvements in transport and telecommunications, the decomposition of production and the use of inexpensive labor power. Except for precision machinery (e.g. video tape recorders and integrated circuits) and industrial machinery (e.g. robots and numerically-controlled machine tools) the "worldwide sourcing strategy" -- featuring a global market for labor forces, industrial free trade zones, offshore plants and enclave factories in East and Southeast Asian countries -- had taken the place of leading sectors in Japan. The outcome within Japan, however, was to place her metropolitan complexes, notably Tokyo and Osaka, with corporate headquarters, research and development and high technological functions, at the apex of a global hierarchy with its base in underdeveloped countries dependent on a narrow range of labor-intensive industries.

Table 6. "The Big Five" Japanese Construction Companies
1978-1979

	Kajima Corp.	Ohbayashi Gumi	Shimizu Eng. Co. Ltd	Taisei Corp Co., Ltd	Takenaka Komuten
1978					
Total(S US m)	3,359.2	-	3,116.8	1,696.2	-
Foreign (%)	6.9	-	5.4	2.0	-
Int'l rank	55	-	69	152	-
1979					
Total(S US m)	3,091.0	2,470.0	3,201.3	n.a.	n.a.
Foreign (%)	3.2	2.7	12.5	n.a.	n.a.
Int'l rank	116	139	44	63	177

Source: *Engineering News-Record*, 1979-1982

Since the early 1970s the Big Five construction contractors based in Tokyo and Osaka had been stimulated sufficiently by these developments to expand their overseas activities (Kaigai kensetsu kihon mondai kentokai, 1982; Nakagawa, 1982; Rimmer with Black, 1985). In 1977 and 1978 they undertook 968 projects worth Y848,000 million. In accordance with Fukuda's Western Pacific Rim Strategy in foreign policy, attention was focused on a broad band of countries ranging from Australia along the Western Pacific Rim to North America (Rimmer, 1988). Specifically, their activities were concentrated on Southeast and Southwest Asia (49 percent of projects in 1977-78). A major departure from Fukuda's policy, however, was their emphasis on the Middle East, notably Iraq, Iran and Saudi Arabia

(47 percent).   Nevertheless, these exports represented only a small part of the business activities of the Big Five (Table 6).

The attention of the Big Five construction contractors was still firmly fixed on the domestic market. Although the government's investment had declined, the Big Five were still able to benefit from private sector developments. These stemmed from the demise of existing industries and their replacement by others using advanced technology and scientific research centered in major cities, particularly in Tokyo and Osaka which were still at the forefront of exports as junctions of international chains of production. Over 50 percent of the work of the Big Five was obtained on a non-competitive negotiated basis, the greater part being derived from the private sector. Design and construct packages accounted for one-third of the total reflecting the Big Five's advantage in research and development. Buoyed by these private sector activities the construction industry was able to offset the decline in government contracts during the first phase of the economic crisis. This proved to be a brief respite as the "second oil crisis" in 1979 plunged the construction industry into deeper trouble. By then, however, Fukuda was no longer prime minister; surprisingly he had been defeated in a ballot for the presidency of the Liberal Democratic Party. Coincidentally, the second phase of crisis had begun.

The Second Phase of Crisis under Nakasone (1982-1987)

The Nakasone prime ministership provides the occasion to examine Smyth's (1985) description of the second phase of the economic crisis. Had the construction industry reached the limits of its flexibility and become an underproducer in a phase of overproduction experiencing a lack of continuous work, a low demand and over-capacity; and had the period been marked by international and social tension?   There is another opportunity for considering the perennial issue: what is the nexus between government and the construction industry?

When Yasuhiro Nakasone became prime minister in 1982 he inherited a sluggish economy and a budget deficit that had not responded to investments in disaster relief, public works and housing construction. During his term, however, the economy exhibited a stable growth pattern. This stability was reflected in a decline in land prices in built-up areas due to changes in social structure (reduced growth of population and households and a decrease in the movement of population) and comprehensive land policies; there was, however, a reversal and a marked upturn in land prices from 1986. This reversal was also apparent in the fortunes of construction contractors. Following a zero growth ceiling on public works and a slump in housing stemming from a decline in personal incomes, they experienced negative growth. A recovery occurred in the construction industry after 1986 as the Nakasone government sought to create internal markets; these were buoyed by increased public works spending and a boom in private housing construction. These contrary trends during Nakasone's term underline the rapidity of changes that first expose and then mask the fundamental economic crisis.

Domestic Construction

Much was expected from Nakasone when he became Prime Minister because of his close affiliations with the construction industry.[1] There was little that he could do when he assumed office, however, to reverse the negative growth recorded by the construction industry. The effects of the past government's ceiling on public works had been aggravated since the "second oil crisis" by a decline in the amount of private work. As the number of construction companies continued to increase, competition between contractors intensified for the declining opportunities that were still focused on the big two metropolitan areas, especially Tokyo.

In 1982, however, an attempt was made by the Nakasone government to boost the regional areas through the creation of 19 technopolis sites as a means of attracting foreign investors to regional areas affected by growing unemployment (Figure 6). The aim of these Ministry of International Trade and Industry (MITI)-inspired developments (based on Silicon Valley, U.S., and Science Park, U.K.) was to revitalize regional economies by creating a base with a resident population of 15,000 for high technology research (e.g. biotechnology, semiconductors, software and new materials science) and industrial production in collaboration with local academic institutions. This program, however, was also perceived as a means of assuaging criticism from the Liberal Democratic Party's power base. As it was matched by the prefectural and local government's continued preference for regional contractors it is not surprising that collusive tendering, preparatory consultation and adjustment were reported among the large national construction contractors, a practice (known as *dango*) aimed at reducing competition and increasing the price of public works (Hippoh, 1983: 234).

Overseas Construction

The lack of public works and intensified competition, aggravated by declining profits, prompted the large construction corporations to "go multinational" in a worldwide search for profits (Table 7). Meanwhile, the Nakasone government sought administrative reform and fiscal reconstruction,

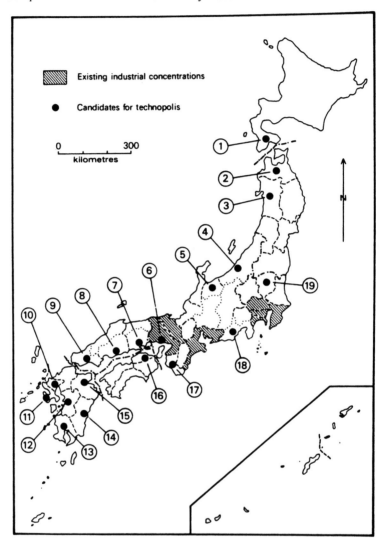

Figure 6: Proposed sites for technopolis (technology-oriented new cities), 1984: 1. Hakodate; 2. Aomori; 3. Akita; 4. Nagaoka; 5.Toyama; 6. Western Harima; 7. Kibi Highland; 8. Hiroshima Chuo; 9. Ube; 10. Kurume-Tosu; 11. Sasebo; 12. Kumamoto; 13. Kokubu-Hayato; 14. Miyazaki; 15. Northern Oita; 16. Western Kagawa; 17. Gobo; 18. Hamamatsu; and 19. Utsunomiya (Source: Tharp, 1982.

Table 7. "The Big Six" Japanese Construction Companies
1982-1986

	Kajima Corp.	Kumagai Gumi Co. Ltd	Ohbayashi Co. Corp.	Shimizu Eng. Co. Ltd	Taisei Corp.	Takenaka Komuten Co. Ltd
1982						
Total ($USm)	4,352.8	3,115.3	-	4,379.8	4,067.0	3,043.8
Foreign (%)	8.4	17.7	-	10.8	11.8	10.2
Int'l rank	77	57	-	67	66	87
1983						
Total ($USm)	3,840.1	3,283.5	3,378.8	4,299.5	4,834.0	3,101.3
Foreign (%)	7.6	22.4	11.1	12.5	9.4	9.8
Int'l rank	77	34	64	44	54	73
1984						
Total ($USm)	3,787.0	3,227.7	3,122.5	3,031.7	4,213.0	3,011.8
Foreign (%)	12.8	26.3	11.5	8.8	6.8	6.4
Int'l rank	39	20	50	55	71	88
1985						
Total ($USm)	4,953.1	4,692.2	4,280.0	4,779.1	4,641.3	3,787.0
Foreign (%)	12.7	46.4	8.8	12.7	5.7	5.0
Int'l rank	30	6	50	34	65	83
1986						
Total ($USm)	5,998.3	6,473.3	5,468.6	7,129.4	6,865.8	5,793.1
Foreign (%)	9.5	29.5	5.1	10.7	5.1	8.2
Int'l rank	34	7	59	23	49	40

Source: *Engineering News-Record* (1983-1987).

including the executive directive "Deregulation for Sake of Promoting Urban Development" (February 1983), as a means of providing long-term relief to the construction industry's problems (Nakamura, 1982, 1985; *Japan Economic Journal*, 1986). Overseas, however, the Middle East had declined as a major market for Japan's international construction contractors after the fall of oil prices and the onset of the Gulf War in 1980. Following Nakasone's broad foreign policy direction pivoted on Japan and focused on East and Southeast Asia and North America -- the Central Axis Strategy -- attention was focused initially on Southeast/Southwest Asia, especially as there was no compensating growth in contracts awarded in Africa and Latin America (Rimmer, 1988). As Asian markets were volatile and highly competitive (particularly with South Korean firms) attention turned to North America and, more unexpectedly, to Australia.

As overseas projects were riskier than domestic contracts the transformation of the Big Five from large national business organizations into multinationals has been protracted. Their reluctance to move offshore has enabled a lesser-known firm, Kumagai Gumi Co., Ltd, to take advantage of the opportunities offered. Thwarted in its ambitions to enter the elite group of domestic construction contractors by client loyalty and the government's practice of doling out public works projects in terms of past turnover, Kumagai Gumi actively sought work overseas as both a construction company and a developer (Rimmer, 1987, 1988). Backed by letters of credit from Sumitomo Bank, overseas earnings amounted to over 46 percent of Kumagai's total contracts in 1985 compared with an average of 10 percent for the Big Five. Indeed, the company's excursion into financial engineering, where it guarantees capital for a project in return for becoming prime contractor, resulted in its accounting for almost half of the overseas contracts won by the fifty-seven members of the Overseas Construction Association of Japan in 1985. As Kumagai Gumi's contracts match those of the leading construction contractors we should think in terms of the Big Six. Nevertheless, Kumagai Gumi was the only truly global company as the attention of the other five construction contractors was still firmly fixed on the Japanese market.

Their behavior was very different from major U.S. construction contractors, such as Bechtel Corporation and Fluor Corporation, which had transformed their firms into global corporations during the 1970s when they followed enterprises engaged in production and property development overseas against the background of a growing trade deficit. Subsequently, high capital costs discouraged their U.S.-based clients from investment in new domestic public works and buildings. When tax cuts boosted demand in the U.S. during the early 1980s the facilities were lacking to satisfy market needs. With the aim of filling this vacuum Japanese manufacturers (e.g.

Toyota, Canon and Nippondenso) and property developers (e.g. Mitsui Real Estate Development Co., Ltd, Shuwa Corporation and Nippon Life Insurance) moved some of their activities to the U.S.; the construction companies followed to attend to their business needs (e.g. Ohbayashi Corporation, with a 50-year business relationship with Toyota, is prime contractor of its plant in Georgetown, Kentucky, U.S.). Once established with the help of their affiliates, the construction contractors moved into business on their own account by targeting major urban areas in the U.S. (notably New York and Los Angeles), a process accelerated by the yen's marked appreciation (*Engineering News-Record*, 1984a, b). Armed with letters of credit from Japanese banks, construction contractors subsequently have established joint ventures with local construction companies and entered the field of public works. Thus, the "hollowing-out" of cities and manufacturing in the U.S. has been matched by the "hollowing-out" of the American construction industry.

Domestic Construction Revisited

These investments abroad seem poised to impose sweeping changes on Japanese cities, which suggests that a similar "hollowing-out" may be occurring in the country's urban-industrial structure forcing its construction industry to work increasingly overseas. The global prominence of Japan's financial sector, the shift toward services (i.e., the "softnomization" of the economy) and increased imports of manufactured goods have been seen as symptomatic of this change (with claims that if direct foreign investment increases by 12 percent annually almost two million jobs will have been created overseas by the year 2000 and 560,000 "lost" in Japan). Employees in regional cities heavily dependent on iron and steel (such as Muroran in Hokkaido and Kumaishi in Tohoku) and shipbuilding (such as Kure in Hiroshima) have been affected adversely by high yen (*endaka*) and the withdrawal of low technology and low-value activities as the economy moves to more sophisticated sectors. Consequently, the fortunes of regional construction companies have declined -- the "Age of the Provinces" is over.

The shift of labor-intensive production from Japan to overseas locations -- prompted by high electricity costs, high labor rates, a strong currency and increased competition from the Newly Industrializing Countries (NICs) in East and Southeast Asia -- was different from the shift of American companies offshore; it was occurring when Japan's current account had a heavy surplus and monetary costs were low. Also, the U.S. had lost key industries such as machine tools. Although Japanese automobile companies (e.g. Honda, Mitsubishi, Nissan and Toyota) have moved offshore, some of their critical components are still being sourced from central manufacturing plants in Japan. Using hyper-efficiency robots and office automation they are competitive even at high values of the yen. Also, their Japanese subcontractors have cut costs to remain competitive through mergers, wage freezes and increased use of part-time, female labor in a bid to avoid the "hollowing-out" of the domestic base. Consequently, there has been a continuation of high investments in the country's domestic industry, particularly in knowledge-intensive industries (*chishiki shuyaku sangyo*) (micro-electronics, biotechnology and new materials), which have provided an important source of contracts for the construction industry. Hence, it is a moot point as to whether Japanese cities (and the country's construction industry) are "hollowing-out" in the same way as their American counterparts or merely experiencing a transitional phase as Japan evolves from an industrial society into an advanced "informationized" society (*johoka shakai*) based on services and high technology. The main effect on the construction industry of shifting from an economy geared to promoting exports and restricting imports (i.e., savings-oriented), to a domestic demand-oriented one that procures raw materials and goods from overseas, has been to draw a marked distinction between the Tokyo market and the rest of Japan.

Tokyo

Tokyo, in contrast to Osaka, experienced a net immigration gain and the concentration of service sector activities, such as personal services, publishing, education and broadcasting (Rimmer, 1986; Inouchi, 1987; Miyao, 1987). Apart from industrial park oases, such as those in Sapporo, Sendai and Kumamoto, regional demand was dampened. Generating 90 percent of the nation's supply of information and 64 percent of all stock exchange transactions in 1986, Tokyo has become a major world financial and information center on a par with London and New York. These activities have been buoyed by distribution systems ranging from value-added computer networks to new, private parcel delivery services. Consequently, there has been a dramatic increase in the demand by foreign corporations (e.g. banks and security companies) and Japanese corporations, particularly those migrating from Osaka, for commercial and office buildings (Miyakawa and Wada, 1987). Just as the amount of floor space required per worker had increased with automation there was now a greater demand for office space. This need boosted prices, which escalated further as part of a "crazy land boom" in downtown locations, the beginning of which has been traced to the sale of surplus land near Shinagawa Station by Japan National Railways (JNR) in 1984. In early 1987, 3.3 square meters of commercial land cost more than Y150 million in the Ginza, a reflection, among other factors, of the ready availability of money for investment and the rapid appreciation of the yen.

Tokyo's explosion, however, has been in many respects a boon to the Big Six construction contractors and the "Big Seven" real estate developers (Mitsubishi Estate Co., Ltd, Mitsui Real Estate Development Co., Ltd, Shuwa Corporation, Nippon Life Insurance, Mori Building Co., Sumitomo Life Insurance and Sumitomo Realty and Development Co., Ltd). The distinction between the two groups, however, has become blurred as the major construction contractors have engaged in property development. In particular, the construction contractors have benefitted from the "real" demand for office space in the central area, especially "fashion" buildings (with shops on the first floor) and "intelligent" buildings, similar to the Ark Hills project which incorporates optical fiber cables for information networks and other systems. The latter's success in attracting foreign financial institutions (including major U.S. security houses such as Saloman Brothers Asia Ltd, Goldman Sachs International Corp. and Shearson Lehman Brothers Asia, Inc.) has prompted the Nippon Telegraph and Telephone Co. to team up with the original Big Five construction contractors and five others to build "smart" buildings (e.g. the Shibaura Shimizu Building completed in April 1987 by Shimizu Construction Co.). Many of these "smart" buildings equipped with the latest telecommunications technology, however, are being located in West Shinjuku rather than the traditional Marounouchi district of Central Tokyo (which the Mitsubishi Estate Co. is eager to redevelop at a cost of Y6 trillion over 30 years).

Given rising property values, the liquidity of Japanese banks (one-third of all loans were channelled into real estate) and declining interest rates, Japanese transnational corporations, which have made capital investments overseas, have been directing their overseas earnings into residential real estate. These investments have augmented their stocks and bonds which have been lodged in special portfolios (*tokkin*). Earnings from their "financial technology" (*zaiteku*) activities have been greater than their productive investments. These developments have pushed up the price of land and housing, first in prime residential areas and then, through the "domino" effect, in other communities in the Tokyo region as displaced inner-city landowners bought new properties to escape punitive capital gains taxes on their sales (the 77 percent increase in residential land prices in 1986-87 eclipsing the 35 percent increase under Tanaka in 1973-74). There was, however, a shortage of vacant lots for construction which reflected the fractionalization of land under the prevailing tax systems (capital gains, inheritance and fixed property imposts). This had the effect of penalizing those who sell land and favoring those who merely occupy it without selling it. Paradoxically, 30 percent of Tokyo is still farmland as this category of land use attracts negligible tax.

As these land use policies hindered redevelopment the Nakasone government sought to overcome the land shortage problem by releasing more land onto the market.   Indeed, the government's privatization (*minkatsu*) program resulted in Japan Railways land, including the large Shiodome Goodsyard, being offered for sale.   As the vendors asked three times the guideline prices published in the National Land Agency's directory the exercise fuelled rising land costs.   The latter, however, were also affected by the activities of "land sharks" purchasing land for sale and resale among land speculators before releasing it onto the market.   Indeed, the return on selling land was so lucrative that eviction specialists (*jiageya*) were employed to "persuade" owners/tenants, safeguarded by the tenancy protection law, to leave so that small lots could be consolidated for development and construction, notably in the Shinjuku and Hamamatsucho areas (i.e., near the Shiodome Goodsyard).

The overheated market was cooled, however, in late 1987 when the government advised banks to curb loans on speculative real estate.   In a bid to stem rising land prices, the Nakasone government decided that in some areas all land deals involving more than 100 square meters (previously 2,000 square meters) would be subject to local government scrutiny from August 1, 1987 (in other areas the minimum was 500 square meters).   A 96 percent tax was also imposed on income accruing from land resold within two years of acquisition after October 1, 1987.   Sale of land in Tokyo belonging to Japan National Railways by the Japan Railways Liquidation Corporation has also been restrained (the sale of the Shiodome Goodsyard has been frozen).   By then, however, the high prices had threatened to undermine domestic growth and, more seriously, social stability through the growing wealth disparities between those with land and those without (owner-occupied houses make up 62 percent of Japan's housing stock). Indeed, the construction industry's position expressed by Rokuro Ishikawa, chairperson of Kajima Corporation (now president Japan Chamber of Commerce), was "that the government should put a lid on private land possession in order to smoothly develop urban districts and increase land available for residential and office building" (*Japan Economic Journal*, August 1, 1987).   Presumably, therefore, the industry would be in favor of introducing new land use and taxation laws to overcome the rigid protection of agriculture and generate space for new housing construction.   Rather than make these politically difficult decisions the Nakasone government encouraged the construction industry's development with loans for public works (roads and bridges) and low cost housing lots, construction being seen as the locomotive pulling large domestic projects.

International Tension

In late 1987, the Nakasone government introduced still another public works and housing program to dampen criticism over its current account surplus, particularly with the U.S.. Funded by profits from privatizing Nippon Telephone and Telegraph (NTT), this latest Y3,600 billion boost to the construction industry coincided with an upsurge in housing construction. This led, in turn, to a shortage of building materials (cement, structural steel and timber) and the illegal employment of foreign workers and clandestine immigrant laborers (*dekasegi-gaijin*) to handle the demand (often involving brokers and crime syndicates). The government's boost for public sector investment was limited, however, in area. Any project involving the built-up area of Tokyo was excluded. This was not a problem as the 20 percent increase in public spending was insufficient to widen or extend a road let alone construct a new one.

Further deregulation and the encouragement of initiatives by the Nakasone government, however, have led to over 40 Tokyo-based construction projects being put forward by a host of ministries (including the Ministry of Construction and Ministry of Post and Telegraph), private developers, and the Tokyo Metropolitan government to boost domestic demand (Cutts and Thornbrugh, 1987). These large projects have included: the speculative "international village" for foreigners; the rebuilding of the inner-circle railway line (*Yamanote-sen*) with a highway on top; the redevelopment of Tokyo Railway Station and the Sapporo Breweries Co's site in Ebisu; the westward shift of the Tokyo Metropolitan government's offices from Marounouchi to Shinjuku (with an underground road to the central government road in Kasumigaseki); and the transformation of Tokyo's urban pattern from a mono-nuclear to a multi-polar arrangement focused on five "core-city areas" (Yokohama-Kawasaki, Tama, Tsukuba, Chiba and Saitama). As reflected in Figure 7A the key projects are located on Tokyo Bay including River City 21, the Tokyo Bay Highway, Yokohama's Minato Mirai [Future Port] 21 teleport and redevelopment project, Chiba's Makuhari Messe and Kawasaki's Seaside Technopia (Table 8). Oriented toward service, leisure and high-technology industries, the express purpose of the "fancy" waterfront projects is to reconstruct Tokyo as a "world city," the emphasis being on sophisticated commercial zones, new telecommunications networks, international convention halls, hotels and residential areas (Rimmer, 1986). Although offering ease of development, the price of the vacated industrial land is still relatively high. Consequently, the resultant private developments are not pitched at low income earners.

As a counterweight to the overwhelming importance of Tokyo

Table 8. Large Waterfront Development Projects under Construction

Project	Date FY	Cost Y tril.	Area ha.	Developer	Notes
		Tokyo Bay			
River City 21 Project	1989		330	Tokyo Mitsui & Co.	
Expansion of Haneda Airport	1993	0.9	1,100	Ministry of Transportation	
Tokyo Teleport (part of larger Tokyo-Manhattan plan)	1995	1.9	98	Tokyo Metropolitan Govt. Mitsui & Co. Mitsubishi Corp.	
Trans-Tokyo Bay Bridge Expy.	1996-97	1.2	---	Trans-Tokyo Bridge Corp.	Public/private mixed finance
Redevelopment of Makuhari City	2000	1.2	438	Chiba Pref., others	Public/private mixed finance
Minato Mirai 21	2000	2.0	186	Yokohama City Mitsubishi Real Estate Co., others	
Seaside Technopia Plan	2001		779	Kawasaki City	
		Osaka Bay and Inland Sea			
New Kansai Int'l Airport	1992	1.0	511	Kansai Int'l Airport Co.	Public/private mixed finance
Rokko Island	1995	1.2	580	Kobe City, others	
Akashi Straits Bridge	1997	0.6	---	Honshu-Shikoku Bridge Authority	
Technoport Osaka	2000+	2.0	700	Osaka City, others	

Source: Tsusansho, 1986; various.

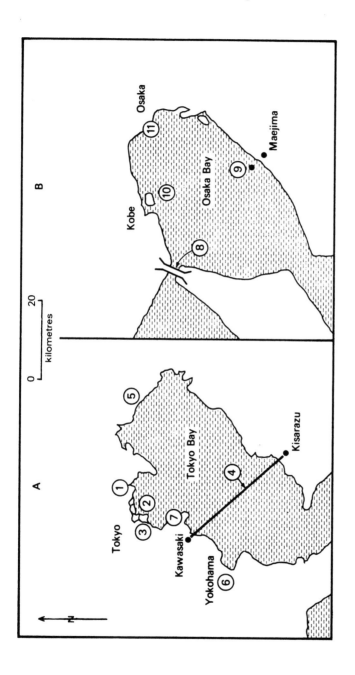

Figure 7: Major waterfront projects. A -- Tokyo; B -- Osaka. Tokyo: 1. River City 21; 2. Expansion of Haneda Airport; 3. Tokyo Teleport (part of Tokyo-Manhattan Plan); Trans-Tokyo Bay Bridge; 5. Redevelopment of Mahakari City, Chiba; 6. Minato Mirai 21, Yokohama; 7. Seaside Technopia Plan, Kawasaki. B -- Osaka: 8. Akashi Straits Bridge; 9. New Kansai International Airport; 10. Rokko Island, Kobe; 11. Technoport Osaka (Source: various)

much attention has been given by national planners to re-establishing the dual focus of the urban system. Under the Fourth National Comprehensive Development Plan (*Yonzenso*) brought down in 1987, the Tokyo region (Kanto) will be developed as an advanced economic, political and international center. The Osaka region (Kansai), still heavily reliant on its "smokestack" industries, will be boosted as an advanced economic, cultural and academic center to compensate for its shortfall as a focus for technological innovation (Osuga, 1987). Much emphasis in revitalizing the Osaka Region as a "new Chicago" is being placed on the "ripple" effects from a series of mega-projects (Figure 7B). They range from Rokko Island in Kobe through Osaka Technoport, the privately-sponsored Y500 billion Kansai Science City on the boundaries of Kyoto, Nara and Osaka prefectures, the Akashi Bridge (the second link between Honshu and Shikoku) to the Y1 trillion New Kansai International Airport scheduled to operate 24 hours a day as a major international passenger and cargo center -- the biggest airport contract in the world (Table 8).

International tension has been caused over the last project as part of a general backlash against Japan's "adversarial trade" which does not favor importing anything it exports (Johnson, 1987). While Japanese construction companies are allowed free access to the U.S. market this right had not been reciprocated in Japan: the last major contract won by a U.S. company was the Tomei Expressway in 1965. Although the private corporation, the Kansai International Airport Co., undertaking the New Kansai International Airport project is influenced by the government, its Phase One contracts for the construction of the seawall, reclamation and access bridge had not been open to public bidding. Consequently, major American companies had been unable to participate in the project. The rationale was that, unlike the U.S. contractors which engage in all activities, their Japanese counterparts undertake only construction work as government or government-sponsored organizations do the planning and design work; the U.S. claim that its firms should engage in planning and design, therefore, was seen as unrealistic by Japanese contractors. As the leading group of Japanese construction contractors are staunch supporters of the ruling party, they do not, according to Johnson (1987: 1.15), want the system changed.[2] Their argument was that all companies, regardless of nationality, are treated equally in the Japanese construction market. Nevertheless, the U.S. government kept up its pressure on this "moral" issue. Although bidding procedures on the New Kansai International Airport were relaxed for American construction companies in 1987 the general matter of access to other projects was unresolved when Nakasone left office; the threat of retaliation, therefore, passed to his successor with the second phase of the economic crisis well underway.

Charting the Crisis under Takeshita (1987-) and Beyond

It is necessary to ascertain whether the fundamentals of the second phase of the economic crisis, isolated by Smyth (1985), have persisted under the Takeshita government. Given the deepening overproduction within the world economy, would the Japanese construction industry be experiencing underproduction without the government's stimulation of the domestic market? Also, are the second phase's hallmarks -- rising economic problems, international tension and social unrest -- still present? Finally, have economic factors been decisive or do political factors also have to be considered?

Before Noboru Takeshita became premier his links with the construction industry were well known.[3] Not surprisingly, his platform in the Liberal Democratic Party's presidential race harked back to Tanaka's plan for remodelling the Japanese archipelago. Takeshita's scheme was entitled "Japan Archipelago: Hometown Theory" (*Nihon Retto Furusato Ron*); it involved the creation of hometowns (*furusato*) to attract people back to the rural areas, particularly through the purchase of second homes for week-end relaxation. Depolarization of industries and urban functions from the metropolitan areas, including the dispersion of central government functions from Tokyo, and a boost to housing production (i.e., by encouraging second homes) had, therefore, been an appealing plan for 15 years. While the revised version was welcomed by regional construction contractors and the rural backers of the Liberal Democratic Party it did not detract from the activities of the major construction contractors or undermine the increasingly important support of white collar workers. Although the appropriateness of its public works thrust (i.e., roads and bridges) in an "informationized society" has been questioned there is no sign of government shifting from its traditional policy. Hence, the question is raised as to what extent this policy can sustain the current upturn in construction activity. A fall in the growth rate of gross national product may trigger a recession in construction and some "hollowing-out" of the economy as corporations seek to escape overproduction.

The fear of unemployment has been intensified by the agreement between Japan and the U.S. on March 29, 1988 to open up the 50 trillion yen domestic construction market to the latter's construction contractors, a direct response of the Takeshita government to the threat of retaliatory action against Japanese construction contractors operating in the U.S. (Masuko, 1988). Besides lengthening the official notification and pre-tendering periods, the accord provides U.S. construction contractors with access to:

1.   Kansai Airport-style projects, based on relaxed bidding procedures agreed in 1987, which include Kansai International Airport, Trans-Tokyo Bay Expressway and Nippon Telegraph and Telephone (NTT) Corporation head office building;

2.   Seven public works projects, including expansion work for Tokyo's Haneda Airport, Tokyo Bay Rim development, Minato Mirai 21 and Osaka's Akashi Straits Bridge and Kansai Science City; and

3.   Private projects related to the public sector contracts such as airport terminal buildings at Haneda, Tokyo Teleport, convention hall at Minato Mirai, Technoport Osaka and Rokko artificial island at Kobe.

Foreign participation in the public sector projects are based on their technical and financial capabilities rather than past performance but the private/public sector projects are reliant on government "encouragement." Construction contractors from China, the European Economic Community and South Korea are expected to demand equal access (though they do not offer Japanese companies reciprocal rights). Apart from relaxation of protectionism under the guise of product quality support, increased foreign participation is dependent upon the Japanese construction industry reforming its traditional business methods, notably pre-bidding collusion (*dango*) and the "planned price system." Under the *dango* system newcomers are excluded by the surreptitious division of work before the contract is made, a practice guaranteeing large and small contractors work on the basis of their past performance. Indirectly, foreigners are also excluded by project representatives deciding the price prior to bidding and then, if it is low, allowing the bidders to negotiate among themselves to decide who might accept the project. Unless these practices are eliminated to permit greater participation, the next dispute over access to the domestic market is likely to be larger in scale and more complicated.

These short-term problems, however, have not prevented the government and the construction industry from taking a long-term view. As part of plans for creating the advanced cities and transport system of the 21st century, policies are aimed at furthering deregulation and introducing private initiatives in urban development under the banner of administrative reform and fiscal reconstruction. Redevelopment of Tokyo and diffusion of its capital-city functions (*sentoron*) to a new location will be of prime importance (Miyao, 1987). As Tokyo's population is expected to grow from 28 million to 34 million by the year 2000 (25 percent of Japan's population) it will attract most attention (though a further 20 percent of the population will live within a 50 kilometer radius of Osaka and Nagoya). Assuming that price controls on land are unlikely, and that other measures, such as giving land owners tax incentives to supply more land to the market and the deregulation of zoning and building codes, will be at best only partially successful, developers in Tokyo will still have to pay a high price for land (Miyao, 1987). Hence, increasing interest is being focused on Tokyo Bay to escape the dilemma. Although this focus runs counter to the shift toward Tokyo's western suburbs, major construction contractors have completed much of their work on rebuilding the existing city and the small area in the northwest corner of Tokyo Bay, and are anxious to have further contracts.

Table 9. Tokyo Bay Development Plans Beyond the Year 2000

Project	Cost Ytrill	Area ha	Population Residential million	Working million
Waterfront Development Plan (Tokyo Metropolitan Government)	3.4	440	0.04	0.15
Tokyo Bay Cosmopolis Plan (ENA)1	55.0	10,000	1.0-1.3	0.6-0.7
New Tokyo Plan 2025 (Group 2025)	238.0	30,000	1.0-1.3	0.6-0.7

Source: Kaneko, 1987.

As shown in Table 9, the Engineering Industry Promotion Association, an affiliate of the Ministry of International Trade and Industry, has outlined the Cosmopolis Plan for reclaiming 10,000 ha. (Kaneko, 1987). An even more ambitious plan to whet the appetites of major construction contractors has been outlined by the "Year 2025 Committee" chaired by Kisho Kurakawa to combat "the Tokyo Problem." In a bold bid to divert the flow of Japanese capital from American securities into the domestic market, Kurakawa envisages a 40-year project which will produce a 30,000-ha man-made island city in the northern part of Tokyo Bay with a population of 4.5 million (with a further 1.5 million on the adjacent land) -- a ready-made symbol of the government's will to boost the domestic economy.   This plan, incorporating the Boso Peninsula Canal and Trans-Bay underground rail and pipeline system, has been criticized as a Nakasone-favored, Tokyo-centered land development strategy.   It is, however, less Tokyo-centric than the Fourth National Land Development Program's (*Yonzenso*) plan for a multipolar city that has earned the ire of the Diet's provincial members; the former would accommodate 1.5 million within Tokyo's existing boundaries whereas the latter would house 2.7 million. (By the year 2010, there may be an estimated 1.5 million foreigners in Tokyo.) Although lacking high-level political and bureaucratic support the scheme is no more adventurous than Tanaka's plans for "Remodelling the Japanese Archipelago" which helped boost the construction industry.   As the project will require 8.4 billion cubic meters of landfill it will involve, in addition to Tokyo's refuse and dredged material from the southern part of the Bay and the proposed canal and levelling mountains in the Chiba Prefecture.   These waterfront plants have been heralded as the wave of the future.   Construction contractors are already gearing up for these projects in a bid to offset the problem of being an underproducer in an age of over-production -- their attractiveness to overseas construction contractors will heighten international tension.

Conclusion

On examination, the trajectory of the Japanese construction industry since the early 1970s has closely mirrored Smyth's theoretical pattern mapped out in Table 2, the main difference between the British and Japanese construction industries being the latter's lag in contractors moving overseas and the upturn in fortunes during the second phase of crisis. Clearly, these findings support Smyth's central contention that the whole crisis "is experienced in all countries although in different ways."

In tracing the history of Japanese construction contracting at critical junctures since the end of the post-war boom, we began with the Tanaka government's attempt to grapple with the falling rate of profit in the late 1960s by injecting capital into the industry which, through inflation, had a detrimental effect on profit rates. Next, we dealt with the first phase of the overproduction crisis under the Fukuda government during which construction contractors and property developers enjoyed more favorable domestic returns than other sectors.   Then, we examined the ways in which the Nakasone government has endeavored to cope with the overproduction crisis (i.e., exporting more than the world economy can absorb) by accommodating new growth sectors and restructuring those that are declining while simultaneously creating a new market for construction contractors. Overall, the declining trend has increased competition among contractors in Japan's shrinking market. Growth within the construction industry is becoming more selective as regards location (e.g. Tokyo) and sector (e.g. "smart" buildings). Because overproduction has continued in the Japanese economy the twin conditions, anticipated by Smyth (1985), have occurred: international tension (particularly with the U.S. and Western Europe) and the implantation of the seeds of future urban social unrest (i.e., between land and non-land owners).

Interwoven with this history has been an emphasis on the production and management of the built environment. On this score, there are fewer signs that the Japanese construction industry, compared with its British counterpart, is reaching the limits of its flexibility as an underproducer in a period of overproduction (Smyth, 1985: 231). Nevertheless, lobbying by the construction industry's associations for more capital expenditure will intensify. Inevitably, the Takeshita government and its successors will have to initiate some of the proposed large-scale infrastructure and telecommunications projects in Tokyo and other areas. Although the Japanese government is trying to persuade the private sector to bear more of the costs of these projects it will not be able to neglect the construction industry as it offers the means of creating employment and mitigating international tensions. The key issue in Japan, however, is whether these measures will resolve the crisis or merely entrench it, particularly as a downturn in domestic construction activity is anticipated in 1990.

Without waiting for the fulfillment of this prognostication the findings of this study on urban change in Japan and the international economy are related to the "new urban sociology," other types of urban political economy, and the literature on "world cities" and "globalization" (Kilmartin and Thorns, 1978; Saunders, 1986, Smith and Tardanico, 1987). Clearly, this study has its roots in the literature on "world cities" which highlights the primacy of the economic variable (Friedmann and Wolff, 1982; Friedmann, 1986). It has, however, moved away from the mainstream of "world city" literature and the principle of economic determinacy through its emphasis on the role of key agents, the construction contractors, engaged in producing and controlling the built environment. The attention given to changing political administrations, and the strong interrelationship between government and the construction industry in this analysis, underlines that a combination of political and economic processes is critical in any explanation. This conclusion brings us to the unresolved issue of degrees of political autonomy and economic determinacy (Saunders, 1983).

The conundrum cannot be resolved, however, on *a priori* grounds, but must be discovered, as this study on Japan suggests, through empirical research. This focus should not only encompass economic dynamics and political administrations but also society by considering the people affected by urban change and the international economy.

Acknowledgements

The assistance of members of Chodai Co., Ltd, the Institute of Human Geography at Tokyo University, International Association of Ports and Harbors, Japan Federation of Construction Contractors Inc., Japan Research Institute for Social Development, Ministry of Construction, Ministry of Transportation, National Land Agency, Overseas Construction Association of Japan Inc., and Shimizu Construction Co., Ltd is acknowledged. Research assistance has been afforded by Barbara Banks, technical assistance by Merv Commons, and logistical support by Chiaki Kuranami. The figures were drawn by Ian Heyward, Cartographic Section, Department of Human Geography, The Australian National University.

Notes

1. Characteristic of interlocking marriages between politics and business in Japan, the Australian Broadcasting Corporation (ABC, 1986) noted Yasuhiro Nakasone's second daughter is married to the son of Takeo Atsumi, Honorary Chairman of Kajima Corporation.

2. According to *Japan Economic Journal* (March 19, 1988), about 80 percent of the 425 Liberal Democratic Party's Diet members are said to receive political funds from contractors' lobby groups. The industry's donation of 340.5 million yen was the second largest to that from banking interests.

3. Takeshita was Minister of Construction under Prime Minister Takeo Miki in 1976. His personal connections come from his birthplace and constituency in Shimane Prefecture, Waseda University, former bureaucrats and economic circles. Ex-Waseda graduates, including the president of Taisei Corporation, have formed an "Encourage Takeshita Group." Among economic circles there is a Builders Group in which the presidents of Takenaka Komuten Co., Aoki Corp., and Fukuda Construction Co. (Mitsuada, 1987). Also, the *Far Eastern Economic Review* (January 7, 1988: 9) reported that Noboru Takeshita's youngest daughter is married to the son of the president of Takenaka Komuten, one of the "Big Six." His eldest daughter is married to the son of Dietman, Shin Kanemaru, ex-Minister of Construction and ex-Secretary-General of the Liberal Democratic Party. Reportedly, Shin Kanemaru is organizing the "Conference on New Capital Problems," inquiring into an alternative location to Tokyo as capital. Another relative is the president of a Shimane construction company.

References

ABC (Australian Broadcasting Corporation) (1986) "Kumagai Gumi and the Japanese Construction Industry." Recorded June 1, Sydney, ABC Talks Programs, Sydney, N.S.W., Australia 2001.

Castells, M. (1972) *La Question Urbaine.* Paris: Maspero.

Cutts, R.L. and Thornbrugh, D. (1987) Redesigning Japan, *PHP Intersect,* January: 6-23.

Engineering News-Record (1979-87) The McGraw-Hill Construction Weekly. New York: McGraw-Hill.

Engineering News-Record (1984a) "Overseas firms closing in on U.S.," August 2, 1984: 10-11.

Engineering News-Record (1984b) "Financial engineering wins jobs," August 2, 1984: 30-5.

Friedmann, J. (1986) The world city hypothesis, *Development and Change, 17*(1): 69-83.

Friedmann, J. and Weaver, C. (1979) *Territory and Function: The Evolution of Regional Planning.* London: Arnold.

Friedmann, J. and Wolff, G. (1982) World city formation: An agenda for research and action, *International Journal for Urban and Regional Research, 6*(3): 309-44.

Harvey, D. (1973) *Social Justice and the City.* London: Arnold.

Hippoh Yasuyuki (1983) *The Construction Industry in Japan: A Survey.* Tokyo: Asian Productivity Organization.

Inoguchi Takashi and Iwai Tomoaki (1984) The growth of zoku: LDP politicians in committees, 1964-1984, unpublished paper presented at the Annual Meeting of the Association for Asian Studies, March 23-25.

Inouchi Noboru (1987) Tokyo and Japan's urban system, unpublished paper presented to the Commission on Urban Systems in Transition, International Geographical Union, Dublin, June.

Japan Economic Journal (1986) "Construction: Domestic demand remains sluggish as government holds down public works spending," Japan Economic Almanac, Tokyo, Nihon Keizai Shimbun: 196, 200, 202.

Johnson, C. (1982) *MITI and the Japanese Miracle: The Growth of Industrial Policy, 1925-1975.* Stanford (CA): Stanford University Press.

Johnson, C. (1987) *Visit to Australia by Professor Chalmers Johnson.* Canberra: Japan Secretariat (c/o Department of Foreign Affairs, Administrative Building, Parkes, A.C.T., Australia 2600).

Kaigai kensetsu kihon mondai kentokai (1982) *Kaigai kensetsu shinko no kihonteki hokoku (chukan torimatome)* (Basic directions and methods for promotion of overseas construction -- interim report). Tokyo: Kaigai kensetsu kihon mondai kentokai.

Kaigai kensetsu kyokai (1980) *Kaigai kensetsu kyokai 25 nendo shi*, (25 Year History of Overseas Construction Association). Tokyo: Kaigai kensetsu kyokai.

Kaigai kensetsu kyokai (1985) *Kaigai kensetsu kyokai 30 nendo shi*, (30 Year History of Overseas Construction Association). Tokyo: Kaigai Kensetsu Kyokai.

Kaneko Hiromichi (1987) "Land development: Tokyo Bay in the year 2050," *Look Japan*, August: 7-9.

Keizai chosa kyokai (1982) *Nenpo keiretsu no kenkyu* (Bank conglomerate studies annual report for 1983). Tokyo: Keizai chosa kyokai.

Kensetsusho (1987) *Kensetsu hakusho* (White Paper Ministry of Construction). Tokyo: Kensetsusho.

Kilmartin, L. and Thorns, D.C. (1978) *Cities Unlimited*. Sydney: George Allen & Unwin.

Kwan, M-P (1987) Transnational capital and urbanization in the Pacific Rim countries: An overview. In M. Douglass and J. Friedmann (Eds), *Transnational Capital and Urbanization on the Pacific Rim: Proceedings of a Conference*. Los Angeles: Center for Pacific Rim Studies, University of California.

Kyoikusha (Ed.) (1980) *Kaishazan shiryo kensetsu gyokai no keiei hikaku -- joi 10sha* (Industry data series: Comparison of management within the construction business). Tokyo: Kyoikusha.

Masuko Takashi (1988) "Construction accord faces test," *Japan Economic Journal*, April 9, 1988: 1, 6.

Mitsuada Hisayuki (1987) "Takeshita -- the well-connected mediator," *Japan Economic Journal*, October 31, 1987: 32.

Miyakawa Tadao and Wada Naohisa (1987) Functions of corporate head-quarters: Concentration in Tokyo, *Japan Economic Studies, 15*(4): 3-37

Miyao Takahiro (1987) Japan's urban policy, *Japanese Economic Studies, 15*(4): 52-66.

Nakagawa, K. (1982) Major constructors scrambling for overseas markets, *The Oriental Economist, 50*: 18-21.

Nakamura Yoshimatsu (1982) *Kensetsu gyokai: gyokaishi No. 316* (Construction industry series). Tokyo: Kyoikusha.

Nakamura Yoshimatsu (1985) *Kensetsu gyokai: gyokaishi No. 417* (Construction industry series). Tokyo: Kyoikusha.

National Land Agency (1985) *The National Land Agency*. Tokyo: Prime Minister's Office, Government of Japan.

Neo, R.B. (1976) *International Construction Contracting: A Critical*

Investigation into Certain Aspects of Financing, Capital Planning and Cash Flow Effects. London: Gower Press.

Nomura Sogo Kenkyusho (1983) *Kokusai konsarutanto no kaigai katsudo sokushin no tameno kihon mondai to choki bijyon sakutei no kenkyu* (A study for consulting engineers of the promotion of their overseas activities and related long-term problems). Tokyo: Kokusai kenstsu gijitsu kyokai.

Osuga Hideo (1987) "Atarashi Kinki no sosei keikaku: Subaru puran no gaiyo" (Plan for creating a new Kinki: Summary of Subaru Plan), *Sangyo ritchi* (Industrial Location), June: 27-35.

Pepper, T., Janow, M.E. and Wheeler, J.W. (1985) *The Competition: Dealing with Japan.* New York: Praeger.

Rimmer, P.J. (1986) Japan's world cities: Tokyo, Osaka, Nagoya or Tokaido Megalopolis? *Development and Change, 17*(1): 121-58.

Rimmer, P.J. (1987) Japan's construction contractors and the regional state: remodelling Australia's structure. In M. Douglass and J. Friedmann (Eds), *Transnational Capital and Urbanization on the Pacific Rim.* Los Angeles: Center for Pacific Rim Studies, University of California.

Rimmer, P.J. (1988) *The internationalisation of the Japanese construction industry: The rise and rise of Kumagai Gumi* (forthcoming).

Rimmer, P.J. with Black, J.A. (1985) Japanese, Korean and Filipino international construction contractors: Structure and performance, *Development Studies Working Paper No. 40.* Canberra: Development Studies Centre (now National Centre for Development Studies), The Australian National University.

Saunders, P. (1983) On the shoulders of which giant? The case for Weberian political analysis. In P. Williams (Ed.), *Social Process and the City.* Sydney: Allen & Unwin: 41-63.

Saunders, P. (1986) *Social Theory and the Urban Question.* London: Hutchison Educational Ltd.

Smith, M.P. and Tardanico, R. (1987) Urban theory reconsidered: Production, reproduction and collective action. In M.P. Smith and J.R. Feagin (Eds), *The Capitalist City: Global Restructuring and Community Politics.* Oxford: Basil Blackwell: 87-110.

Smyth, H. (1985) *Property Companies and the Construction Industry in Britain.* Cambridge: Cambridge University Press.

Tanaka Kakuei (1973) *Building a New Japan: A Plan for Remodelling the Japanese Archipelago* (trans by Simul International Inc. of Nippom Retto Kaizo-Ron). Tokyo: Simul Press.

Tharp, M. (1982) Gaijin in the backyard, *Far Eastern Economic Review, 25* June, 47-49.

Tsusansho (1986) *Johoka mirai toshi koso* [Information on New City Plans]. Tokyo: Tsusansho [Ministry of International Trade and Industry].

Yamaguchi Takashi (1986) National policies and urban system: The Japanese experience, Proceedings of the Department of Humanities, College of Arts and Sciences, University of Tokyo, 84 (*Human Geography Series, 9*): 27-46.

Yanaga Chitose (1968) *Big Business in Japanese Politics*. New Haven and London: Yale University Press.

GLOBAL PRODUCTION AND REGIONAL "HOLLOWING OUT" IN JAPAN

Kuniko Fujita and Richard Child Hill
Michigan State University

The magnitude of Japanese overseas manufacturing investment since the currency exchange rate adjustment in 1985 is unprecedented in Japan's postwar history. Industrial globalization threatens Japan with contraction in domestic production, plant closings and manufacturing job losses paralleling the past experience of the U.S. This paper investigates the internationalization of Japanese manufacturing and the manner in which the Japanese state is responding to the threat of industrial and regional hollowing out, principally through a case study of the automobile industry, Toyota Motor Corporation, and Toyota's home territory, Aichi Prefecture.

In September, 1985, financial ministers from the five major industrialized countries (the "G5") met in New York and agreed to increase the value of the yen against the dollar. Exchange rate adjustment was a technical response to an underlying political problem. History and ideology prevented administrations in the U.S. and Japan from altering the financial and industrial practices at the root of Japan's huge trade surplus with the U.S.. Trading manufactured goods for raw materials, food and energy has long been considered a matter of national survival in Japan, and the Reagan administration's free trade ideology hampered the direct imposition of U.S. import restrictions on Japanese goods.

The 1985 exchange rate adjustment steeply appreciated the value of the yen against the dollar (from 265 in summer 1985 to 130 in summer 1988). Japanese industrialists are countering the rising yen by sharply accelerating overseas production. Japanese corporations have been locating production sites abroad since the 1960s and they stepped up direct foreign investment in the early 1980s to circumvent trade barriers. But the speed and scale of the transnationalization of Japanese firms since the G5 meeting in 1985 is simply unprecedented in Japan's postwar history.

The transnationalization of production has been most remarkable in Japan's automobile industry. By 1989, eight Japanese car companies will have put nearly S5 billion into the construction of 10 assembly plants in North America alone. By 1989, these transplants will be capable of producing 2.16 million cars and light trucks inside the North American market

(*Japan Economic Journal*, September 5, 1987; Snyder, 1987). Replacing the export of finished vehicles, transplant production is a new phase in the internationalization of the Japanese automobile industry.

Industrial globalization poses a potentially serious social issue for Japan. As Japanese manufacturing companies assemble more cars in North American transplants, as they source more components and materials from newly industrializing countries (NICs) on the Pacific Rim, and as they export fewer finished commodities from Japan, won't domestic production contract, jobs in supplier and affiliated companies decline and plants close? In short, won't Japan experience deindustrialization paralleling the past experience of the U.S. and the U.K.? How are national and local officials in Japan responding to the hollowing out threat?

Japan's mining, shipbuilding, iron and steel industries contracted in the 1970s. But industrial layoffs were not massive, companies managed to keep workers employed by shifting them around, and Japan's vaunted social stabilizer -- the big company, lifetime employment system -- was largely kept intact. Today's highly valued yen could be writing a different story. Japan's heavy industrial complexes, often organized into "corporate castle towns," are in decline; some are even disappearing (Ministry of Labor, 1987; Shima, 1987).

Manufacturing for export has long been the engine of Japan's most dynamic regional economies. Regional cities, those outside the Tokyo-Osaka "world city" orbit, have largely depended upon tax revenues from export-led manufacturing firms. As Table 1 shows, Japan's top 20 cities, by value of shipped products, are heavily engaged in industrial exports, such as cars and consumer electronics. Will shifting production facilities from Japan's regional cities to Pacific Rim NICs, the U.S. and the European Economic Community (EEC) lead to a spiral of plant closings, layoffs, and regional deindustrialization?

In this paper we investigate the internationalization of Japanese manufacturing and the manner in which the state is responding to the threat of industrial and regional hollowing out, principally through a case study of the automobile industry, Toyota Motor Corporation, and Toyota's home territory, Aichi Prefecture.

The Transnationalization of Japanese Industry

The globalization of Japanese auto production signals a third phase in the postwar transnationalization of Japanese industry. Overseas investment took off in the 1960s, a period of rapid growth in Japan. During the 1960s, Japanese direct foreign investment flowed mainly into textile and miscellaneous goods factories located in Asian countries on the Pacific Rim.

Table 1. Japan's Top 20 Cities Ranked by Value
of Manufacturing Shipments, 1985

City	Primary Product	Total Shipments (10,000,000 yen)	Primary as % of Total
1. Tokyo	Publication and Printing	1,253,499	31.1%
2. Osaka	Chemical Products	747,067	12.6%
3. Kawasaki	Electrical Machinery	676,291	23.1%
4. Toyota	Automobiles	632,291	89.6%
5. Yokohama	Electrical Machinery	607,335	25.3%
6. Nagoya	Transport Machinery	489,421	18.8%
7. Kurashiki	Petroleum and Coal	370,880	28.9%
8. Ichihara	Petroleum and Coal	323,235	47.8%
9. Kobe	Food Products	283,451	19.9%
10. Kitakyushu	Steel	273,020	37.7%
11. Sakai	Petroleum and Coal	268,114	25.0%
12. Kyoto	Textiles	264,929	15.8%
13. Amazaki	Steel	190,743	21.4%
14. Hiroshima	Transport Machinery	184,362	49.3%
15. Fujisawa	Transport Machinery	173,892	30.1%
16. Himeji	Steel	172,309	50.4%
17. Yokkaichi	Chemical Products	170,752	50.4%
18. Hamamatsu	Transport Machinery	169,339	34.8%
19. Higashi-Osaka	Metal Products	162,113	17.4%
20. Yokosuka	Automobiles	146,936	80.6%

Source: Statistics Bureau (1986)

Labor-intensive and export-oriented, Japanese textile companies had already reached maturity during the prewar period. They went offshore principally in search of cheap labor (Ozawa, 1979).

The industrial space left by outgoing textile and miscellaneous goods companies was filled by basic materials producers: iron and steel, nonferrous metals, petrochemicals, pulp and paper. Japan's leading economic actors during the late 1960s and early 1970s, basic materials companies were capital intensive, energy consuming, export dependent and relied heavily upon imported, cheap, raw materials, including crude oil, iron and copper ore, bauxite and lumber.

The 1973 oil crisis undermined the profitability of Japan's basic materials industries and citizen's movements challenged their role in despoiling Japan's environment (Miyamoto, 1983). With financial assistance from the Japanese state, basic materials companies responded to the crisis by launching a second phase in the transnationalization of Japanese industry: they set up processing transplants in thinly populated areas of the raw materials producing countries of southeast Asia (Ozawa, 1979). The one exception was iron and steel, a basic materials industry which managed, by adopting innovative technology and organizing government sanctioned pricing cartels, to renew its international competitive strength without going offshore.

The rise of auto, consumer electronics, office equipment and telecommunications industries in the 1970s compensated for the contraction of Japan's basic materials sector. Like their industrial forerunners, though, these advanced assembly companies were also highly dependent on export markets.

The Transnationalization of Japanese Auto Production

Japanese auto companies are now leading a third phase in the transnationalization of Japanese industry. Several structural features of Japan's motor industry set the stage for globalization.

The Context for Globalization

Centrality to the Economy. Auto manufacturing is Japan's largest export industry and has held that status for over a decade. In 1985, the year the G5 Ministers were meeting in New York, Japan exported 6.8 million motor vehicles, worth S44.4 billion and amounting to 19.6 percent of the value of all Japan's exports. Altogether, Japanese companies manufactured 12.4 million motor vehicles in 1985 -- 30 percent of total world production. Eleven percent of Japan's work force and 18 percent of Japan's manufacturing investment were directly employed in auto production. Japanese passenger car imports, on the other hand, came to just 55,000 cars in 1985, 80 percent of German vintage (Kitazawa, 1987).

Export dependent growth.   Exports accounted for nearly all of the growth in Japanese auto production between the mid-70s and mid-80s. Production for the domestic market barely increased (from 4.9 million units in 1973 to 5.6 million units in 1985) while exports nearly tripled (from 2.1 million motor vehicles in 1973 to 6.8 million in 1985).   The ratio of exports to total vehicles produced ballooned from 29 percent to 55 percent during the same period of time.

A falling profit rate.   Motor vehicles exported to the North American market provided a considerably higher profit margin for Japanese manufacturers than cars produced for home consumption.   Before the G5 conference in 1985, Japanese car companies were averaging $2,000 gross profit per exported car (Kitazawa, 1987).   But with the rise of the yen since October 1985, profit margins on exports have fallen sharply; so much so that price competitiveness in the less expensive car lines has shifted from Japan based companies to producers located in the newly industrializing countries and Yugoslavia (Suzuki, 1987).

Surplus capacity.   The production capacity of Japanese transplants in North America will reach an estimated 2.6 million by 1989 (Snyder, 1987).   When transplant production is added to the 2.3 million exports from Japan under the voluntary restraint agreement, the sum comes to 4.5 million Japanese cars in the U.S. market plus another 650,000 or so from South Korea.   U.S. consumers currently purchase 11 million vehicles each year, including six million small cars.   The outcome is predictable: surplus capacity, and even fiercer international competition for the North American market, the world's largest.

The trade deficit.   As Japan's North American assembly transplants come on line, imports of auto parts and components from Japan will likely increase, the U.S. trade deficit with Japan will likely rise, as will pressure for further increases in the value of the yen.

Transnational Strategies

All the contextual factors thus far surveyed -- the centrality of auto production to Japan's economy, export dependency, a falling profit rate, overcapacity, fiercer international competition, and the threat of further yen appreciation due to a rising U.S.-Japan trade imbalance -- have persuaded Japanese auto manufacturers to adopt a new global strategy.

It is useful to draw a distinction between horizontal and vertical transnational strategies (Gilpin, 1987: Ch. 6).   Companies pursuing a horizontal, "company town" strategy organize spatially concentrated and integrated manufacturing complexes at strategic regional points around the globe. Companies organizing international production according to a vertical, "global factory" strategy divide the manufacturing process into multiple pieces, spread them out over many countries and coordinate the relationship among pieces from specialized centers of control. Both production strategies and variations in between can be seen in the world auto industry today (Porter, 1986: ch. l; Hill, 1987).

Japanese car manufacturers have excelled at organizing highly efficient, horizontally integrated, export oriented manufacturing complexes (Cusumano, 1985). Japanese companies started out as exporters of completed vehicles to world markets from the highly concentrated and integrated manufacturing complexes that dot Japan's Pacific basin. Overseas transplants in North America and the EEC were then launched in the early 1980s, first by Honda and eventually by all of Japan's major auto manufacturers, largely to circumvent growing political obstacles to trade (see Table 2). Thus far, Japanese transplants have been primarily assembly operations rather than full-fledged, integrated manufacturing complexes along the model of Toyota City in Japan or Ford's Rouge in Dearborn. The major, higher value automotive components have continued to be supplied from Japan (Luria, 1986).

But under conditions of the appreciated yen, the trend among Japanese auto producers today is decidedly toward a vertically organized, global factory division of labor. In order to make up losses on the exchange rate, to secure adequate profits on U.S. investment, to bypass U.S. export restrictions, and to protect against too large a U.S. trade imbalance with Japan, Japanese car manufacturers are reducing exports of finished cars and components from Japan and transferring parts manufacturing operations to low-cost suppliers in Korea, Taiwan, Mexico, and other nations along the Pacific Rim (*Japan Economic Journal*, March 21, 1987; Misawa, 1987; Rother, 1987; Takeuichi, 1987). This emerging Pacific Rim division of labor is organized through a complicated set of joint production and ownership arrangements among Japanese, U.S. and NIC companies. Parts produced in Pacific Rim NICs will be sent to assembly transplants in North America and to domestic operations in Japan.

Toyota Motor Corporation and Aichi Prefecture

Toyota Motor Corporation illustrates the change in global strategy among Japanese auto manufacturers.

Table 2. Japanese Transplants in North America and Britain: Investment, Annual Production Capacity, Production Start Year

Company	Investment	Annual Production Cap.	Production Start Year
U.S.			
Honda Motor	S530 mil.	360,000	1982
Nissan Motor	745 mil.	240,000	1983
Toyota-GM (NUMMI)	400-500 mil.	250,000	1984
Mazda Motor	550 mil.	240,000	1987
Toyota Motor	800 mil.	200,000	1988
Mitsubishi-Chrysler.	600 mil.	240,000	1988
Fuji Heavy-Isuzu	500 mil.	240,000	1989
Honda Motor	380 mil.	150,000	1989
Canada			
Honda Motor	200 mil.	80,000	1986
Toyota Motor	400 mil.	50,000	1988
Suzuki-GM	615 mil.	200,000	1989
Britain			
Nissan	350 mil.	240,000	1986
Isuzu-GM	na	19,000	1987

Sources: Japan Automobile Manufacturers Association (1987); *Japan Economic Journal* (August 29, 1987; September 26, 1987)

Map 1.   Aichi Prefecture, Japan

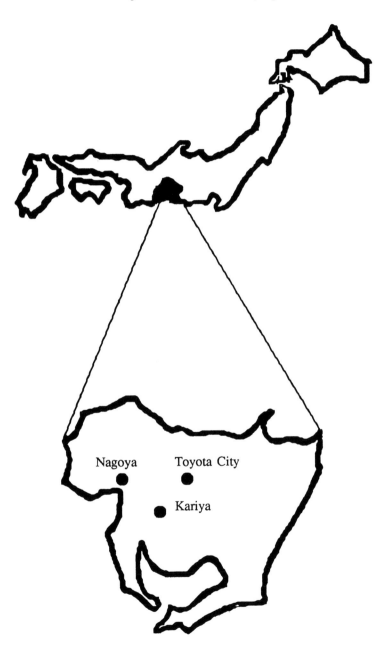

Figure 1: The Japanese Auto Production System

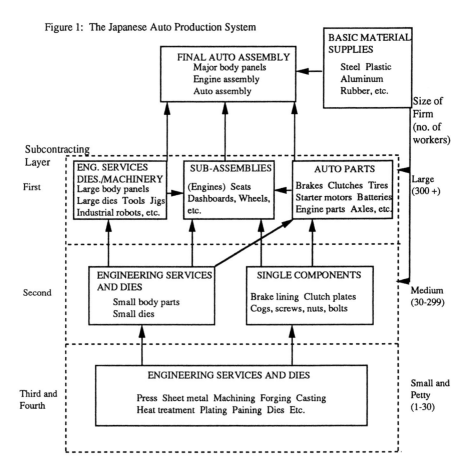

Source: Sheard (1983)

Toyota's Company Town

Toyota's production system is firmly planted in Aichi Prefecture, the heart of Japan's central industrial belt (see Map 1). All of Toyota's major plants are concentrated in Aichi Prefecture as are most of the company's principal suppliers.

Toyota's production system includes its own assembly and components plants; suppliers of basic materials; subcontractors directly supplying subassemblies, parts, dies, and engineering services; and a myriad of small- and medium-sized firms indirectly linked to the production process through the supply of parts and services to the automakers' direct subcontractors. Toyota and its subcontractors are organized into a hierarchically-specialized production chain, tiered according to productive capacities, capital intensity and wage costs (see Figure 1). The Toyota production system interlinks small workshops with businesses of various sizes and descriptions all the way up to the parent Toyota company (MITI, 1977; Kaneko, 1982; Fujita and Hill, 1989).

Toyota Motor Corporation exerts a high degree of control over its production system. Two suppliers' organizations, Kyohokai and Eihokai, help coordinate the relationship between the Toyota parent and its first-tier subcontractors. Each first-tier supplier has between two and three hundred second-tier subcontractors and each second-tier subcontractor has many smaller-sized, third-tier suppliers. Subcontractors at each tier level must accept strict conditions and controls over price, quality, and delivery from their parent company in the tier above. Subcontractors seek a place in the Toyota chain of command to secure the benefits that a parent company can provide: stable markets, access to investment funds, stable supplies of good quality raw materials, technical and managerial guidance in plant layout, and so on (Cusumano, 1985: ch.5).

In spatial terms, Toyota has amplified the classic Ford system of conveyor belt production within plants to a regional production system tying together assembly plants and suppliers (Sheard, 1983). Toyota's "just-in-time" delivery system integrates the production lines of subcontractors with the parent firm. Just-in-time delivery in small batches requires close contact between parent and subcontractors and promotes spatial concentration of production. Spatial proximity further reduces transportation costs, minimizes possible disruption or delay in delivery and allows for quick changes in delivery schedules (Sugimori, 1977; Ohno and Monden, 1983).

Through their production networks, Toyota and nine first-tier "Toyota Group" companies manufacture 70 percent of the value of an automobile (Higgins, 1987). Once a part of Toyota Motor Corporation, the nine companies in the Toyota Group became independent in the 1950s. The

Table 3. Toyota Group Companies
Location, Major Products and Number of Firms
in Their Supplier Associations

Company	Location	Major Products	# Firms in Suppliers Association	# Suppliers in Aichi Prefecture
Aichi Steel	Tokai	Speciality steel, die casting	48	46
Toyoda Automatic Loom Works	Kariya	Engine parts gas & diesel engines	54	51
Toyota Auto Body	Kariya	Assembly	84	62
Aishin Seiki	Kariya	Transmissions, engine parts, clutch disks	93	87
Toyoda Machine Works	Kariya	Power steering, crank shafts, machining	67	56
Nippondenso	Kariya	Engine & electrical parts	67	53
Toyoda Gosei	Nagoya	Engine parts, brakes and seals	72	57
Chuo Spring	Nagoya	Springs	67	57
Aisan Industry	Taifu	Engine parts, carburators, valves	23	21

Source: Kaneko (1982)

Toyota Group includes Aichi Steel, Aishin Seiki, Asian Industry, Nippondenso, Toyota Auto Body, Toyota Automatic Loom Works, Toyoda Gosei, Toyoda Machine Tools, and Chuo Spring (see Table 3).[1]

Toyota Motor Corporation's headquarters and major production facilities -- final assembly, engine, transmission, casting, machine tool and parts manufacturing -- are all located in Aichi Prefecture; most are located in Toyota City, a municipality bounding one of the world's largest manufacturing complexes (Fujita and Hill, 1989). Six of the nine Toyota Group companies are located in neighboring Kariya City whose well-developed machine tool industry is closely tied to Toyota City's assembly lines. Other Toyota Group companies are located in the nearby Aichi cities of Nagoya, Tokai and Taifu. The Toyota group produces a range of subassemblies and parts including crank shafts, power steering, transmissions, clutch disks, brake cylinders, air conditioners, and condensers. Materials industries which supply auto production -- steel, rubber, plastics -- have grown up around the parts manufacturing operations.

Each Toyota Group company has its own supplier association with membership lists ranging from 23 to 93 subcontractors per association (see Table 3). These third-tier subcontractors are also concentrated within Aichi Prefecture as are the fourth-tier subcontractors that supply them. The 30 percent of the car not produced by the Toyota Group is manufactured and assembled through the networks of Toyota's remaining first-tier suppliers. Of those, 63 are located in Aichi Prefecture and 102 are headquartered in Tokyo, Osaka and other parts of Japan. In conformity with the just-in-time system, first-tier suppliers headquartered outside Aichi Prefecture maintain branch plants and warehouses in Toyota City or surrounding Aichi Prefecture.

Toyota's Global Factory

In response to the steep appreciation of the yen, Toyota is shifting emphasis from a spatially concentrated, horizontally organized, "company town" production strategy to a spatially dispersed, vertically organized, "global factory" division of labor. There are two dimensions to Toyota's current global strategy. The first is a Pacific Rim division of labor whereby Toyota is using NICs of East Asia as export platforms for low value added parts and economy cars targeted principally for markets in Japan and the U.S. The second is Toyota's transplant production strategy in North America.

Toyota's Pacific Rim division of labor. In the 1960s, Toyota's overseas production activities were largely limited to knock down (KD) assembly plants. Parts and components were manufactured in Aichi

Prefecture and exported to the host countries for assembly. In the 1970s, Toyota built parts manufacturing facilities in Indonesia, Thailand, Australia and Brazil in response to national car development programs with local content requirements. As production technology in each host nation advanced, Toyota began exporting components to countries neighboring the host nation. By 1982, Toyota was exporting engines manufactured in Australia to Japan (Toyota Motor Corporation, 1982).

Many first-tier Toyota suppliers followed the parent company overseas. A few suppliers engaged in direct manufacturing but most limited their activities to technical assistance and sales operations. Of the suppliers who initially accompanied Toyota abroad, most were headquartered outside of Aichi Prefecture, mainly in Tokyo and Osaka. They included Yazaki Corporation, Kayaba Industry, Yuasa Battery, NHK Spring, and Bridgestone. These companies produced low value added products, such as batteries, tires, glass and wire harnesses to meet the local content requirements of host nations. Imasen Electric Industries and Aoyama Seisakusho were among the few Aichi-based, Toyota suppliers to engage in offshore production in the 1960s. They were producing auto parts in Taiwan and Thailand. In the 1970s, Nippondenso, Aishin Seiki and Meiwa Industry began offshore production of electric parts, auto parts, piping and casting products in Thailand, Taiwan and Indonesia.

Since the appreciation of the yen in 1985, Toyota has greatly extended the global reach of its production system. Taking advantage of its long-term foothold in the Asian NICs, Toyota has upgraded its subsidiaries, expanded its production facilities and encouraged its suppliers to come along. Thus far, the Toyota parent has primarily focused on the production of trucks for local Asian markets but the Toyota family of overseas suppliers is increasingly using the Asian NICs as export platforms for markets in Japan, the U.S. and other parts of the world.

As can be seen from Table 4, Japanese auto suppliers have sharply increased overseas production since 1985. While Japanese parts makers have a presence all over the world, they are concentrated mostly in Taiwan, South Korea and other Asian nations on the Pacific Rim. As can be seen from Table 5, Aichi-based Toyota suppliers have followed the same overseas trajectory.

Toyota's production operations in Taiwan, Thailand and Indonesia illustrate the company's Pacific Rim strategy.

Taiwan. There are seven auto makers in Taiwan. Most are joint ventures between Taiwanese and Japanese or U.S. car manufacturers. One is the Toyota-Taiwanese venture, Kuo Zui Motor Ltd, a truck and passenger car assembly operation. As auto production has grown in Taiwan, local demand for parts has become stronger. But the strong yen has made parts

Table 4. Japanese Auto Parts Suppliers in Overseas Markets

Region and Country	Total	Manu-facturing	Sales	Technical Assistance	R&D	NA	# Starting After 1985
Asia	360	141	11	201		5	90
China	12		12	12			8
Korea	65	19		46			31
Taiwan	86	42	1	43			21
Thailand	62	28	3	29		2	6
Malaysia	33	17	1	15			6
Indonesia	37	13	1	23			7
India	30	6		24			10
Oceania	49	8	9	32			12
Australia	46	7	8	31			10
New Zealand	3	1	1	1			2
North America	148	59	56	33	1		45
U.S.	135	54	49	32	1		40
Canada	13	5	7	1			5
Latin America	49	18	4	28			7
Mexico	21	4	2	15			5
Brazil	15	11		4			---
Europe	78	12	26	32			18
England	20	3	9	8			6
Spain	13	2	1	10			4
W. Germany	18	2	12	4			2
Africa	16	2		14			3
Middle East	2		1	1			---
Total	702	240	151	341			175

Source: Automotive Herald, Ltd. (1987)

Table 5. Overseas Mfg. by Toyota Suppliers based in Aichi Prefecture

Company	Ownership*	Country	Start Year	Product
Aishin Seiki	J	Taiwan	1979	Auto parts
	F	U.S.	1988	Pressed parts
Aoyama Mfg.	F	Thailand	1965	Nuts & bolts
Arakawa Autobody	J	Taiwan	1987	Auto bodies
Imasen Electric	J	Taiwan	1968	Auto parts
Inoue T.P.M.	F	U.S.	1987	Tooling, exterior parts
	J	U.S.	1988	Inst & door panels, consoles
Chuo Seiki	J	U.S.	1988	Wheels
Hayashi Telemp	J	U.S.	1983	Floor carpets, door trim
Maruyasu Industry	J	U.S.	1984	Fuel and brake pipes
Meiwa Industry	J	Indonesia	1975	Piping & other casting prod.
Nippondenso	J	S. Korea	1976	Auto meters
	J	Taiwan	1987	Altntrs, starters, air c o n d s .
	J	Thailand	1972	Electrical parts
	J	Malaysia	1980	Electrical parts, radiators
	J	Malaysia	1983	Air conditioners
	J	Indonesia	1975	Radiators, spark plugs, air conditioners
	F	U.S.	1971	Electrical parts, air cond.
	F	U.S.	1984	Radiators, htrs, condensors
	F	U.S.	1987	Electrical parts
	J	Brazil	1980	Compressors
	J	India	1984	Alternators
	J	Australia	1972	Heaters, meters, radiators
Ryobi	J	U.S.	1987	Aluminum diecast parts
Tokai Rika	J	Canada	1986	Seat belts
	F	U.S.	1988	Switches, locks
	J	S.Korea	1985	Switches
Tokai Rubber	F	U.S.	1987	Motor mounts
Toyoda Gosei	J	Taiwan	1985	Urethane parts
	J	Canada	1986	Weatherstrips
	J	U.S.	1987	Steering wheels, plastic prts
Tatematsu Mould Wks	J	U.S.	1988	Plastic parts, instruments
Sango	J	U.S.	1986	Mufflers

*J = Joint Venture; F = Full Ownership   Sources: Aichi Keizai Kenkyujo (1987); Arnesen, et al. (1987); Automotive Herald Ltd (1987); Toyota Motor Corporation (1986); *Japan Economic Journal*, various issues imported from Japan very costly. Toyota's strategic response has been to request Nippondenso, a central member of the Toyota Group, to go to Taiwan and help upgrade the facilities and product quality at Kuo Zui Motor. In 1988, Nippondenso began production of air conditioners and auto electric equipment in a joint venture arrangement with local Taiwanese firms.

In like manner, Toyota first-tier suppliers, Arakawa Autobody and Toyoda Gosei, have joined forces with local Taiwanese firms to produce auto bodies, interior equipment, plastic and rubber products.   Imasen Electric Industrial Co., a Toyota supplier in Taiwan since 1968, is shifting its entire production of automotive horns to Taiwan in a joint venture with local interests. Nittan Valve and Fuji Valve, operating in Taiwan since the late 1960s, are expanding their local joint venture facilities and raising their exports of engine valves to Japan by 50 percent (*Japan Economic Journal*, March 21, 1987).

Thailand.   With the strong yen rendering exports from Japan increasingly less profitable, Toyota's affiliated corporation, Toyota Motor Thailand, has emerged as an important supplier of parts and components to the Toyota Group (Hasegawa, 1987). The Thailand-based company exports metal molds to Indonesia, Taiwan, Malaysia and Australia where they are used in the production of inexpensive pressed parts for export to Japan and the U.S.. Toyota Motor Thailand is also about to produce diesel engines for small trucks in a joint venture with Siam Cement Company, Thailand's largest manufacturer. This joint venture will export diesel engines to West Germany where Toyota, in a joint venture with Volkswagen, is about to begin assembling small trucks.

Most of Toyota's 19 suppliers in Thailand began production for the Thai domestic market in the 1960s and 1970s. Since 1985, many have expanded their production facilities to export to Japan and the U.S.. Yazaki Corporation, for example, has tripled the wire harness production capacity of its Bangkok subsidiary, Thai Arrow Products Company, primarily for export to U.S. based auto sub-assemblers (*Japan Economic Journal*, November 7, 1987). Yuasa Battery is exporting batteries to the U.S. from its expanded production facilities in Thailand. And Stanley Electric Company, a top maker of automotive lighting systems, is relocating all of its metal molding facilities to Thailand (*Japan Economic Journal*, March 21, 1987).

Indonesia.   Toyota's local Indonesian joint venture, Toyota Astra Motor, recently exported its first shipment of 14 Toyota Astra Kijangs to Thailand, Brunei and Fuji. Toyota has been manufacturing the Kijang for the local Indonesian market for several years, but only recently has the joint venture company achieved sufficient technical prowess to make a car that is marketable beyond Indonesian borders. Possessing a low level of automobile technology, Indonesia has not attracted many parts suppliers.

Toyota's ten Indonesian-based suppliers are all engaged in low value added production, principally tires, batteries, shock absorbers and piston rings.

Yuasa Battery, a Toyota supplier, established its own Indonesian joint venture, PT Yuasa Battery Indonesia, in 1975 in response to a threatened ban on imported batteries and tires by the Indonesian government. The domestic demand for automobiles in Indonesia, however, has not grown as fast as originally expected and the production of batteries has grown slowly. With the rise of the yen, though, Yuasa Battery Indonesia has begun exporting batteries to Japan as part of Toyota's strategy to offset a disadvantageous exchange rate (Komaki, 1987).

Toyota's transplant strategy in North America. Toyota has three transplants in North America. NUMMI, a joint venture with General Motors in Fremont, California began production in 1984. Toyota Motor Manufacturing USA in Georgetown, Kentucky started manufacturing cars in 1988. And Toyota Motor Manufacturing Canada, in Cambridge, Ontario, will start up in 1989.

Prior to 1985, only a handful of Toyota suppliers had located production facilities in North America. At the NUMMI plant, Toyota shipped in most of the auto parts from Japan and used GM suppliers for the rest (Krafcik, 1986). But as the rise of the yen escalated the cost of parts imported from Japan, and as political pressure to increase local U.S. content grew stronger, the number of Japanese auto suppliers in the U.S. mushroomed from 28 in 1984 to 97 in 1987 (see Table 6). Of Toyota's 55 transplant suppliers, 42 have come to the U.S. since 1985 (see Table 7).

Table 6. Japanese Suppliers Manufacturing Auto Parts in the U.S., North- and Southeast Asia.

Country	# of Japanese Suppliers	# of Toyota Suppliers	# of Plants Established after 1985 Total	Toyota
U.S.	97	55	69	42
South Korea	19	12	7	2
Taiwan	43	25	9	4
Singapore	9	7	0	0
Philippines	5	4	0	0
Thailand	23	23	0	0
Indonesia	13	10	1	1
Malaysia	17	14	3	2

Sources: Automotive Herald, Ltd (1987); Arnesen et al. (1987); Toyota Motor Corporation (1986); *Japan Economic Journal*, various issues.

Table 7. Toyota Suppliers Manufacturing Auto Parts in the U.S.

Company	Start Year	Ownership*	Products	Location
Aishin Seiki	1986	F	Pressed parts	IN
Akebono Brake	1987	J	Brake systems	KY
Asmo	1986	F	Plastic parts	MI
Asahi Glass	1986	J	Car windows	OH
	1986	J	Window assembly	OH
Bridgestone	1967	F	Tires	TN
Chuo Seiki	1988	J	Wheels	KY
Clarion	1987	F	Car radios	KY
Daikin Mfg	1983	F	Clutches	MI
Diesel Kiki	1984	J	Heat exchangers	TX
Fujitsu Ten	1986	F	Car radios	IN
Furukawa Electric	1988	F	Cables	GA
Hayashi Telemp	1983	J	Floor carpets	MI
Hitachi	1985	F	Auto parts	KY
Hitachi Metal	1973	F	Permanent magnets	MI
	1988	F	Aluminum wheels	OH
Ichiko Ind.	1984	J	Lighting equipment	IL
Inoue M.T.P.	1987	F	Tooling	KY
	1988	J	Instrument panels	KY
Ishikawajimia Harima			Turbocharge housing	IL
Izumi Motors	1977	J	Steering wheels	NY
Japan Storage Battery	1988	F	Batteries	na
Jidosha Kiki	1986	J	Brakes	TN
	1988	J	Batteries	TN
Koito Mfg.	1983	J	Weatherstrips	IL
Koyo Seiko	1958	F	Bearings	SC
Matsushita Elec.	1987	F	Car telephones	GA
Maruyasu Indust.	1985	J	Fuel & brake pipe	CA
Mitsuboshi Belt.	1985	F	Fan belts	IL
NHK Spring	1987	J	Coil springs	KY
Nifco	1987	J	Plastic parts	OH
Nishikawa Rubber	1987	J	Door seals	IN
Nippon Cable	1975	F	Control cables	MI
Nippon Glass	1988	J	Windshields	na
Nippon Seiko	1962	F	Ball bearings	MI
Nippon Oil Seals	1980	F	Oil seals	GA

(continued on next page)

Table 7. Toyota Suppliers Manufacturing Auto Parts in the U.S.
(continued)

Company	Start Year	Ownership*	Products	Location
Nippondenso	1971	J	electric parts	CA
	1984	F	radiator, heater, condensor	MI
	1987	F	electric parts	CA
NTN Toyo Bearing	1971	F	bearings	IL
	1985	F	bearings	MI
Ogihara Iron	1986	F	pressed panels	MI
Ryobi	1986	J	aluminum diecast	IN
Sango	1987	J	mufflers	IN
Showa Mfg.	1987	F	shock absorbers	OH
Stanley Electric	1986	J	lamps	MI
	1981	F	lamps	OH
Sumitomo Electric	1983	F	optical fibers	NC
	1979	J	PC twisted wires	CA
	1988	J	disc brakes	na
Tachi-S	1986	F	seats	MI
	1988	J	seats	TN
Tatematsu Mould	1988	J	plastic parts	KY
Tokai Rubber	1987	F	motor mounts	MA
Tokai Rika	1988	F	switches	MI
Topy Industries	1986	F	small wheels	KY
Toyoda Gosei	1986	J	rubber parts	MO
Toyo Radiator	1988	J	radiators	IL
Yazaki	1987	J	meters	VA
Yuasa Battery	1977	J	batteries	PA

*J=Joint Venture; F=Full Ownership

Sources: Automotive Herald, Ltd (1987); Arnesen et al. (1987); Toyota
Motor Corporation (1986); *Japan Economic Journal*, various issues

Additional Aichi Prefecture-based Toyota suppliers are now setting up production facilities near Toyota's Kentucky plant. Toyota projected 60 percent local content at the start-up of the Kentucky plant with parts, materials and services procured from more than 200 U.S.-based firms (Toyota Motor Corporation, 1987). By 1990, Toyota plans to be producing 200,000 cars a year in Kentucky and 500,000 altogether in its three North American plants (Sorge, 1987).

Toyota's North American investments may dovetail with a Toyota transplant strategy in Latin America. It has been reported that Toyota is contemplating a massive, $2.4 billion investment in car and components operations in Brazil (Turner, 1987). Brazil's car and light truck industry is dominated by European (Volkswagen, Fiat) and American (GM, Ford) companies and the Brazilian government has been actively seeking Japanese investment. With the rising yen, a Brazilian production base would provide Toyota with a lower-cost source of parts and small cars for local and North American markets. Japanese parts and vehicles sourced from Brazil would also enable Toyota to circumvent voluntary restrictions placed on Japanese car exports to the U.S. With nearly $40 billion of Brazil's foreign debt held by U.S. institutions, the U.S. government is likely to support any export-led Brazilian recovery. Japan's MITI is also encouraging Japanese firms to make investments in nations with debts outstanding to Japan, including Brazil and Mexico.

Toyota has yet to build a strong foothold in Europe. But with mounting trade frictions over Japanese car exports to EEC countries, Japanese automakers are rushing to build a production platform in Britain for export into the EEC market. Nissan, Isuzu and Honda have already located production facilities in the U.K. and Japanese auto part suppliers are following (see Table 4).

Aichi Prefecture

In addition to Toyota's production system, Aichi Prefecture hosts headquarters and plant operations for Mitsubishi Motors and many Nissan suppliers. Aichi's neighbors in the Tokai region include Mie Prefecture, location for Honda's Suzuka plant, and Shizuoka Prefecture, headquarters for Suzuki Motors. The auto industry drives the Tokai regional economy. Motor vehicle production accounted for 38.5 percent of the total value of products shipped out of Aichi Prefecture in 1985, and directly employed 192,237 people, 21.3 percent of Aichi's manufacturing work force (MITI, 1987).

The globalization of Toyota Motor Corporation poses a potentially serious employment issue for Aichi Prefecture. A recent survey of Japanese car companies estimated that a two million decline in motor vehicle exports to the U.S. could result in the loss of nearly half a million domestic jobs (Ozaki, 1987).

Toyota's factories in Aichi Prefecture have remained busy thus far supplying engines and transmissions to the company's North American transplants. But as stiffening competition in the North American market has led to more plant closings and laid-off workers, the United Auto Workers and American supplier associations are challenging the low local content of Japanese transplants (United Auto Workers Research Department, 1987). To maintain access to the North American market, Toyota and other Japanese auto companies eventually will have to produce engines and transmissions in the U.S. and Canada.

Toyota's first-tier transplant suppliers are also under pressure to increase North American content. The Toyota group must either recruit more second-tier suppliers from Japan or increase their use of indigenous, North American companies. Either way, Aichi-based suppliers will lose export orders and face production cutbacks. And by channeling parts produced in Mexico and Asian NICs into its North American operations, Toyota is even further reducing business for lower-tier, Aichi-based suppliers.

High-quality, low-cost parts produced by small and medium-sized subcontractors have underpinned Toyota's price competitiveness in world markets. Nearly 90 percent of the 4,700 second-tier companies are small or medium-sized, as are nearly 98 percent of the 31,600 companies filling in the third and lower tiers of Toyota's production system (MITI, 1977). But the rising yen is eroding Toyota's protective commitments to its family of subcontractors. Smaller subcontractors, without technology attractive to the parent maker, are threatened with abandonment. While Toyota encourages its suppliers to invest overseas, the company does not provide financial assistance, nor does it guarantee success in the North American market. Most small subcontractors do not have the resources to follow their parent abroad.

Toyota's revenues declined in 1987, the first time in 13 years. Operating profits also decreased 24.5 percent over the previous fiscal year. Declining profits stemmed primarily from an 8.4 percent drop in exports. The rising yen reduced Toyota's exports to the U.S. by 5.1 percent, to Saudi Arabia by 21.7 percent, and to Australia by 50.7 percent. Toyota managed to offset the exchange rate loss by further rationalizing its production system and through increased domestic sales spurred by an expansionary government fiscal policy. Toyota employed workers idled by the export slump by transferring them to company subsidiaries and suppliers.

According to a recent Prefecture study, there is no sign yet of a hollowing-out of Aichi's economy, as indicated by deep production cuts or large-scale layoffs. The study acknowledges factors, such as those detailed above, that may bring about the future deindustrialization of Aichi's economy, but the report emphasizes that only a small percentage of Aichi suppliers have shifted production operations overseas thus far. By increasing outlays on research and development, Toyota and local supplier companies are hoping to create new products for the domestic market to compensate for the contraction in overseas exports. Right now, the report concludes, Aichi companies are less interested in government-designed policies to stem capital flight overseas than they are in programs to reduce business taxes and expand public subsidies for industrial parks (Aichi Keizai Kenkyujo, 1987).

Global Production and Hollowing Out

The transnationalization of Japan's automobile industry has not resulted thus far in the hollowing out of auto dependent industrial regions. Nonetheless, deindustrialization remains a serious national issue in Japan. As noted above, Japanese industrial corporations are moving production operations overseas at an unprecedented pace and that movement will continue. Manufacturers have turned to global production to offset exchange rate losses and to alleviate international frictions brought on by Japan's trade surplus. Japanese manufacturing companies with a foothold in Asian NICs will continue to expand their production bases there. North America and Europe will continue to attract Japanese transplants.

According to a survey by the Japan Industrial Location Center, 65 percent of the companies listed on the Tokyo Stock Exchange plan to build or add to their overseas plant capacity (*Japan Economic Journal*, January 2 and 9, 1988). The ratio of overseas to domestic production will likely increase from five to ten percent by 1990 and the number of overseas jobs in Japanese transplants will correspondingly rise -- from about 1.06 million to 2.12 million during the same period of time. Roughly 80 percent of Japanese employment overseas is in the manufacturing sector and direct overseas manufacturing investment is projected to increase 14 percent annually through the year 2000 (Industrial Structure Council, 1987).

Japan will continue to import more manufactured goods from the Asian NICs. As local production technology has improved, NIC-based producers are closing the quality gap with Japan. Japanese manufacturers are contracting with local NIC firms to lessen the foreign exchange risks connected with overseas production. Products from these plants, sold under Japanese brand names, are pouring into Japan. (Shibayama, 1988). Manufactured goods already account for 45 percent of Japan's total imports and the ratio seems certain to rise in the future. "Reverse imports" to Japan from North American transplants will also increase following the path already laid down by Honda (motorcycles) and Sony (consumer electronics).

The rising yen is forcing Japan's older, "sunset" industries -- mining, shipbuilding and steel -- to further restructure and reduce employment. Japan's Ministry of Labor (1987b) estimates that as many as 1.65 million workers may be forced to leave the manufacturing sector between 1986 and 1993. Although there are an estimated 900,000 surplus workers in Japan's manufacturing industries now, massive layoffs have been avoided. Like Toyota, Japanese steel companies have been able to avoid layoffs by deploying workers internally, dispatching workers to subsidiaries and suppliers, and asking older workers to retire early. But as the globalization of Japanese auto manufacturing proceeds, domestic demand for steel will decline, and steel companies will experience added pressure to lay off surplus workers.

State policies

What role has the state played in the globalization of Japanese manufacturing and how are public officials responding to the deindustrialization threat? Following the G5 meeting in 1985, the Nakasone administration set up a blue ribbon civilian commission headed by the former governor of the Bank of Japan, Haruo Maekawa, to recommend an economic course that would reduce Japan's trade surplus while guaranteeing continued economic growth. The "Maekawa Report," as the commission's proposals came to be called, recommended a reorientation in Japan's growth strategy from export to domestic led expansion. To reduce the trade surplus, the report encouraged firms to set up more transplants abroad and consumers to spend more money on imports at home.

The Makeawa report was received with considerable skepticism on both sides of the Pacific (Dower, 1987), but the report did help shape a consensus among the Japanese that they could no longer rely so heavily upon an export driven economy. Japan had to assume responsibility for creating a more balanced system of international trade. The report linked the working out of restructuring conflicts among different interests -- industrialists, labor unions, local and central state officials -- to a national goal, remaking Japan's role in the world economy.

The Maekawa report was followed by the "new Maekawa Report" containing specific recommendations to curtail the mounting trade surplus. To spur domestic consumption, the report emphasized new land use and housing construction policies, shortened working hours, and modifications in food import controls. New forms of international cooperation to facilitate transplant production were also recommended. The state backed the Maekawa recommendations with a six trillion yen emergency expenditure package, including five trillion in public works and one trillion in individual tax reductions.

The new Maekawa report acknowledged that the national industrial restructuring program might well generate local plant closings but it offered no specific measures to counteract that possibility. To soften the pains of restructuring, the report did recommend priority allocation of public works projects to structurally depressed regions. Economically troubled localities were also encouraged to upgrade their information and transportation infrastructure so as to attract new industries.

Implicit in the new Maekawa report, as in the industrial policies of most advanced capitalist societies today, is the assumption that high technology and service industries can absorb workers displaced from the manufacturing sector. This hope is echoed by the various Ministries concerned with employment issues in Japan, including MITI, the Economic Planning Agency, and the Ministry of Labor. State technocrats are optimistic about the future of Japan's economy, at least in the short and medium term. To the extent there is a concern over hollowing out, it has to do with a "mismatching" of supply and demand for jobs among various categories of workers and among regions, a problem state officials think can be resolved through employment adjustment policies.

MITI is simultaneously championing domestic development of high value industrial products and advising export-led industries to shift more routine production overseas. Executives heading Japan's principal export industries -- auto, machine tools, electronics -- agree on the general strategy of producing low value added products overseas (particularly in the Asian NICs) and high value added products at home (MITI, 1987b). But the immediate interests of state officials and corporate executives don't always coincide. MITI officials want to reduce international trade frictions by reducing Japan's trade surplus with the U.S. Export industry executives want to cut production costs to remain internationally competitive. If production costs or market considerations favor producing high value goods elsewhere in the world, companies will follow that course, arguing their own survival necessarily takes precedence over MITI's vision of Japan's role in the international division of labor. Japanese electronics companies, for example, are locating research and development facilities in regional headquarters' centers, like Singapore and Hong Kong, to be closer to their production bases in the Asian NICs (Lau, 1987). For similar reasons, Japanese automakers in North America are now building research and development complexes along Michigan's "Automation Corridor."

State officials in Japan, like their counterparts in the U.S., are also pinning their employment hopes on a growing service sector. According to the Economic Planning Agency (EPA), job opportunities in high value added services (e.g. information software, health, leisure) will become a major "replacement" sector in Japan by the turn of the century. But there are hazards connected to this sort of projection. High value services, like high technology, are linked to the production process and are likely to follow rather than replace developments in manufacturing (Cohen and Zysman, 1987).

State officials locate Japan's main restructuring problem in a geographical "mismatching" between employment growth in the service sector in a handful of big cities (principally Tokyo and Osaka) and declining manufacturing jobs in outlying regional cities. According to the Industrial Structure Council, an advisory body to MITI, employment in primary and manufacturing industries will decline by 3.3 million between 1984 and 1995 but the decrease will be more than offset by a 4.4 million increase in service sector employment (Industrial Structure Council, 1987).

To curb employment concentration in Tokyo and prevent the hollowing out of regional economies, MITI proposes to establish regional development centers designed to attract investment in information and related service industries. To attract new regional investments, the plan requires local governments to construct "core" industrial parks and facilities in the targeted areas. Companies locating in the target areas are to receive tax breaks and other public subsidies (*Japan Economic Journal*, October 17, 1987). MITI has also set up "relocation centers" in each Prefecture's Chamber of Commerce and Industry to exchange information on job opportunities and to mediate employment transfers between different companies and regions.

Service decentralization, like high-tech decentralization, may not be a genuine planning option in Japan (Fujita, 1988). Take, for example, the Depressed Areas bill which passed the Diet in 1987. Under that bill, the government provides development funds to "third sector," public/private organizations to spur regional economic revitalization (Economic Planning Agency, 1988). According to the government, public works priority is to be given to the 175 officially designated depressed areas in Japan, but project initiative is to rest with private firms. Since private companies in depressed areas are already reeling from industrial restructuring, it is questionable whether the private sector can or will take the initiative to boost declining regional economies.

Japan's public investments on science parks, information centers and the like are overwhelmingly concentrated in the Tokyo, Nagoya and Osaka metropolitan areas. As Table 8 shows, wages are much higher, unemployment is lower, and research facilities more populous in Tokyo than in the rest of Japan. Contrary to the plans drafted by MITI, Tokyo will likely

Table 8. The distribution of research and development centers,
income and unemployment between metropolitan Tokyo (Kanto region),
metropolitan Osaka (Kinki region) and other regions of Japan

Area	# of R&D Centers* 1986	Income Per Capita (in 1000 yen, 1984)	Rate of Unemployment 1987
Tokyo	78	3,019	2.5%
Kanto Area	274	2,117	2.5%
Osaka	57	2,335	na
Kinki Area	103	1,985	3.5%
Hokkaido	3	1,827	4.2%
Tohoku	17	1,684	3.4%
Tokai	46	2,026	2.0%
Hokuriku	2	1,911	2.4%
Chugoku	22	1,817	2.6%
Shikoku	4	1,692	3.8%
Kyushu	13	1,699	4.0%
Okinawa	0	1,477	5.2%
Japan	484	2,058	2.8%

*R&D centers separately located from their company headquarters with a
capitalization of more than 50 billion yen.

Sources: Economic Planning Agency (1987); Ministry of Labor (1987);
Statistics Bureau (1987)

226 Comparative Urban and Community Research

host an even larger percentage of Japan's high value services and research facilities in the future. As a preeminent "world city," Tokyo has become a powerful magnet for high level business and government services. And the globalization of Japanese manufacturing makes Tokyo even more attractive to the world's transnational corporations.

Conclusion

Japan's policy responses to the hollowing out of domestic manufacturing are tentative and still mostly on hold. Government-stimulated domestic demand has compensated for declining exports thus far but over the long run government fiscal measures are not likely to contain regional deindustrialization. In a multi-centered, interdependent world economy, one nation's economic policy must respond to the interests of other nations. But responsiveness to interests abroad invariably runs counter to interests at home. Hailed as a progressive policy, the Maekawa report defines a new role for Japan in the world economy and responds to the long-neglected needs of Japanese consumers. But while the Maekawa Commission helped build a policy consensus among public and private sector elites, it did not bring new groups into the policy making process. The most vulnerable segments of Japanese society -- less skilled workers and small subcontractors in declining industries, regions and localities -- have largely been left to fend for themselves.

Notes

1. Established in 1937, Toyota Motor Corporation was originally named Toyoda Motor Corporation after the founding family. Executives later changed the company name from Toyoda to Toyota because the "ta" ending sounded more melodious to the Japanese ear. Some of the companies in today's Toyota Group also reflect the name change (e.g. Toyota Auto Body) while others retain the family name (e.g. Toyoda Machine tools).

References

Aichi Keizai Kenkyujo (1987) Auto parts makers and the test of internationalization (kokusaika no shiren o mukaeru jidosha buhin gyokai), *Aichi Keizai Jiho, 153*, 1-22.

Arnesen, Peter J., Robert E. Cole and A. Rama Krishna (1987) *Japanese Auto Parts Companies in the U.S. and Japan: Implications for U.S. Competitors.* Ann Arbor: University of Michigan - East Asia Business Programs Report #32.

Automotive Herald Company, Ltd. (1987) *Production Operations and Technical Aid to Japan's Parts and Components Suppliers in Overseas Markets: Supplement to Facts and Information '87--Guide to Japan's Auto Industry.* Tokyo: Automotive Herald.

Cohen, Steven S. and John Zysman (1985) *Manufacturing Matters: The Myth of the Post Industrial Economy.* New York: Basic Books.

Cusumano, Michael (1985) *The Japanese Automotive Industry.* Cambridge, MA: Harvard University Press.

Dower, John W. (1987) America's Japan: The end of innocence, *The Nation, 245*(7), 224-228.

Economic Planning Agency (1987) *White Paper in 1987.* Tokyo: Economic Planning Agency.

Economic Planning Agency (1987) *1987 Regional Economy Report* (Endaka o norikoe aratana hatten o mezashite). Tokyo: Economic Planning Agency.

Economic Planning Agency (1987) *1987 Kenmin Keizai Keisan Nempo.* Tokyo: Economic Planning Agency.

Economic Planning Agency (1988) *Regional Economy in the Process of Structural Adjustment* (Kozo chosei no shintensuru chiiki keizai) Tokyo: Research Bureau, Economic Planning Agency.

Fujita, Kuniko (1988) The technopolis: High technology and regional development in Japan, *International Journal of Urban and Regional Research, 12*(4).

Fujita, Kuniko and Richard Child Hill (forthcoming) Toyota's City: corporation and community in Japan, *Regional Studies.*

Gilpin, Robert (1987) *The Political Economy of International Relations.* Princeton, NJ: Princeton University Press.

Hasegawa, Kiyoshi (1987) Toyota Thailand plans major expansion, *Japan Economic Journal*, October 17.

Higgins, James V. (1987) Toyota group shows that GM may be wrong, *Detroit News*, January 21.

Hill, Richard Child (1987) Global factory and company town: The changing division of labor in the international automobile industry.

In Jeffrey Henderson and Manuel Castells (Eds.), *Global Restructuring and Territorial Development*. London: Sage, 18-37.

Industrial Structure Council (1987) *A Report Outlining the Nature of Japan's Industrial Structure in 1995*. Tokyo: Industrial Structure Council, Ministry of International Trade and Industry.

Japan Automobile Manufacturers Association (JAMA) (1987) *The Motor Industry of Japan 1987*. Tokyo: JAMA.

Japan Economic Journal (March 21, 1987) Auto parts makers build up Taiwan plants as export base.

Japan Economic Journal (September 5, 1987) Japanese auto production plants in North America.

Japan Economic Journal (October 17, 1987) Firms shifting product development to Asian NICs.

Japan Economic Journal (October 17, 1987) MITI plans to boost regional economies.

Japan Economic Journal (November 7, 1987) Yazaki plans to raise Thai production.

Japan Economic Journal (January 2 and 9, 1988) Industries hope high-tech will cure hollowing out.

Kaneko, Yoshiro (1982) Research on auto related small and medium sized industries report 2" (jidosha kanren chushyo kogyo jittai chosa, dai 2 ho) *Aichi Keizai Jiho, 125*, 65-166.

Kitazawa, Yoko (1987) Setting up shop: The hollowing of Japan's economy, *AMPO: Japan-Asia Quarterly Review, 19(4)*, 10-15.

Komaki, Toshihisa (1988) Japan shifts production to ASEAN states, *Japan Economic Journal*, January 2 and 9.

Krafcik, John (1986) Learning from NUMMI, International Motor Vehicle Program Internal Working Paper, Massachusetts Institute of Technology, 15 September 1986.

Lau, Minerva A. (1988) Manufacturers scramble to open Singapore bases: pool of skilled technicians attract high-tech firms fleeing strong yen, *Japan Economic Journal*, January 2 and 9.

Luria, Daniel (1986) New labor-management models from Detroit, *Harvard Business Review*, September-October, 22-29.

Maekawa, Haruo, et al. (1986) *The Report of the Advisory Group on Economic Structural Adjustment for International Harmony*. Tokyo: Advisory Group on Economic Structural Adjustment.

Maekawa, Haruo, et al. (1987) *Action for Economic Restructuring*. Tokyo: Special Committee on Economic Restructuring, Economic Council, Prime Ministers Office.

Ministry of International Trade and Industry (1987a) *Census of Manufactures in 1985*. Tokyo: MITI.

Ministry of International Trade and Industry (1987b) *Research on the Division of Labor in the Auto Industry* (bungyo kozo jittai chosa: jidosha sangyo hen). Tokyo: Small and Medium Sized Enterprises Agency.

Ministry of International Trade and Industry (1987) *The Interim Report of the Forum on the Future Prospects of the Machinery and Information Equipment Industries.* Tokyo: Machinery and Information Equipment Industries Bureau, MITI.

Ministry of Labor (1987a) *1987 White Paper.* Tokyo: Ministry of Labor.

Ministry of Labor (1987b) *Shokugyo Anteigyomu Tokei.* Tokyo: Ministry of Labor.

Misawa, Mitsuru (1987) Mexico provides low-tariff route to U.S., *Japan Economic Journal*, May 30.

Miyamoto, Ken'ichi (1983) Environmental problems and citizens' movements in Japan, *The Japan Foundation Newsletter, 11*(4), November, 1-12.

Ohno, Taiichi and Yasuhiro Monden (1983) *New Development in Toyota's Production Method* (Toyota seisan hoshiki no shin tenkai). Tokyo: Nihon Noritsu Kyokai.

Ozaki, Iwao (1987) Japanese auto production in the U.S. (America ni okeru jidosha genchi seisan), *Journal of the Japanese Institute of Labor.*

Ozawa, Terumoto (1979) *Multinationalism, Japanese Style.* Princeton, NJ: Princeton University Press.

Porter, Michael (1986) *Competition in Global Industries.* Boston: Harvard Business School Press.

Rother, Larry (1987) "Plants in Mexico Help Japan Sell to U.S.," *New York Times*, 26 May.

Sheard, Paul (1983) Auto production systems in Japan: Organizational and locational features, *Australian Geographical Studies, 21* (April).

Shibayama, Shigehisa (1988) More Japanese companies sign OEM deals to cut costs, make cheaper products, *Japan Economic Journal*, March 5.

Shima, N. (1987) Unemployment Tragedies of an Economic Superpower, *Tokyo Business Today* (June): 24-28.

Snyder, Jesse (1987) Japanese Speed New Products to U.S., *Automotive News*, July 27.

Sorge, Marjorie (1987) Toyota Builds Solid Future for U.S. Plants, *Detroit News*, July 15.

Statistics Bureau, Management Coordination Agency (1986) *1985 Population Census of Japan, Volume 3: Results of the Second Basic Complete Tabulation.* Tokyo.

Statistics Bureau, Management Coordination Agency (1987) *A Report on the Labor Force Survey.* Tokyo: Management and Coordination

Agency.

Sugimori, Y., et al. (1977) Toyota production system and Kanban system -- Materialization of just-in-time and respect for the human system, Fourth International Conference on Production Research, Tokyo (reprinted by Taylor and Francis Ltd, London, England).

Suzuki, John (1987) Toyota Profits Down 21% for Fiscal Year, *Automotive News*, August 27.

Takeuchi, Hiroshi (1987) Japan fuels rocketing economies of Asian NICs, *Japan Economic Journal*, July 25.

Toyota Motor Corporation (1982) Overseas KD Plants (Toyota no kaigai KD kyoten). Tokyo: Toyota Motor Corporation.

Toyota Motor Corporation (1986) Toyota and Toyota Group's Major Suppliers (Toyota Group kakusha no shyo kyoryoku kojo). Toyota City: Toyota Motor Corporation.

Toyota Motor Corporation (1987) *News From Toyota*, no. 47, September 24.

Turner, Rik (1987) Toyota Seen Eyeing Huge Brazil Stake, *Automotive News*, August 16.

United Auto Workers (1987) *U.S. Auto Jobs: The Problem is Bigger than Japanese Imports.* Detroit: UAW Research Department, September 2.

"THE TECHNOPOLIS STRATEGY" VS. DEINDUSTRIALIZATION: HIGH-TECH DEVELOPMENT SITES IN JAPAN

Jeffrey Broadbent
University of Minnesota

Through a policy to help the growth of regional centers of advanced electronics and computer research, called the "Technopolis Plan," the Japanese government plans to spur research in this field, slow down the movement of high-tech firms overseas, and redistribute population away from the big urban centers to regional cities. However, the Plan runs counter to current trends of capital internationalization, which are leading to the loss of manufacturing capacity in Japan, its "hollowing out." Through a case study of the Oita Technopolis, this paper tests the ability of the Japanese national state to bend economic trends to national and regional purposes. Since the Technopolis Plan is falling short of expectations, it concludes that this ability is not very strong. Nevertheless, personalistic connections between the Oita governor and high-tech companies enabled Oita Prefecture to become one of the more successful technopolises.

National Industrial Policy and Overseas Investment: Economic Trends vs. Social Needs

With the growing tendency of corporations to invest abroad, the relationship of the international economy and domestic social growth and problems has received increasing attention (Smith and Feagin, 1987). The movement of capital abroad, which the Japanese call the "hollowing out" (*kūdoka*) of their national economy, has generated tremendous socio-economic problems in the industrially-advanced capitalist countries, and has been a mixed blessing for the recipient countries. In the "First" World, deindustrialization has thrown workers into unemployment, reduced national economic competitiveness, and contributed to urban fiscal crisis and population imbalance (Bluestone and Harrison, 1982; Nihon Kaihatsu Ginko, 1987: 62), even as in the Third World "dependent development" has increased internal stratification, squatter urbanization, and the North-South economic gap (Evans, 1979; Timberlake, 1987: 41).

This economic restructuring results from the increased profitability of foreign production for re-import for multinational corporations (MNC) (Feagin and Smith, 1987: 10). Geographic and economic theory contends that industry locates near the cheapest factors of production: transportation, production costs, and economies of scale (Alonso, 1964: 3-25; Webber, 1984: 67). Given the growing international communications and transportation potentials of MNCs, the "global assembly line" is ever easier to achieve.

But this trend also has to do with state policies (Feagin and Smith, 1987: 20). Through tariff barriers, industrial consortium leadership and other mechanisms, the state intervenes to alter economic conditions. This couples economic restructuring with state theory, in particular recent debates about the strength of the state as a political actor, autonomous of the will of the dominant social classes (Evans, Reuschmeyer, and Skocpol, 1985). Capital flight poses a crisis for the state because it undercuts the economic vitality of a nation. If the state, as contended, has considerable autonomous power, it should make a decisive appearance here. Political logic would push it to intervene to preserve national economic strength.

Especially Japan, with its well known reputation of "Japan, Inc.," the strong state, should exhibit state intervention. Depending upon the purposes of the state, this intervention could appear not only in the successful maintenance of national capital accumulation, but also in the handling of social problems, such as the type and style of urbanization and employment restucturing. In the logic of social science, Japan provides a natural "crucial test case" for studying the autonomy of the state, via the more concrete problem of the impact national industrial policy can have upon the effect of global economic restructuring in capitalist societies.

The Technopolis Development Plan of the Japanese Ministry of International Trade and Industry (MITI), officially promulgated in 1983, supports the construction of advanced technological reserach, development and production sites throughout Japan. MITI followed this up with the Regional Research Core Concept, intended to strengthen the research component of technopolis and other sites and other related policies. These policies represent a direct governmental effort to slow down the hollowing out of the economy, as well as to redistribute population away from the crowded cities (Tatsuno, 1988: 3). How successful they are is another matter.

By looking at one of the Technopolis development sites, this paper examines the relative success of the economic and social goals of the Technopolis policy, and through this, the relative strength of the Japanese state, both local and national. Field research was conducted on the Oita Technopolis site in 1988, and this research extends an earlier work there on the politics of its "heavy" industrialization (Broadbent, 1986, 1988).

Besides the typical political and economic determinants, the study of the relation between the state and big business in Japan requires confronting some other sociological elements. Political-economic analysis has traditionally given motivational priority to economic and coercive incentives, not social or cultural ones. The latter have been considered "soft" and secondary (Johnson, 1982: 9).

Yet, studies of Japanese social organization often emphasize the strength of networks of specific social relationships in channeling information, influence and decisions. Under various colorful terms, such as "human veins" (*jinmyaku*) or "root-binding" (*nemawashi*), "backstage" personalized relations are given great prominence in popular discussion and social science. Emphasizing the importance of pre-existing social relations, recent extensions of network research refer to the social "embeddedness" of political and economic relations (Granovetter, 1985: 504).

The exceptional strength of these in Japanese society, if such is the case, may derive from the cultural value system, which emphasizes intense group solidarity (Nakane, 1970) and strong sense of reciprocal obligation (*on* and *giri*) (Lebra, 1976: 93 and Chp. 6, passim.). Such values, if strong enough, would support government efforts to stem the tide of overseas investment by leading Japanese firms to prefer to locate with Japan. That is, the cultural system, apart from policy and economic determinants, might have some autonomous determinative effect on industrial location plans.

Overseas Investment

In recent years, Japan has increasingly followed the outward tide of capital internationalization. Traditionally, Japan's industrial strategy has been the opposite. Like a skilled surfer, the economic ministries have sought to "ride the wave" of technical progress, keeping the advanced and profitable industries to support the domestic economy and allowing declining industry to flow abroad. But now the forward swell of the wave is going abroad too. This includes the most "high-tech" and presumably competitive Japanese products, such as semiconductors and computers, which may slowly "soften" the economy, leaving it a vulnerable service economy, such as England or the U.S. already show in more advanced stages.

Because of the increasing value of the yen, the high cost of domestic labor, and other factors, Japanese industry has increasingly built new factories in the competing New Industrial Countries (NICs), such as Korea, Taiwan, etc. or in the U.S., behind its potential tariff barriers. Some of these re-export their products back to Japan, but most are for further export to Europe, the U.S. and other destinations. The trend is accelerating. According to one estimate, direct foreign investment (DFI) in 1980 totaled S4.7 billion, but by 1987 totaled S33.4 billion. Of this, the proportion invested in Western Europe, the U.S. and Canada grew from about 45 percent to about 65 percent of the total, while investment in Asia shrank

rapidly (*The Economist*, August 13, 1988: 21).   According to another estimate, DFI totalled $32.2 billion in 1983 and $105.9 billon in 1987
(Inoguchi, 1988: 27).   Because of this trend, the sectoral structure of the
economy has been changing; while manufacturers have been laying off
workers in Japan, service sector companies such as hotels, housing, transport and leisure have been picking them up (*The Economist*, August 13,
1988: 22).

Domestic critics charge that this trend undermines the productive
strength of the Japanese economy, leading to its "hollowing out," leaving
only an empty shell.   They predict that capital "flight" will lead Japan to
the same socio-economic problems this has led to in the U.S. and England:
weakened economic competitiveness, urban fiscal crisis, and unemployment.
The Japan Development Bank recently reported such fears, and many other
groups within the nation, capital, labor, and intellectuals alike, echo the
same forebodings (Nikkeiren, 1987; Jidosha Soren, 1986; Asahi Shimbun,
1987).   Indicative of its fears, the Bank formally defines "hollowing out" as
follows: "All productive industries lose competitiveness, important industries leave the country and flow to foreign countries by direct investment,
only service industries remain within the country, and development strength
weakens."   It predicts that this fate awaits Japan if it allows overseas
investment to continue unimpeded (Nihon Kaihatsu Ginko chosa bu, 1987:
62).   In the same vein, an academic critic blames U.S. import dependency
on the internationalization of its capital investment and, worried about
Japan's fate, concludes, "The employment problem cannot be left to individual firms.   The government must intervene.   If there really is a 'Japan,
Inc.,' it is time for it to step forward" (Sato, 1986: 38).   So strong is the
trend that even the conservative critics have doubts about the ability of the
Japanese State to intervene and slow it down.

On the other hand, Japanese liberals support the trend.   They argue
that growing overseas investment will reduce trade frictions with developed
countries through job transfers and will help developing countries through
technology transfer.   The worries of the critics are overstated, they say.
After all, one liberal article points out, Japan's share of recent overseas
investment still lags far behind that of other advanced countries (Sakamoto,
1988: 9).   In 1986, it notes, the U.S. made 33.5 percent of all such investments, England 18 percent, West Germany 9.5 percent, Holland 8.5 percent,
and Japan 7.5 percent.   Overseas manufacturing, figured by dividing the
total sales value of national firms incorporated overseas by the total domestic sales value, is even more skewed: West Germany 19.2 percent, U.S.
18.1 percent, and Japan, only three percent.   The article recognizes that the
trends are accelerating, with overseas production ration expected to double
to 6.2 percent of total by 1992.   This is interpreted, however, as part of

Japan's necessary new international role and responsibility.

That the semi-official Development Bank is sending out worried criticisms of capital outflow (as cited above) indicates widespread elite concern. The Development Bank has considerable indicative influence over the economy (Johnson, 1982: 200), so its pronouncements may be seen as a direct attempt to slow down the pace of overseas investment. To the contrary, however, the pace has not only increased, but the nature of it has also changed toward more highly technological firms.

Development and Social Crisis

Throughout the post-World War II period, Japan has suffered from an unprecedented and immense flow of population toward the few big cities, especially Tokyo. This has led to the "over-population/depopulation" (*kamitsu-kaso*) problem: cities have burgeoned and rural towns and villages have dwindled. The statistics on urbanization demonstrate this trend. Between 1955 and 1980, total national population grew very slowly, but the distribution changed radically. The three metropolitan areas of Japan increased from 36.9 to 47.8 percent of the entire population. Tokyo alone held 25 percent of the entire population (compared with 5 percent for New York). At the pre-war urban peak (1940), 29.4 percent of the Japanese national population lived in cities over 100,000 (Fukutake, 1982: 21). In 1980, this figure had increased to 56.4 percent (Fukutake, 1982: 101).

This tremendous urbanization means much for the quality of social life in both city and country. On the one hand, urban areas are hard-pressed to build enough new schools, roads, and sewers (Fukutake, 1982: 103). Tokyo dwellers find apartments tiny and rents extremely high, with neighborhood parks scarce and baseball fields requiring reservations a month in advance. Land prices have tripled in the last four years. Currently, the total land value in the Tokyo metropolitan area, collateralized at 80 percent of market value, is worth $8 trillion, a sum greater than the worth of all U.S. real estate plus all U.S. companies listed on U.S. stock exchanges (Ohmae, 1989). On the other hand, declining populations in country towns and villages have led to empty schools and an aged population with nobody to care for them. Recent research reports that the internationalization of capital has withdrawn industries from the small towns and hinterland areas, worsening their financial and social situation (Murayama, 1988).

A solution to this is seen in moving industries out of the major metropolitan areas and back to the hinterlands. There, they would provide jobs for local youth, and so induce them to stay. Eventually, they might support a massive "U-turn" phenomenon, inducing city dwellers to move back to rural areas, thus redistributing the greatly over-concentrated population of Tokyo and other major urban areas.   The solution of this problem has been the stated goal of Japanese national industrial redistribution plans for most of the post-World War II period.

Over the post-World War II period, in an effort to minimize social problems and maximize national capital accumulation, the Japanese government has issued a number of national industrial structure, industrial distribution and land use plans.   Which, if any, of these have had much effect is the subject of much debate.   The series of national land use plans produced by the National Land Agency (Kokudocho) or its precursors, such as the Comprehensive National Development Plan of 1962 (Zenkoku Sogo Kaihatsu Keikaku) (Uchino, 1978: 116), the New Comprehensive National Development Plan of 1972 (Uchino, 1978: 190), and the Third National Comprehensive Development Plan of 1977 have all emphasized the need for such redistribution.   However, these plans have had little success to date (Sargent, 1986: 230).

Industrial redistribution is not easily accomplished.   Bringing industry to a rural area, not to speak of research facilities, runs directly counter to the tendency of hollowing out.   Why should industry go to rural Kyushu, to face the problems of rural development in expensive Japan?   In a less-developed country, they could enjoy cheap labor, tax breaks, and other benefits.   Recent sociological studies have begun to show that under some circumstances, industrial location does not conform to these predictions, in one case in the emergence of new firms (Reynolds, 1988).

In keeping with the desire of big business to follow the logic of "capital accumulation," other state agencies and plans have actually facilitated concentration in big city areas near their major markets.   The Ikeda Cabinet's "Income Doubling Plan" of 1960, for instance, supported continued industrial concentration in the Pacific Belt Region, near the big cities where most industry already existed (Uchino, 1978: 116).   An official of the Japanese government's National Land Agency commented on this:

> The Ikeda Cabinet pushed growth in the Pacific Coast Belt area.   But we [bureaucrats at the National Land Agency]...pushed for the New Industrial Cities (NIC) law to reduce regional differences in income and stop the over-concentration of population. There were two opposing [forces], economic efficiency and regional growth.   Two different opinions.   All the regional Diet representatives were totally opposed [to further concentration on the Pacific Coast belt].   The big business leaders (zaikai) need the [political] support of all the (LDP) Diet representatives, so they let them ask for (the NIC law).   (The zaikai) asked the bureaucrats to put on a

good act [that investment was going to the outlying regions], but to put all the real investment into the Pacific Coast Belt area....In actuality, most of the growth did take place in that [Pacific Coast Belt] area...MITI had guidance power, but did not use it (Interview data, 1979).

MITI's industrial structure plans and indicative "visions" give priority to industrial efficiency too, and tend to ignore social consequences (Johnson, 1982: 253). The Economic Planning Agency issues economic development plans, which since 1970 have been called "Social and Economic Plans," but have had little social effect (Fukutake, 1982: 185-6). In its various development policies, then, the state takes self-contradictory stances.

The Technopolis Development Plan

The Technopolis Development Plan (*Saido Gijitsu Kogyo Shuseki Chiiki Kaihatsu Sokushinho*), officially promulgated in 1983, aims at developing regional small-scale Silicon Valley-type "technopolises" (Tsusho Sangyosho, 1988; Glasmeier, 1988; Hiramatsu, 1983: 212-220). The plan is the brainchild of MITI, although during its creation they incorporated recommendations from the other related ministries and from Diet politicians in the ruling Liberal Democratic Party. The plan supports the relocation or new construction of advanced electronics and computer industries, moving them from the big cities to create local sites for more intensified high-tech production and research. One of the plan's major purposes, according to MITI, is countering the overseas investment trend in these industries (Tsusho Sangyosho, 1988: 52). Since 1983, 24 technopolises have been designated throughout the Japan by the Ministry of International Trade and Industry, many in less-developed or hinterland areas of Kyushu and Tohoku, and more are under consideration.

The Technopolis Plan is viewed with alarm in the West, where it is seen as another step toward Japanese technological superiority. A recent popular book published in the U.S. sounds the alarm on this effort (Tatsuno, 1986). It sees the Technopolis Plan as a key link in Japan's strategy to master the high-tech economy, thus contributing further to U.S. economic defeat. To the extent that the Technopolis Plan has this effect, it adds fuel to those who argue that the U.S. government should take on more of the functions of MITI that "guide" and protect high-tech growth (Vogel, 1985: 281-82).

In Japan, the plan is seen in much broader terms than simply facilitating high-tech growth. It also includes many social goals, which make the Technopolis Plan sound quite similar to previous national social development plans.   By bringing both research and production facilities to the countryside, the plan seeks to develop three aspects of the rural site: production (*san*), education (*gaku*), and residential quality of life (*ju*).   It should provide jobs locally, expand the local educational system to include better high-tech training opportunities, and make a modern lifestyle with all the amenities of the big city, plus the bucolic attractions of the countryside.

Besides spurring competitiveness in high-tech industry, the government hopes such sites will become centers for rural economic revitalization, dispersing population and income more equitably throughout the country (Tsusho Sangyosho, 1988: 46; Oita Ken Kikaku Soshitsu, 1985: 2-4).   In this way, it is hoped, a new rural culture can be developed that will eventually draw the urbanized youth back to their home towns.   If not for that social need, high-tech growth could proceed just as well around the big cities, as it has around Boston or Minneapolis.

The methods extended in the plan to help technopolis sites achieve these goals include tax incentives, depreciation allowances, special loans from the Japan Development Bank or Hokkaido-Tohoku Development Corporation, and insurance guarantees.   As part of the plan, MITI also supports and encourages related activities such as venture capital in high-tech fields, research institutes, and professional services in these sites (Tsusho Sangyosho, 1988: 48; Tatsuno, 1988: 6-8).

Specifically, four types of national level aid are available to the sites (data from MITI interview, October 12, 1988):   1) plants that locate there get a 15 percent reduction in the first year's building tax and a 30 percent reduction in machinery (*setsubi*) tax; 2) cities, towns and villages within a technopolis area can reduce the real estate tax on plants and be compensated by the national government for that portion of revenue loss; 3) companies which buy land within a technopolis for the purpose of building a plant will not be subject to certain other land taxes (*tokubetsu tochi hoyuzei*); and 4) technopolis sites are expected to make a "third sector" (*dai san sekuta*) corporation, investing prefectural government and private capital to support research facilities, technology training institutes, and venture capital.   Private capital invested in this way will not be taxed.

Viewed from either economic or social purpose, the technopolis sites, like the sites of previous plans, have achieved some success.   For the 14 early designated technopolis sites, the industrial location rate for the three years after the designation was 1.2 times that of the three years before it, and was also above the national rate (Nakano, 1988: 38).   Some sites have shown considerable growth in high-tech industries and have established software and other research facilities (Tsusho Sangyosho, 1988: 49).

Even the successes in redistributing production facilities achieved by the technopolis sites are unexpected, however.   They run counter to the predictions of industrial location theory, the objective economic logic of optimal location, especially under conditions of hollowing out. May these successes, though relatively small, be attributed to the power of state planning or guidance, or is some other factor at work influencing the locational decisions of industry?

Two Types of National Planning

National development plans provide the major means of state intervention. Chalmers Johnson has emphasized the strength and importance of these, especially those formed and implemented by MITI (Johnson, 1982). Over the decades following the end of World War II, the Japanese government announced a large number of national economic and social development plans. To Americans, this succession of national plans sounds more socialistic than capitalistic.

Actually, the plans are more indicative than commanding. The Japanese government produces two types of plans, economic and social. The former concern industrial restructuring. The latter attempt to handle the social impact of the first: urban crowding and loss of community. Johnson's famous characterization of Japan as a "plan rational" society, with economic development proceeding under MITI's guidance, applies best, if at all, to the explicitly economic plans. Even these, in fact, do not usually have much enforcement power over industry. They are most potent in the case of specific task forces set up by MITI, such as the inter-industrial consortium for developing the VLSI computer chips. Social development plans have less priority with more powerful central ministries such as MITI and the Ministry of Finance, and hence have even less impact. What counts most to the powerful ministries is winning the economic war. The social amenities will follow, they believe.

No matter how comprehensive and sweeping the national plans may sound, then, Japan is not really a planned society or economy. Much is left up to the initiative of the prefectural governments (Samuels, 1983: 251). They work out arrangements, especially for social development plans, with industry on an individual and ad hoc basis. Thus, one should have no illusions that national economic and social development plans constitute the heart and main engine of the Japanese economy.

Careful perusal of the preceeding characterization of the goals of the Technopolis Plan, then, leads one to the conclusion that, from the national point of view, this is not simply an economic development plan. It is also a plan for rural social development. This, then, is a different class of plans than the famed industrial structure plans of MITI. As such, one would not expect it to have much impact on actual rural development. As before, most would be left up to the initiative of the individual prefectural governors.

A number of factors, then, militate against a poor rural prefecture being able to attract front-line industry. The weakness of the planning system has been mentioned. Furthermore, the current tendency for Japanese business to locate production facilities overseas militates against industrial location in the domestic rural areas. How was Oita able to counter these negative forces and, to some degree, develop a successful technopolis?

The Oita Technopolis

The technopolis in Oita Prefecture, on the eastern shores of the southernmost island of Kyushu, exemplifies the effort to bring population back to the rural areas. During its earlier "New Industrial City" phase of heavy industrialization, Oita was known as one of the "best students" (*yuto-sei*). It is living up to that reputation in its technopolis efforts as well. Since MITI is currently reviewing the success of the technopolises and helping them prepare for a "new era," exact statistical data on individual sites is not publicly available. However, according to the qualitative assessment of a MITI official working on plan, compared either to the total 24 sites thus far designated (1988), or to the 14 early designated sites, the Oita Prefecture Technopolis stands out as doing very well ("hijoni yoku yatteiru dewa naika"), as having drawn in a large amount of high-tech industry. Measured either by total value of output (*kogyo shukkagaku*) or number of plants (*kensu*), it is among the top five technopolises (Vogel, 1985:122).

Despite the success on the production (*san*) aspect of the technopolis project, the Oita Technopolis is only average on the educational (*gaku*) and residential (*ju*) aspects (MITI interview data). In general, the technopolises, like their predecessors the NICs, have had relatively little success on the social aspects. Given the highly automated nature of high-tech production, they have done virtually nothing to draw in people from big cities to redistribute population.

In addition to previous industries, a number of "high-tech" (electronics and computer-related) companies located in Oita in the 1980s. They produce electronic cameras and high-capacity computer chips: assembly, not research. Hence, they don't really fulfill the Technopolis Plan's vision of research in the countryside. But in light of the hollowing out tendency, even these limited accomplishments are surprising. While the U.S. complains of deindustrialization and plants moving overseas, how can the Japanese Technopolis Plan achieve even this amount of success?

The current technopolis project must be seen as an extension of Oita Prefecture's long history of attempts to industrialize and generate local jobs. Oita was an agricultural prefecture until the end of the 1950s. It suffered from low relative income and standard of living, few jobs, and an outflow of youth to the cities. After World War II, the population swelled artifically with returnees from the disbanded colonies. But by the early 1950s, with industrialization in the big cities, youth flowed out in search of employment and the population began a rapid decline. In the hopes of creating local jobs, Oita Prefecture started plans for a "Seaside Industrial Area" in the mid-1950s (Broadbent, 1988: 134). Quickly receiving designation under the auspices of the national government's "New Industrial Cities" plan of 1962, this project expanded into a vast steel and oil refining complex. Because of its highly automated character, it did not provide the hoped for volume of employment for local youth, but by the mid-1970s had helped to stabilize the population at about 1.25 million. However, due to its concentrated nature, it reproduced the same "depopulation/overpopulation" problem on the prefectural scale (Broadbent, 1987).

By the late 1970s, riding the tide of the times, the governor turned in a new direction. He hoped that bringing in high-tech industries would be a new and better strategy for improving prefectural welfare. In this effort too, the prefectural government came under the auspices of a national plan, the Technopolis Development Plan. In an ebullient book, the governor outlines how high-tech industrialization coupled with agricultural and other forms of development can bring progress to Oita (Hiramatsu, 1983). MITI has not yet collected statistics on comparative growth plan achievement rates for the 24 technopolises (direct interview data), but in sheer volume of output, the four most successful technopolises are probably Okayama, Hiroshima, Yamaguchi, and Kumamoto. These big cities, however, started with a strong and diversified industrial base. In terms of percentage increase in high-tech investment, Oita is probably one of the most successful technopolises.

Despite the weakness of central government support coming through the Technopolis Plan, the Oita Technopolis succeeded in drawing in a number of well-known high-tech companies: Sony, Canon, Matsushita, Nihon MRC, Daihen Tech, and others. In addition, some factories already there, such as the Toshiba computer chip factory, increased their level of production. These new factories are not concentrated in a single industrial park, but spread out among the hamlets of the rural Kunisaki Peninsula. What enables this unusual locational pattern is proximity to the large prefectural airport. Governor Hiramatsu, in an analogy to the earlier "Seaside Industrial Area" created in Oita City twenty years earlier, calls this an "Airside Industrial Area" (*Rinku Kogyo Chitai*).

In all, 32 factories have been built within the technopolis area as a result of the project, or at least have increased their production since the project began. They all make products related to computers, such as large-scale integrated circuits (LSI), very large-scale integrated curcuits (VLSI), micro-motors, boards, and other parts. The Toshiba Oita factory, the largest VLSI factory in Oita, is outside the technopolis area and was established earlier. It employs 2,200 people and produces half the world's (1,000 K) VLSI computer chips. It has expanded in the 1980s, perhaps partly under the stimulus of the technopolis project. This kind of production forms the heart of the technopolis. As such, it provides some jobs and technical training to local people, but does not radically change the proportions or size of the local work force.

The employment potential of high-tech development is limited by its own application. The advanced automation used in the new factories reduces the number of workers needed. The Canon Oita factory is a good example. They have a partly robotized factory. Automated conveyor cars run by demand-call along regular walkways supplying robotic and human run production stations with pieces for assembly.

Together, the 32 factories employ 4,688 people. The two biggest employers among these, Kyushu Matsushita Denhin and Texas Instruments, were established in 1970 and 1973, respectively, long before the technopolis project. If their workers are subtracted, the employment total shrinks to 3,508 (Oita Ken, Jan. 1988). Among this number, many came from Tokyo and other places to work in the upper managerial and techical divisions of the factories. Ultimately, employment for locals in the factories probably does not come to more than 2,500 jobs. Compared to the total working population of 580,588 for Oita Prefecture in 1980, this is not very large, only about 0.4 percent. If additional jobs indirectly generated in the service industries are included, this still totals not more than one percent of the work force. Hence, one cannot say that the technopolis project is having a major impact on Oita's employment problem.

The employment goals of the Plan include not only additional jobs, but also a change toward more knowledge-intensive work. Work on a production line, assembling computer chips, does not qualify, as this. The first signs of such a change in the Oita workforce have appeared, ironically, outside the actual technopolis area of the Kunisaki Peninsula. Within Oita City itself, following MITI's support for "third sector" research entrepreneurialism, a consortium of local businesses and government contributed funds to build a "Soft Park" where training in and the actual writing of software is going on. Japan largely lacks U.S.-style free-wheeling venture capital support for start-up entrepreneurs, but this kind of state-guided investment seems to be its functional equivalent.

The Fujitsu Systems Laboratory, one main factory in this park, employs 200 persons. Fujitsu has a tele-conferencing room where collaborative research can go on between people in Oita and elsewhere. In this way, modern technology carries the possibility of overcoming the problems of distance that historically have made the cities sites for research and innovation.

Extensive workforce change in this direction awaits a flourishing of research and development facilities. As is already evident, the high-tech industries in the Oita Technopolis carry on production, not basic research. All but one of the six plant managers I talked with predicted it would be hard to establish significant research facilities in Oita. One of them (Canon) agreed with the governor's hope that in the future, with the increasingly free flow of information of all kinds, this might be increasingly possible. Certainly, the Fujitsu facilities indicate that possibility. But most predicted that basic research would continue to be centered in the Tokyo area.

The Oita Technopolis, despite its relatively weak economic and employment effect, is considered a model of successs. Judging from this, on the whole the Technopolis Plan must not be having much effect on regional economic development or population. Basic research is still concentrated in big cities, where sufficient colleagues, excitement and information exist for researchers to do good work. The long-term dream of redistributing population throughout the country is not much closer to realization due to it.

Locational Factors in the Development of the Oita Technopolis

Compared with other sites designated by the Technopolis Plan, the Oita Technopolis has drawn in relatively many high-tech production facilities. What explains its comparative success? In explaining industrial location, scholars have traditionally emphasized material economic factors such as land, labor and resources, as well as facilities and geographical features. On the other hand, in Japan, it could be that personal social networks and loyalties strongly affect locational decisions. Here, first the material and then the socio-cultural factors are examined.

Material factors

A number of typical locational factors such as good harbor and airport, availability of labor, and Oita's previous history of development as an NIC during the 1960s and 1970s, seem to play some role, as one would expect. Of particular importance is timing: how much do the requests from the prefecture synchronize with the indications from the international economy, which make the construction of new factories possible?

As for timing, Governor Hiramatsu asked those industries to come in the early 1980s, right after Oita's designation by MITI as a technopolis. In this way, he got commitments earlier, whereas now those industries are going overseas and other technopolis sites are not able to attract them.

The notion of internationalization of production encourages one to think that all production facilities can be readily moved to places where labor is cheap. Under those conditions, workers in industrialized countries lose their attractiveness to industry. This seems especially true for workers in rural areas in developed countries; they have neither the skills of their urban country-fellows, nor the low rate of pay of the Third World. Under these circumstances, it seems almost impossible for the rural hinterland of an advanced country to offer its own industry any inducement to come.

It turns out, however, that Oita workers had their own attractive features to domestic industry. They were not viewed simply as production workers that could be easily replaced by moving overseas "so they'd better not ask for a raise." In the companies' estimation, different types of labor skills exist: some jobs can be sent overseas, but others cannot, even if labor is cheaper. As I was told at Toshiba Oita (1/19), foreign labor is hard to train up to the level required for IC chip production (the "front-end" process), while packing them in little brown plastic chip boxes and bending the legs down (the "back-end" process) can be done in other countries. The Japanese labor force has the requisite qualities for the more technically exacting front-end process: high education, loyalty to the company and stability (working in one place for a long time). This adds up to a work force of consistently high quality. When recruiting new workers in Oita, Toshiba, for instance, does not feel it necessary to be selective. Their recruitment process is simple: when they need 60 new workers, they send out a request for 80 candidates [*gureenu boizu* -- "green boys"] who are seniors in the Oita technical high schools, and choose the 60 from that lot.

This consistently high quality supports the more complicated work processes, such as that required for the production of VLSI chips. The Toshiba IC company has a "back-end" assembly factory in Malaysia, where such a high degree of work quality is not needed. The upshot is that there seems to be a continuing strong attraction for factories producing knowledge-intensive products to locate in rural areas in Japan. Such industries will not move all their facilities overseas.

Presently, the main functions of the technopolises are to bring together rural labor and high-tech industries, and to redistribute industry, which is too urbanized and concentrated. High-tech industries can make special use of these two functions because, for the first, they need the industriousness of rural labor and, for the second, they can ship their light-weight but expensive products through airports. Hence, the material factors of labor and transportation convenience available in rural Japan have some drawing power. The materially-related factor of technological research and development, however, militates against industrial redistribution. The predominant opinion of most Oita respondents was that a critical mass of competing experts and companies is necessary to drive creative people to their fullest expression, and only the big city has this.

Social factors

These material factors, while specific to Japan, are not specific to Oita Prefecture. They could be found in other prefectures, too. To explain why industry chose Oita, rather than some other prefecture, one must turn to other factors. The web of personal connections between the current governor and the presidents of many of the companies proved to be of great importance. The governor of Oita, Mr. Hiramatsu, is a retired top official of MITI. He was one of the innovators of Japanese development strategy. The intense reliance on personal contacts is, sociologically speaking, the most important and striking aspect of Oita's Technopolis development process.

The importance of Hiramatsu's personal connections arises because of his former career with MITI. In the 1960s, when Japanese knowledge-intensive industries, particularly computer companies, were still in their fledgling stage, he helped fend off their U.S. competitors. He helped devise and impose MITI's well-known restrictions on the entry of U.S. computer companies into the Japanese markets (Vogel, 1985). In this way, he made a lot of friends among the presidents of those companies. Later, Mr. Hiramatsu retired from his MITI position early in order to return to his home prefecture of Oita, becoming first its vice-governor, and then its governor. In doing so, he knowingly sacrificed a chance to rise to the highest post within MITI (the Jimujikan or Executive Director). He did this, according to one of his top officials, because he was concerned about spurring the social and economic development of the rural areas within Japan, and wanted to help his own home prefecture, Oita, become a model case of that. His attitude indicates the strength of sentiments of love for one's "hometown" in Japanese culture.

When asked by Governor Hiramatsu to locate in Oita, the presidents of the high-tech companies he once protected and supported felt obligated to respond to his request even though from a strictly profit and loss ("bottom line") point of view, the location was not ideal. In Japanese, this sense of repaying favors is referred to as "ongaeshi," a notion loaded with heavier moral implication than in the West.

The SONY Oita plant is a good example. This plant is located about 15 minutes from the airport in the Kunisaki Peninsula, on 86,000 square meters of land and employs 150 people. Every month it produces and tests two million LSI (large scale integrated circuits of 256K). A manager of the plant related the circumstances of their decision to move to Oita as follows:

> President Morita [of Sony] and Governor Hiramatsu are very close friends. When Texas Instruments wanted to locate in Oita 15 years ago, MITI would only allow [foreign companies to enter Japan as] joint ventures, and refused permission. So SONY and Texas Instruments went 50/50 on the venture. At that time, the person who put them together was Mr. Hiramatsu. He helped President Morita see the necessity of that....Because of the close relation established at that time, Oita Prefecture was able to pull SONY to the prefecture later.

The manager's words testify to a close personal relationship that helped pull the plant to Oita. However, from the point of view of at least the theory of industrial location in the U.S., and probably common practice too, it is amazing that the plant came to Oita despite less than optimal location conditions. He went on to speak about these factors:

> The locational conditions are not so good for them. The sea is close by, and when you make integrated circuits [computer chips], the salt breeze is not so good. For SONY, it was neither the best nor the better location. But we owed Governor Hiramatsu a favor and couldn't refuse him....But now we are glad we came here. The prefectural government is very helpful, in finding good workers, providing electricity, reducing taxes, and making a good road to the airport.

This testimony indicates the striking degree to which the sense of interpersonal obligation, of responsible reciprocity for favors received, motivates even supposedly "hard-nosed" economic activity in Japan. Actual economic loss may be incurred by major corporations in order to repay favors received in the past. The governor prefers to emphasize the good locational features of Oita, but most of the officials and managers I spoke with emphasized these personal connections as key in attracting industry.

This points to an economy woven together very differently from that of the West, where short-term economic rationality and calculability is the ruling principle. In Japan, the major decision-makers see economic growth as occuring not through the invisible hand of anarchic competition, but as always mediated and facilitated by human connections. These human connections are of great importance, for they provide the way of negotiating differences and working out reciprocities and avoiding problems. While sometimes perhaps not economically rational in the short run, in the long run this "negotiated growth" pays off for both the individual companies and the economy as a whole. By making organizations run more smoothly, the trust created more than compensates, even in hard economic terms, for any short-run losses.

To Americans used to the hard-headed world of business contracts, making decisions on the basis of honor seems unlikely, counter-intuitive, and even suicidal. However, sociologists contend that friendship and the trust it engenders is crucial for business connections, even in the U.S. In Japan it is common practice and is enshrined in traditional culture as a central virtue. Modern Japanese youth are losing their sense of this virtue, but among the generation born before the end of World War II, such as Governor Hiramatsu and the company presidents, it still retains its symbolic grip.

Creative Aspects of Negotiated Development

The path of development of the Oita technopolis eloquently demonstrates that the plans of the central government have little coercive or regulatory power. In fact, their very openness to creative input from any of the actors in the system makes them flexible and responsive, a situation best called "negotiated development." National government has a "tutelage" relationship over local government, which allows for flexibility on some points, particularly when the governor is an OB ("old boy" or retiree) of the ministry (Samuels, 1983: 102). For example, the original MITI technopolis plan envisioned concentrating all the industries in a concentrated industrial park of about 2,000 hectares (4,000 acres). According to an Oita prefectural official, Governor Hiramatsu foresaw that this would recreate the typical pattern of urban sprawl around the industrial park and give little benefit to the villages further away.

Aware of that problem, and having experienced it within Oita Prefecture as a result of the New Industrial City, Governor Hiramatsu conceived of a radically new format for rural industrial development; scattering the industries around a wider area throughout Kunisaki peninsula (130,000 hectares). This prevents over-urbanization, yet they are all still within ready access of the airport. It also permits an unusual employment pattern. Workers in the new industries are usually young, and can migrate to jobs. In this case, though, the people still living in their traditional villages can find work in the modern sector. In some cases (at Sony, at least), the factories have made special effort to employ the elderly for part-time work. This benefits both parties; low-wage, loyal workers for Sony and jobs for those who had little hope to find them.

Culture and work are deeply intertwined. Modern factory work, with its accompanying urbanization, has destroyed the traditional customs of the agricultural villages wherever it has spread throughout the world.

Village customs, despite their negative aspects which reflect centuries of oppression and class exploitation, also have their positive side. They allow a deeply felt sense of commmunity, or mutual aid and belongingness, to coalesce around common symbols. Modern society, many scholars have complained, suffers acutely from the lack of this. In Japan, the transformation from traditional to modern society has occured rapidly, over the short span of 100 years. In the rural areas, traditional community customs still remain.

By scattering modern factories among traditional villages, the Oita technopolis plan provides the opportunity for traditional villages to become economically prosperous once again, and to retain their youth. Thus, the positive, joyful and fulfilling aspects of village culture need not become merely the pastoral dreams and children's bedtime stories of an alienated urban middle class. Some Japanese politicians and ministries recognize and value solidarity as a characteristic of their own culture. Given the opportunity, they try to perpetuate it despite the dissolving effect of industrialization and urbanization.

To find these modern factories spread out throughout the ancient lands of Kunisaki Peninsula, dotted in a landscape known as "Buddha's home town" (*Hotoke no sato*) along with 1,000-year-old Buddhist temples, is truly astonishing. It is a situation full of cultural contradictions. A striking example is the Canon factory, which makes the popular Autoboy camera, perhaps the best middle-priced camera now on the market. Near this modern factory is an ancient Buddhist temple. Long black fringes of hair, accumulated in the temple over hundreds of years, hang down the inner walls, the shorn locks of women, hung there in earnest prayer that some misfortune be remedied.

The illustrates the enormous contrasts between tradition and modernity engendered here. In the process of Oita's Technopolis development in the Kunisaki Peninsula, some local beliefs, such as in the beneficial effects of shaving one's locks off, may lose their potency. But others, such as the rituals of the villages which foster solidarity, may not. For instance, at the end of August in the festival of Obon, villagers gather to hold hands and dance in large circles, to entertain the spirits of departed ancestors who have returned for a visit. Then, after three days of festivities, they send them back to Heaven, lighting their way with candles. In another ritual around this time, the young men of the village bring the village Shinto God (*ujigami*) out of its usual shrine and put it into a portable shrine (*omikoshi*) which they carry on their shoulders. Having drunk much sake (rice wine), they stagger from house to house of the village to bring the annual greetings of the God directly to each door. Working in a factory producing computer chips, even designing them as an electrical engineer, need be no barrier to participating in these rituals of joyous solidarity. Here in the

Kunisaki Technopolis, in a unique way, it is made possible.

Conclusion

This perspective on urbanization and industrial distribution, looking at the State from its ability to make and implement economic and social plans, is not of much relevance in the "weak-state" U.S., where most recent urban theory has been born (Smith, 1984). Indeed, most industrial "location theory" has supported an opposite theory, free market principles where industry follows the cheapest "factors of production." The ecological and central place theories of urbanization have similar implications (Logan and Molotch, 1987: 4). However, some urban theorists doing research in the European context have noted some impact of national state policy in defining the central and regional urbanization process (Zukin, 1985: 358; Body-Gendrot, 1987: 250). The general conclusion seems to be that, under some conditions, local (prefectural or state-level) governments have unexpected power to take policies which affect their own urbanization and industrialization fates (Feagin and Smith, 1987: 17-23).

The Technopolis Plan and its outcomes reveal both strengths and weaknesses in the capacity of the Japanese state to plan for economic and social needs. If the Japanese state is as "strong" as often reputed, national plans such as the Technopolis Plan should succeed quite admirably. In that case, the Japanese state would be an exemplar of the "autonomous" state, rising above the conflicts of classes and interest groups to chart the long-run course of national development for its own purposes. But the fact that the plans do not succeed so well indicates that this popular image is not very accurate. The state does not seem so autonomous.

The locational movement of industry is usually thought to be the product of economic factors related to wages, taxes and resources. In Japan, these factors certainly influence industrial movement; the "hollowing out" internationalization of the Japanese economy is one result. The success or failure of the Technopolis Plan depends in part on such factors, too. That is, it relies on the skill and cultural readiness of workers in the Japanese "internal periphery" to attract high-tech industry from the center. These factors keep some of that industry within Japan, contributing to economic growth in rural areas, rather than sending it overseas.

In some cases, however, social and cultural rather than material reasons draw industry to the internal periphery, or at least determine which among the choices they will take. In part due to his previous connections with industry as a MITI bureaucrat, Governor Hiramatsu was able to draw them to Oita. They did not forget. This confirms the hypothesized importance of solidarity and reciprocal obligation in Japanese culture. These values reflect a tightly knit social world in which favors are seen in a long time span.   This solidarity provides the conditions wherein business and political actors think of economic relations as a collective, long-term process.   To prove this assertion, a survey of all techopolises, detailing their industrial growth or investment and the "OB" connections of their governor with central economic ministries, would be necessary.   Lacking that, this single case study, coming from one of the more successful sites, provides prima facie evidence for it.

The Japanese state is thus revealed as not very strong in the face of broad world economic trends.   These trends affect the investment logic of individual companies, causing them to respond in ways similar to that in the West, leading to ever greater international investment.   Under certain conditions, however, a limited amount of at least marginally-economically logical investment will flow to internal hinterland sites.   These are distributed, not so much at the behest of central government plans such as the Technopolis Plan, but rather as the result of the personal connections so important in Japanese politics.   In the 1980s, the data indicate that the planning capacity of the state, even in economic structural areas, has weakened greatly.   Even when domestic economic vitality is at stake, the logic of firm-level capital accumulation can rarely be constrained.

These conclusions, coming as they do from a crucial test case, that of "strong state" Japan under conditions of incipient economic crises, marshall against the thesis of the autonomy of the state.   Rather, they indicate that the short-run investment decisions operate with effective freedom, largely unhindered by the Japanese state, despite the social concerns enunciated in its national plans.   At its strongest, the Japanese state flows with and helps give more effective focus to this tide.   The strength of the state, at this point, is more indicative than coercive, based in part on moral appeal embedded in solid social networks and cultural identities.

References

Alonso, William (1964) Location theory. In John Friedmann and William Alonso (Eds.), *Regional Development and Planning.* Cambridge, MA: Ballinger.

Asahi Shimbun, Dec. 14, 1986; Nikkei Shimbun, Nov. 17, 1987.

Bluestone, Barry and Bennett Harrison (1982) *The Deindustrialization of America.* New York: Basic Books.

Body-Gendrot, Sophie (1987) Plant closures in socialist France. In Michael P. Smith and Joe R. Feagin (Eds.), *The Capitalist City: Global Restructuring and Community Politics.* New York: Basil Blackwell.

Broadbent, Jeffrey (1988) State as process: The effect of party and class on citizen participation in Japanese local government. *Social Problems, 35*(2). 131-144.

Broadbent, Jeffrey and Yoshiaki Kobayashi (1987) Positive social breakdown: Migrant youth, urbanization, and political change in regional Japan. Working Paper No. 2, Center for Life Course Studies, Dept. of Sociology, University of Minnesota.

Chie Nakane (1970) *Japanese Society.* Berkeley: University of California Press.

Evans, Peter (1971) *Dependent Development.* Princeton: Princeton University Press.

Evans, Peter, Dietrich Reuschmeyer, and Theda Skocpol (1985) *Bringing the State Back In.* Cambridge: Cambridge University Press.

Feagin, Joe and Michael Peter Smith (1987) The new international division of labor. In Michael Peter Smith and Joe R. Feagin (Eds.), *The Capitalist City: Global Restructuring and Community Politics.* New York: Basil Blackwell.

Glasmeier, Amy (1988) The Japanese technopolis programme: High-tech development strategy or industrial policy in disguise? *International Journal of Urban and Regional Research, 12*(2), June.

Granovetter, Mark (1985) Economic action, social structure, and embeddedness, *American Journal of Sociology, 91*(3) (November): 481-510.

Hiramatsu, Morihiko (1983) *Technoporis e no Chosen* (The Challenge of Technopolis). Tokyo: Nihon Keizai Shibunsha.

Inoguchi, Takeshi (1988) The ideas and structure of foreign policy: Looking ahead with caution. In Takeshi Inoguchi and Daniel Okimoto (Eds.), *The Political Economy of Japan, Vol. 2: The Changing International Context.* Stanford: Stanford University Press.

Jidosha Soren (Confederation of Japan Automobile Workers Unions) (1986) *Undo Hoshin* (Movement Policies), July 1.

Johnson, Chalmers (1982) *MITI and the Japanese Miracle*. Stanford: Stanford University Press.

Lebra, Takie Sugiyama (1976) *Japanese Patterns of Behavior*. Honolulu: University Press of Hawaii: 93 and Chp. 6, passim. For the conterargument, see Mouer and Sugimoto.

Logan, John and Harvey Molotch (1987) *Urban Fortunes The Political Economy of Place*. Berkeley: University of California Press.

Murayama, Kenichi (1988) Teiseichoka ni okeru Chiiki Sangyo no Genjo to Kadai (The Current Situation of Regional Industry under Conditions of Slow Growth). In Shinshu Daigaku, Jinbun Kagaku Ronshu. 22.

Nakano, Takayuki (1988) Tekunoporis Kensetsu wa Aratana Sozeiki e (A New Beginning for Technopolis Construction). Sangyo Ritchi. 27: 6, 37-40.

Nihon Kaihatsu Ginko chosa bu (1987) *Sangyo to Kudoka-Eikoku in okeru kaigaitoshi to kokunai keizai e no eikyo* (Industry and hollowing-out: The effect of English overseas investment on its internal economy). Tokyo Nihon Kaihatsu Ginko.

Nikkeiren (1987) RoDo Mondai Kenkyu Iinkai Hokoku, Sangyo to Kudoka, Koyomondai e no Taisho in tsuite (Industry and hollowing-out, responses to the labor problem). Jan. 21

Ohmae, Kenichi (1989) "Remove the fuse -- but quitely please." *Japan Times*, January 23: 19.

Oita Ken Kikaku Soshitsu (Oita Prefectural Government Planning Office) (1985) *Toyono Kuni Tekunoporis Keikaku* (The Technopolis Plan of "Toyonokuni" [a colloquial name for Oita Prefecture]). Oita: Oita Prefectural Government.

Oita Ken (Oita Prefectural Government) (1988) Ken Kitakunisaki Teknoporis Kaihatsu Keikaku no Gaiyo (Outline of the Prefectural Northern Kunisaki Technopolis Plan) (January).

Reynolds, Paul (1988) "Organizational births: Perspectives on the emergence of new firms." Unpublished manuscript.

Sakamoto, Haruo (1988) Deta de miru Anbaransu Okoku Nippon (The Unbalanced Big Country Japan as Seen through Data), *Asahi Janaru*, September 2: 9.

Samuels, Richard (1983) *The Politics of Regional Policy in Japan*. Princeton: Princeton University Press.

Sato, Sadayuki. (Hitotsubashi University) (1986) Un'nyuizon ga Unda Bei no "Akujunkan" (The Vicious Circle that American Import Dependency has Produced). Nihon Keizai Kenkyu Senta Kaiho (Japan Economic Research Center Report). 518 Go, August 15.

Smith, Michael P. (1984) *Cities in Transformation*. Beverly Hills: Sage.

Smith, Michael P. and Joe R. Feagin (Eds.) (1987) *The Capitalist City: Global Restructuring and Community Politics*. New York: Basil

Blackwell.
Tatsuno, Sheridan (1986) *The Technopolis Strategy.* New York: Prentice Hall.
Tatsuno, Sheridan (1988) Building a Japanese technostate: MITI's technopolis program. In Raymond W. Smilor, George Kozmetsky and David V. Gibson, *Creating the Technopolis: Linking Technology, Commercialization and Economic Development.* Cambridge, MA: Ballinger.
Tsusho Sangyosho (1988) Tekunoporis no Kensetsujokyo (The Construction Situation of the Technopolises. *Sangyo Ritchi.* 27(2): 46-52.
Vogel, Ezra (1985) *Comeback.* New York: Simon and Schuster.
Webber, Michael T. (1984) *Industrial Location.* Beverly Hills: Sage.
Zukin, Sharon (1985) The regional challenge to French industrial policy, *International Journal of Urban and Regional Research,* 9(3).

JOB AND HOUSING DISPLACEMENT:
A REVIEW OF COMPETING POLICY PERSPECTIVES

Todd Swanstrom
SUNY-Albany

Robert Kerstein
University of Tampa

Despite an outpouring of research on deindustrialization and gentrification in recent years, fundamental disagreements persist about the nature of the phenomena and what, if anything, public policy should do about them. This article traces these disagreements to two basic approaches: the market approach and the conflict approach. The market approach, which is shared by liberals and conservatives alike, views deindustrialization and gentrification as fundamentally healthy phenomena; to the extent that costs are involved, they should be handled after the fact by compensatory programs. The conflict approach views deindustrialization and gentrification as manipulated by political interests; conflict theorists advocate public planning of housing and job markets to prevent the costs of deindustrialization and gentrification from occurring in the first place. The paper concludes by criticizing the trade-off between equality and efficiency that is central to the market perspective. By breaking down the separation between economic and social policy, the conflict perspective argues that it is possible to achieve growth and equity at the same time -- thus pointing the way out of a basic dilemma in American public policy.

Deindustrialization and gentrification would appear to be very different, even opposite, phenomena: gentrification, after all, is due to *reinvestment*; deindustrialization is the result of *disinvestment*. In fact, however, deindustrialization and gentrification are closely allied processes. Gentrification, in many ways, is the flip side of deindustrialization: deindustrialization is caused, in no small part, by the shift of employment from goods production to services, and it is the concentration of certain types of service employment in the CBDs of older cities that is at the heart of gentrification. Moreover, deindustrialization and gentrification present analogous problems of policy analysis and prescription. In both cases, the policy issues revolve around displacement; in one case, the displacement of families from their homes, in the other, the displacement of individuals from their jobs.

Even though there is now a massive empirical literature on deindustrialization and gentrification, scholars still disagree on the causes, consequences, and desirability of the phenomena. On one side, scholars argue that gentrification is a healthy and beneficial process for cities; overall, the benefits outweigh the costs (Nathan and Schill, 1983: 133). In the long run, everyone benefits from gentrification, proponents argue, because it boosts the tax base of the city. According to the U.S. Department of Housing and Urban Development (HUD) *Displacement Report* "displacement is a common and continual process in housing markets" and does not present a serious problem that requires federal intervention (U.S. Department of HUD, 1979: 4; see also Sumka, 1979).

Similarly, some analysts, such as Charles Schultze, argue that the present rate of economic transition from industry to services is appropriate (*Business Week*, 1983). The benefits of industrial change, such as lower prices and greater efficiency, outweigh the costs. Market-oriented analysts argue that the costs of deindustrialization are exaggerated by left-wing critics (McKenzie, 1984). Others, of a more liberal persuasion, go further and argue that the rate of economic change in the U.S. is too slow and recommend that the government intervene to accelerate the movement from sunset to sunrise industries (Thurow, 1980; Reich, 1983).

On the other side, scholars argue that economic change in both housing and jobs is too rapid and involves unacceptable social costs. Far from viewing gentrification as a normal and beneficial process, Richard LeGates and Chester Hartman emphasize "its connections with fundamental housing market pathology, and the subtle connections with government action...." (1981: 231). They view the extent of displacement as excessive. The HUD *Displacement Report*, they argue, was "systematically biased to understate both the extent and seriousness of displacement" (LeGates and Hartman, 1981: 211). The actual number of people displaced annually, they estimate, was 2.5 million, almost twice the HUD estimate (p. 236; see also Hartman, 1979).

Similarly, some scholars argue that the speed of transition from industry to services in the U.S. is too rapid. Barry Bluestone and Bennett Harrison, for example, argue that the American economy is "hyper-mobile." In *The Deindustrialization of America*, they maintain that 32 to 38 million jobs were lost due to private disinvestment in the 1970s (Bluestone and Harrison, 1982: 9). More recently, they have expanded their critique of deindustrialization by arguing that secure, well-paid blue collar jobs are being replaced by insecure, low-paid service sector jobs (Bluestone and Harrison, 1986; Harrison, Tilly, and Bluestone, 1986).

Fundamental disagreements, such as those described above, will not be solved by collecting more data. Behind these empirical disagreements lie different explanatory frameworks which guide research and shape the interpretation of the data. The policy debate is not purely ideological -- your conclusions do not depend entirely on what is brought to the subject matter, or on values and assumptions. (For a discussion of the role of ideology in the understanding of gentrification, see Beauregard, 1985.) Facts do matter. At the very least, however, facts do not "speak for themselves" but must be interpreted within a theoretical framework. The primary purpose of this essay is to make explicit the implicit theoretical frameworks behind the deindustrialization and gentrification policy debates.

Many have attempted to classify the literature on neighborhood change (London, Bradley, and Hudson, 1980; Schwab, 1981; Solomon and Vandell, 1982; Schwirian, 1983; Zukin, 1987) and industrial change (Congressional Budget Office, 1983; Plotkin and Scheuerman, 1984; K. Dolbeare, 1986). Our effort differs from past efforts, however, in several respects. Unlike most earlier classifications, we are centrally concerned with policy implications. We argue that the explanatory frameworks establish the very criteria that are used to judge public policies. (For a closely related discussion of policy paradigms, see Dunn, 1981: 2-4 and Anderson, 1978.) We hope to show how clearly distinguishing the primary theoretical approaches and baring their assumptions can clarify often muddled policy debates and contribute to a more coherent relationship between empirical analysis and policy recommendations. Finally, we also differ from earlier efforts in our attempt to distinguish the market approach from what we call the "conflict approach." While drawing on neo-Marxism, the conflict approach can be differentiated from a strictly Marxist analysis. In the conclusion, we argue for the superiority of a loosely structured conflict approach.

Market and Conflict Approaches: An Introduction

The market model does not require much explanation. It is so much a part of our thinking that we are usually unaware of it. As the late Louis Hartz argued, politics in the U.S. is dominated by a liberal-Lockean consensus (Hartz, 1955). The values that Americans generally use to judge policy options are the utilitarian values of the marketplace. The debate between conservatives and liberals, we will argue, is a debate that takes place *within* the market paradigm.

While often uncritically accepted, the power and logic of the market paradigm should not be underestimated. Every economic system must answer three questions: 1) *What* to produce? 2) *How* to produce it? and 3) *For whom?* These three questions represent a simultaneous equation of mind-boggling proportions. Amazingly enough, market theory claims to have an answer to the equation that does not depend on a master mathematician or government planners.   The final result is not intended by any of the actors in the system; no actor has the power to determine the final outcome.   Economic outcomes are the result of a complex interaction between supply and demand, producers and consumers (Novak, 1982). Each actor is assumed to be an independent decision maker seeking to maximize his or her own utility.   Theoretically, markets allocate resources in the most efficient manner possible, maximize economic growth, and lead to the highest consumer satisfaction possible within the constraints of technology.

Market theory also purports to answer a fourth question, which is especially pertinent for our purposes: *Where*?   The most influential application of market theory to locational issues is the Chicago school of human ecology.   The basic idea is that human beings, like all other living creatures, must compete for space in a kind of geographical social Darwinism.   The dominant interests win control of the choicest land, contributing, in the long run, to the well-being of the entire community.   While using the language of biology, the ecological approach is firmly rooted in market economics (Logan and Molotch, 1987: 5-7; Cummins, 1986: 180-82). Dominance is represented by the ability of some actors to outbid others for land, which is priced according to its desirability.   For producers, land is viewed as an element of capital, like any machine.   Production takes place at the most efficient geographical locations -- which change according to changing technology and consumer demand.   The price of land, or land rent, reflects the efficiencies of one place over another.   Companies must move to the most efficient location for production or face the competitive consequences. The whole process is guided by a kind of "hidden hand" that allocates each parcel of land to its highest and best use.

Two general points about the market model need to be stressed. First, no one intends the final outcome.   The outcome is the result of autonomous decisions by individuals and firms seeking to maximize utility and profits.   Power is not exerted in the market model.   Each actor is free to reject any particular exchange; markets achieve what Milton Friedman has called "unanimity without conformity" (Friedman, 1962: 23).   Markets involve competition, not conflict: individuals meet their own needs by exchanging with others, arriving at a state of Pareto Optimality where no individual can be made better off without someone else being made worse off.[1]

Second, mobility of both capital and residents is a key mechanism for adapting urban land use to changing technology and consumer demand (Miron, 1982).   Barriers to mobility restrict consumer sovereignty and prevent urban land from achieving its highest and best use.   The ideal of market theory, then, is a "frictionless" economic system.

Compared to market theory, the conflict approach is not as easy to understand; it does not come easily to most Americans. The unit of analysis is the collectivity, not the individual; the action is power, not exchange. Unlike the market model, the conflict model does not have a long established logical and deductive form. Since the conflict model is still evolving and is not as neat and logical as the market model, we will need to take more care in developing it.[2]

While it is impossible to define a strictly orthodox conflict approach, it is possible to identify the conflict approach negatively: purely economic explanations, whether market or Marxist, are rejected. Michael P. Smith puts the matter well in his recent book, *City, State and Market:*

> [P]aradoxically, structural Marxism resembles the economistic thinking of the New Right devotees of market capitalism. Both attribute too much historical significance to the material forces of production, i.e., to technical and economic processes, while failing to acknowledge how deeply these processes are imbedded in historically specific national and local social and political processes (1988: 6).

According to the conflict approach, there is no such thing as an "economy" with its own imminent logic, whether that logic be the rational structure of neo-classical economics or the "laws of motion" of capital.[3]

The conflict approach is built on the notion that markets are shaped by power. The "free" market is a myth; markets are always socially constructed according to particular values and interests.[4] The location of jobs and residents is not the result of independent actors pursuing narrow economic self-interest in an anonymous market. Land use outcomes are viewed instead as the result of powerful actors who intentionally seek to shape markets in their own interests. The agency for asserting this power over the market is often the economic institutions themselves. Through monopoly, uneven sharing of information, or collusion, economic institutions can exert power over the market. In addition, economic actors are often socialized into ideological beliefs or values that override rational calculations of profit or utility. Redlining, conflict theorists charge, is based on such biased institutional values (see Smith, 1988: 12-14).

The most important agency for exerting power over the market, however, is government. The conflict approach stresses the role of the state and emphasizes the "*under*determination of political outcomes by economic relations" (Jessop, 1982; cited in Gottdiener, 1987: 115). While market and structural Marxist analysts usually view the state as reacting to economic forces, conflict theory views the state as shaping those forces. Conflict theorists borrow heavily from neo-Marxists who stress class struggle and who analyze policy outcomes as at least partly contingent and dependent on political and social conflict.   While stressing state action, however, some neo-Marxists reduce political conflict over the location of jobs and residences to strictly economic conflicts between workers and capitalists. Thus, once again, political outcomes are derived from economic relations.[5] Conflict theorists, on the other hand, stress that classes are not the dominant political actors; in the U.S., at least, class consciousness is generally low, both among the workers and capitalists.[6]   The American "broker" or "contracting out" state apparatus, including the separation of power between branches of government and division of power between federal, state, and local governments, stimulates access by class factions and interest groups to state power, which is used to manipulate market outcomes (Alperowitz and Faux, 1984: Ch. 2; Smith, 1988: Ch. 2-3).

In short, the conflict model focuses on human *agency* as well as economic structures.   Conflict theory should not be confused, however, with pluralism; the state is not a neutral arbiter between competing interests. The most sophisticated conflict theorists acknowledge a complex interaction between agency and structure (Smith, 1984; Gottdiener, 1985).   Political outcomes tend to be biased in the direction of the interests of economic dominants, in part because of the constraints of the economic system, or least people's perceptions of those constraints.   In the political sphere, unintended political effects may mean that the final outcome is not strictly the intention of any one group; nevertheless, the outcome is shaped more by power assertions than by independent exchanges.

Under the conflict approach, land plays a special role.   Market theory views land as simply another factor in production.   Land, however, is a unique commodity that fits only with difficulty into a pure market perspective.   First, the supply of land is fixed (Logan and Molotch, 1987: 24).   Fixed supply gives land, especially when it possesses certain characteristics, such as centrality, "an inherent monopolistic quality" (Harvey, 1973: 168).   Moreover, the value of land is determined not so much by its intrinsic character as by its relation to other parcels of land around it.   As the saying goes, land has three important characteristics: location, location, location.   Fundamentally, land is accessibility -- to jobs, to markets, to raw materials.   More than any other commodity, land values are determined by externalities.   The conflict model does not view land externalities as randomly distributed (Swanstrom, 1985: 23-25).   Real estate interests are able to use public policies to manipulate land values.   At the local level, for example, land values can be manipulated by zoning laws (Gottdiener, 1977) and by the location of public improvements (Harvey, 1973: Ch. 2).   John Logan and Harvey Molotch call those who manipulate land values in this way "structural speculators" (Logan and Molotch, 1987).

Under the conflict approach, mobility of capital and residents is not viewed as mainly a vehicle for promoting growth and consumer satisfaction. The question *Where?* is not simply a technical question of efficient supply. Since the value of land, and indeed of life chances, depends on these mobile factors, mobility is an instrument for redistributing wealth, not just expanding it. Conflict theory views residential mobility (e.g. suburbanization) as a method for distributing scarce resources, not simply as a way of responding to changing transportation technologies and consumer demand (Danielson, 1976; Ashton, 1978; Markusen, 1978; Schneider, 1980; Jackson, 1985).

Market theory is both an empirical theory of how the world works and a normative theory of how it ought to work. Besides the empirical approach outlined above, conflict theory also has an underlying normative framework. Conflict theory views the free market not so much as undesirable, as impossible. Power and conflict are necessarily involved in economic change (Kuttner, 1984). If conflict is necessary, then it should be regulated by the set of rules that have been refined over the centuries to resolve irreconcilable differences fairly and equally: political democracy. Political decision making in markets should not be hidden behind the veil of free market theory. Political democracy should be extended to the market. The goal is not simply better policies but wider democratic participation in policy-making, especially by the lower classes who are presently excluded. Since conflict theory views the market as already shaped by political power, it is not necessary to socialize private property. Rather, the goal is to subject the political determinations to democratic control. The normative standard behind the conflict approach is compatible with the emerging theory of economic democracy (Carnoy and Shearer, 1980; Bowles, Gordon, and Weisskopf, 1983; Dolbeare, 1986; Center for Popular Economics, 1986).

The Market Approach to Gentrification

As discussed earlier, the most prominent application of the market approach to urban development has been the Chicago school of human ecology. The ecological approach has been used to explain the characteristic sprawled development pattern of American cities. The best known application is the concentric zone model of Ernest Burgess, originally published in 1925 (Park, et al., 1967). Urban areas tend to expand, Burgess explained, outward from a CBD (CBD) with each inner zone invading and succeeding the uses in the outer zone as technology and growth expand the city. The invasion-succession model of ecological theory dominated research on neighborhood change for decades.

The basic insights of the ecological approach have been applied to cities with increasing technical sophistication in the developing fields of urban economics and geography. Suburbanization, for example, is explained as the result of changing consumer demand interacting with improvements in technology. The basic explanation is simple: improvements in transportation technology increase residential choice by making it possible for people to live further from where they work. At the same time, increasingly affluent households choose to trade off increased commuting time for improvements in housing in the form of lower costs per square foot of living space, due largely to improvements in home construction technology and lower land costs (Kain, 1962; Alonso, 1964; Muth, 1969).

Market theorists use the bid rent curve (Figure 1) to explain changing land use patterns -- in particular, the process of suburbanization. The downward-sloping bid rent curve represents the fact that households are willing to pay less for land the further it is located from the CBD. Not everybody has the same bid rent curve, however. Suburbanites, it is argued, have a flatter bid rent curve (Figure 1, line BB) and therefore are able to outbid others for land that is distant from the city center. The poor, on the other hand, value more the low transportation costs and access to jobs near the city center and by living in high density are able to generate land rents that enable landlords to outbid others for inner-city land (line AA).

Given the market explanation of suburbanization, gentrification would seem to pose a problem for market theorists; gentrification, after all, is a complete reversal of the outward pushing invasion-succession model that dominated ecological analysis for 60 years. Market theory is not static, however. By taking into account changing patterns of supply and demand -- changing technology and consumer tastes -- market theory is capable of developing a logical and coherent explanation of gentrification.

The most important factor in the market explanation is changing demand for residential space close to the CBD. A number of demographic trends are cited as causes of this changing demand: decreased household size, increased divorce rate, increased number of childless couples, and increased involvement of women in the workforce (see London and Palen, 1984: 14-15). Empirical research demonstrates that inmovers tend to be young professionals of relatively high income living in small households (for a review of the evidence see Gale, 1979; and LeGates and Hartman, 1986: 179-84). The basic idea is that the number of career-oriented households has been growing and they tend to value more the cultural amenities, consumption opportunities, and historical architecture available in upscale central-city neighborhoods. Another major factor is that inferior central city schools are not a drawback for childless couples (Nathan and Schill, 1983: 17). As a result, market theorists argue, gentrifiers have a

Figure 1. Bid Rent Curve

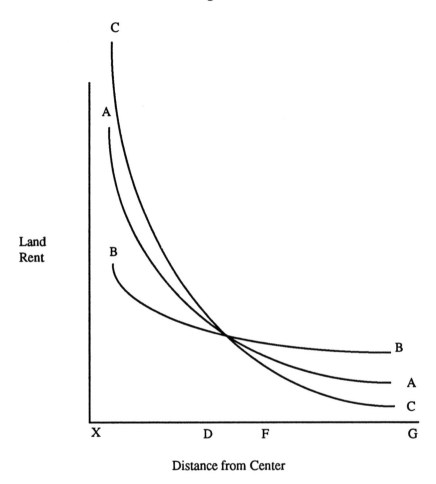

Distance from Center

AA lower-income household
BB upper-income suburban dweller
CC inmover to center city

Source: Nathan and Schill (1983)

much steeper bid rent curve than family-centered suburban households (Figure 1, line CC) and thus are able to outbid other households for residential space close to downtown.

Early Marxist analysis of gentrification criticized market explanations for relying on consumer preferences and ignoring the movement of capital and jobs. As Neil Smith put it: "Gentrification is a back to the city movement all right, but of capital rather than people" (Smith, 1979: 539). The market approach, however, is fully capable of integrating the movement of capital, or supply side considerations, into its demand side explanation of gentrification.[7]

In the full market explanation, changing patterns of consumer preference for inner-city housing are shaped by changing markets for capital and jobs. Most important, of course, is the growth of downtown professional office employment (Berry, 1985: 91-95). In market models, this is explained primarily by the agglomeration economies associated with concentrating a wide array of business and information processing functions in the CBD (Manners, 1974; Stanback, et al., 1981; Daniels, 1982; Gottman, 1983).

Another important supply side factor is the length of the average commute. As suburbs have sprawled out, people who work downtown have had to tolerate longer and longer commutes, in terms of both time and cost. Eventually, some are no longer willing to accept the trade-off of longer commutes for increased living space. According to market theory, the gentry are basically those downtown office workers, with the demographic characteristics described above, who accept higher levels of housing density in exchange for increased leisure time. Research has shown, in fact, that gentrification is positively correlated with high levels of white collar employment in the CBD and long commuting distances (Lipton, 1980).

Market theorists of gentrification generally applaud it as a positive development for older central cities (Sumka, 1979, 1980; Black, 1980; James, 1980; Sternlieb and Hughes, 1983; Nathan and Schill, 1983: 133). Gentrification provides a counterbalance to suburbanization that potentially benefits all citizens by improving the city's fiscal health and its capacity to provide services. While market theorists acknowledge that gentrification causes displacement, they argue that it should not be viewed as a serious national problem (Sumka, 1979: 486; U.S. Department of HUD, 1979; President's Commission, 1980: 31) and that it does not usually cause significant hardship on those who are forced to move (Nathan and Schill, 1983: 7). Market theorists concentrate on the system benefits of mobility, not its distributive consequences. Residential mobility is a method for adapting society to changing technologies and consumer demand and helps bring each parcel of land up to its highest and best use.

The policy recommendations of market theorists are based on their overall assessment of gentrification. Because gentrification is a basically healthy process, government policy should not impede it. Rent control and condominium conversion restrictions, for example, are undesirable because they might discourage investment (Kasarda, 1980: 394; Nathan and Schill, 1983: 140-42). To the extent that government is involved in housing markets, it should stimulate market trends, not retard them (Black, 1980: 119; James, 1980: 155). Pro-market policies include stimulation of the CBD through such devices as tax abatement and tax increment financing. Policies also could be targeted to specific neighborhoods and involve such measures as improved service delivery and rezoning to encourage exclusive residential use in some sections and mixed uses in other areas to allow development of restaurant-residential-boutique districts (Nathan and Schill, 1983: 129).

Although market theorists admit that gentrification causes displacement, they emphasize that policies to deal with displacement should not intervene into markets to stop it. By slowing reinvestment in central cities, interventionist policies will do more harm than good. As the McGill Commission Report argued, policies should be people-oriented, not place-oriented. "Sensitivity to the housing needs of low-income and elderly city residents could be better shown by assisting them to gain access to the transforming housing market rather than by implementing policies aimed at preventing displacement" (President's Commission, 1980: 31). In other words, policies should aid residential mobility, not impede it. Certainly, housing referral systems to make individuals aware of vacancies are acceptable. In general, policies to increase the housing options of the displaced are also acceptable, including supply-side policies to encourage the provision of low-income housing or, more preferably, demand-side subsidies, such as housing vouchers, to help the displaced find their own housing in the marketplace (Nathan and Schill, 1983: 141; President's Commission on Housing, 1982). Though market theorists support some public initiatives, the resources devoted to these program should be relatively meager because most of the displaced do relatively well in finding alternative housing (Nathan and Schill, 1983: Ch. 5).

The policy options described above fit into what we call "market conservatism." "Market liberalism" can be distinguished from market conservatism by its particular policy recommendations. At the same time, however, market liberals and market conservatives share fundamental assumptions about the efficacy of private markets. Market liberals agree with conservatives that markets are efficient allocators of resources and that market outcomes are determined by the impersonal forces of supply and demand, and not, as in the conflict model, by intentional power. Market liberals acknowledge that markets generate unequal burdens and social costs but, like market conservatives, they view these as the unintended effects of efficient markets.   Public policies, then, for both market liberals and conservatives, are designed not to plan markets but to compensate those who are injured by market transactions after the fact.

The main difference between market liberals and market conservatives is that market liberals are more concerned about the unequal distribution of the external costs generated by market transactions.   Because of their concern with inequality, market liberals generally view displacement as a more serious problem than market conservatives (Clay, 1979: 32-33); the consequences of displacement can be severe, including the loss of social and institutional ties and employment opportunities (Gale, 1984: 99). Housing markets should not be planned to prevent displacement, but policies should be implemented to help the displaced.   Market liberal policies are generally reactive to the market, not proactive.   In some circumstances, ironically, market liberals defend redistributive programs on the grounds that they are necessary to prevent more radical intervention into the marketplace. Some scholars, for example, defend increased compensation for displaced households on the grounds that, without these policies, lower-income community groups might fight displacement and succeed in slowing the gentrification process itself (Lang, 1982: 92; Houstoun and O'Connor, 1980: 298-99).[8]

The Conflict Approach to Gentrification

Conflict theorists adamantly disagree with the assumptions underlying the market perspective on urban development.   Market-oriented ecological and "bid-rent" explanations of urban growth assume that the form of the built environment is determined primarily by the preferences of individual actors, constrained by changing technologies and available resources.   Conflict theorists admit that consumers influence land use patterns, but they contend that institutional actors, both private and public, are more important determiners of urban form (Form, 1970).

The conflict approach can be understood by contrasting its explanation of suburbanization with the market explanation.   Using the bid-rent curve (Figure 1), market analysts argue that middle income suburban residents outbid low-income inner-city dwellers for low density suburban housing.   Conflict theorists, on the other hand, maintain that a free market for land does not exist.   Low-income households cannot even bid for suburban housing, conflict theorists argue, when suburbs engage in exclusionary practices, such as zoning laws prohibiting the construction of multi-family housing (see Foley, 1975; Danielson, 1976; Ashton, 1978; Markusen, 1978;

and Jackson, 1985).   Similarly, inner-city neighborhoods will decline, regardless of consumer demand, if banks redline them or offer mortgage loans
only on less desirable terms (Schafer, 1980; Listokin and Casey, 1980;
Avery and Buynak, 1981; Black and Schweitzer, 1985).   In addition, the
federal government, through such policies as the interstate highway program,
Federal Housing Administration (FHA) loan guarantees, and grants for suburban sewer and water systems, powerfully promoted suburbanization
(Vaughan, 1977; Fainstein and Fainstein, 1978; Savitch, 1979; Glickman,
1980; Feagin, 1983; Jackson, 1985).   In short, conflict theorists argue that
institutional practices, not individual preferences, best explain suburbanization, the dominant post-World War II metropolitan land-use trend in the
U.S.

As they later would criticize gentrification, conflict theorists
criticized urban renewal for claiming to benefit the whole city.   In reality,

Market and conflict analysts differ not only on how to explain
suburbanization, but also on how to interpret the efforts by government to
counter the negative effects of suburbanization on central cities through such
programs as urban renewal.   The market liberal rationale for urban renewal
is that inner-city decline will not reverse itself without government intervention.   Basically, negative externalities and interdependencies in inner-city
land markets create a Prisoner's Dilemma situation: it is not rational for
individual landowners to invest in a particular parcel of land unless
investment also occurs in surrounding parcels of land.   The federal government's Urban Renewal Program, enacted in 1949, was designed to reverse
this negative investment psychology by giving grants to local governments
to assemble large parcels of land using eminent domain, clear it, and sell it
to private investors at greatly subsidized rates.   The idea was that the whole
city would benefit from the new jobs and investment.[9]

As they later would criticize gentrification, conflict theorists
criticized urban renewal for claiming to benefit the whole city.   In reality,
they argued, the benefits accrued to only a small sector of real estate
interests, while the costs were borne by the poor and minorities.   According
to conflict theorists, it was not local elected officials representing the
interests of inner-city voters who pushed urban renewal (cf. Dahl, 1961).
Rather, growth coalitions, representing corporate interests with large land
holdings in central cities, pushed urban renewal in order to bolster declining
central city property values (Domhoff, 1978; Mollenkopf, 1983; Kleniewski,
1984).   The winners were the growing white collar service employers in the
city, including corporate offices, medical complexes, and universities.   The
losers were the poor, especially minorities.   As evidence, conflict theorists
cite the displacement of low-income inner-city residents by urban renewal,
which destroyed many more housing units than it built (and those housing
units that were built often went to upper-income professionals) (Gans, 1966;
Edel, 1971; Senate Committee, 1973).

Conflict theorists stress the continuities between urban renewal and gentrification; the winners and losers in the two cases are essentially the same. The conflict explanation of gentrification, then, is very similar to earlier conflict explanations of urban renewal. A conflict explanation of gentrification would appear to be more difficult to construct, however, since gentrification appears to be a private market phenomenon. Displacement from gentrification is seldom caused by government officials using the power of eminent domain. Conflict theorists argue, however, that appearances are misleading: eminent domain has been replaced by a complex configuration of federal, state, local and private actions that buttress and shape the gentrification process. While these actions may be more subtle than the "federal bulldozer" (Anderson, 1964), they can be just as effective.

Conflict and market analysts differ not just on the primary causes of gentrification (institutional power versus independent market behavior), they also differ on what precisely needs to be explained. Conflict theorists accept the market notion that changing demographics and consumer tastes have created an increased demand for housing close to downtown employment. What is at stake for conflict theorists, however, is not the general fact of gentrification but its particular timing and location, the booms and busts of neighborhood change. Certain neighborhoods become overwhelmed by what Rolf Goetze calls a "tidal wave" of gentry, while only a short distance away disinvestment can still be the rule (Goetze, 1979). The costs and benefits of uneven neighborhood development are, themselves, unevenly distributed.

Conflict theorists stress that neighborhood investment and disinvestment are not antithetical processes, but mutually reinforcing (Marcuse, 1986). Where and when reinvestment occurs is related to where and when disinvestment occurred. Neil Smith has introduced the concept of an inner-city "rent gap": the difference between the actual ground rent realized from a parcel of land and the potential ground rent given a more profitable use (see Smith, 1979; 1986). Disinvested residential areas near downtown with older historically significant structures have large rent gaps and are prime targets for gentrification. Institutional actors seize on areas with high rent gaps to reap windfall profits in housing appreciation. Such behavior helps explain the vicious rapid gentrification of select areas and the disequilibrium between overheated and underheated housing markets not easily accounted for by market theory.

The identification of stages in the gentrification process has been central to empirical research on the topic (National Urban Coalition, 1978; Clay, 1979; Gale, 1979; National Association of Neighborhoods, 1980; DeGiovanni, 1983; Pattison, 1983). In the early stages of gentrification, as identified by researchers, independent risk-oblivious "pioneers" buck negative investment trends by moving into a neighborhood and upgrading deteriorated structures. The early stages of gentrification thus fit with the idea of independent decision-making in the market. The later stages, however, fit better with a conflict perspective, as independent decision-making is replaced by interdependent decision-making coordinated by institutional actors. Risk-averse, well-off investors are able to make large profits in housing appreciation in the later stages of gentrification. Public and private institutions take actions, such as using Community Development Block Grant (CDBG) funds for housing rehabilitation, which reduce the risk of investing in housing. As part of this process, the displacement of poor residents by wealthy gentry ensures rising real estate values.

Throughout, conflict theorists stress the actions of private institutions, local governments, and the federal government in shaping the gentrification process. Conflict theorists argue that if developers are big enough and are able to pump enough money into a particular area, they can by their own actions (in violation of market theory) create a self-inflating market that will guarantee them windfall profits. "A survey of thirty cities found developers to be important at a relatively early point in 40 percent of the gentrifying neighborhoods" (Feagin, 1983: 96; survey in Clay, 1979). Private lenders are another key institutional actor. After disinvestment, lenders may be in a position to greenline neighborhoods and boost the gentrification process. Roman Cybriwsky, David Ley, and John Western show how banking interests played a key role in the civic coalition that initiated the gentrification of Society Hill in Philadelphia. The Philadelphia case study gives a concrete sense of the myriad ways that human will can shape markets, highlighting the "often overlooked ability of organized interest groups to define the character of urban revitalization" (Cybriwsky, et al., 1986: 117).

Local governments are a central component of the "growth machine" that feeds gentrification (Molotch, 1976). Infrastructural amenities, such as brick sidewalks and old-fashioned streetlights, have often been used by local governments to stimulate gentrification. The most common method, however, is tax subsidies. In New York City, the J-51 tax abatement program for housing rehabilitation had given away $1.66 billion in subsidies by 1983 (Parker, 1983: 11); as of 1987, under the 421a program, over $551 million had been given away for new residential construction (Hinds, 1987). In both programs, the bulk of the subsidies have gone to high-income, gentrified housing in Manhattan (Domurad and Messinger, 1983). Stimulated by such subsidies, many single room occupancy hotels (SROs) have been converted into luxury condominiums or apartments for the urban gentry. In New York City, between 1970 and 1983, the number of SRO units dropped 89 percent, from 127,000 to 14,000 (Coalition for the

Homeless, 1985: 5). Tax-stimulated conversion of SRO housing is a major cause of homelessness in American cities (Hoch and Slayton, forthcoming).

The federal government has also promoted gentrification through its grants to cities. Urban Development Action Grants (UDAGs) have often subsidized downtown office employment, and sometimes have been used for higher income housing (Hartman, Keating, LeGates, 1982: Ch. 13; Marcuse, 1986: 174). CDBG monies have been used by localities to fuel gentrification (Hartman, Keating, LeGates, 1982: Ch. 12), a practice that has been made easier by the loosening of regulations which required targeting the funds to the poor. In 1978, the Carter Administration issued new regulations for CDBG which required that "75 percent of the program funds... be used for projects and activities which principally benefit low- and moderate-income persons...." (*Code of Federal Regulations*, 24, April 1, 1978, 570.02). In 1981, however, the Reagan Administration eliminated the specific percentage requirements and made it easier for block grant funds to be used for economic development and gentrification (*Housing and Development Reporter*, 1981: 1081-82). The Reagan Administration also rescinded Carter's policy on urban displacement (Executive Order 811). Finally, Historic Preservation Tax Credits, which require local initiative for district designation, have subsidized gentrification in many neighborhoods. In 1984 these credits were worth $320 million (C. Dolbeare, 1986: 266).

The federal government's own policies have also boosted the gentrification process. The most important federal policy is homeowner tax deductions for mortgage interest and property taxes. In 1986, for example, homeowner tax deductions totalled $42.4 billion in subsidies. By contrast, direct outlays on all low-income housing programs totalled only $10.0 billion (Low Income Housing Information Service, 1987). While in some cities, such as New York, gentrification is primarily a rental phenomenon, in most cities gentrification converts rental units for lower-income households into owner-occupied units for wealthy professionals. Federal policy has fueled this. In particular, the tax code has fueled condominium conversion, a prime method of gentrification in many cities (Goetze, 1981).

In conclusion, the conflict analysis of gentrification views residential mobility as primarily a distributive mechanism, not a growth mechanism. The benefits of mobility are seen as being bottled up among a small corporate and professional elite, not spreading widely to society as a whole. While the benefits of urban reinvestment are highly visible, the costs are not. A chic new neighborhood may be created in one place, but the displaced poor may only be creating an overcrowded ghetto somewhere else. Gentrification almost never results in racially or economically mixed neighborhoods (LeGates and Hartman, 1986: 194-96). In fact, according to the conflict perspective, the process is intended to displace the poor and create a homogenous submarket, where investor-owners will capture the benefits of living in a middle- and upper-class enclave (Smith and LeFaivre, 1984).

The policy recommendations of the conflict school follow directly from their explanation of gentrification.   Because housing markets are viewed as already marred by massive political interventions and inefficiencies, conflict theorists are much more open than market theorists to using government to address problems such as displacement.   Conflict theorists go further than market liberals, however; they believe in proactive planning, not reactive planning.   Conflict theorists recommend that government plan housing and prevent displacement instead of simply compensating the victims after the fact.   The goal is to make government policies responsive to existing residents, not to financial interests and mobile gentry.

The concrete policy goal of conflict theorists is what Chester Hartman has called "the right to stay put" (Hartman, 1984a: 306-308).   This goal is pursued through policies that protect renters and homeowners from forced displacement.   Rent control is one common method for achieving this goal (Hartman, 1984: 313-14).   Another method is guaranteed tenure for certain classes of renters, such as the elderly.   The right of first purchase helps to protect renters from condominium conversions but obviously does not go far enough because many renters cannot afford to buy their unit.   One way of dealing with this is to prohibit conversions unless a certain percentage of the tenants agree (Lauber, 1984: 294). General restrictions on condominium conversions are also compatible with the conflict perspective.

Other policies that limit displacement involve proactive planning of housing markets to varying degrees.   Rolf Goetze, for example, calls for spreading out housing demand in order to prevent overheated housing markets from causing extensive displacement (Goetze, 1979).   By targeting housing subsidies to marginal neighborhoods and formulating affirmative marketing programs for them, local governments can spread out housing demand and cool-off overheated gentrifying neighborhoods.[10]   Taxes on speculative gains in real estate can also help to dampen investment in overheated housing markets (Hartman, Keating, and LeGates, 1982: Ch. 4; Mills, 1983).   In general, housing subsidies, such as CDBG housing loan funds, should be targeted to declining neighborhoods or existing residents of neighborhoods facing gentrification pressure and not be used to aid in-movers (Auger, 1979).

Conflict policies are generally targeted to places, not to people; they are designed to improve and stabilize neighborhoods, rather than help individuals after they have been displaced.   Certainly neighborhoods need capital investment in both housing and commercial ventures, but profit-seeking investment designed to change the class structure of neighborhoods is not desirable. Rather, community development corporations, controlled by neighborhood residents, that reinvest profits within the neighborhood for the benefit of the existing residents are the vehicles favored by conflict theorists (Harrison, 1974: 167-84; Bowles, Gordon, and Weisskopf, 1983: 318-22). Government should support these organizations. Limited equity coops should also be supported as a way of helping tenants become owners while at the same time preventing displacement due to speculation (Lauber, 1984: 295-98).

The Market Approach to Deindustrialization

The debate on deindustrialization is remarkably similar to the debate on gentrification. In both cases, market and conflict approaches diverge sharply. As in gentrification, students of deindustrialization disagree not so much on a description of the phenomenon as on how to evaluate its costs and benefits for society as a whole and the distribution of these costs and benefits across space and among different social classes.

Deindustrialization refers to the loss of industrial jobs throughout the American economy, but especially in older central cities. Two processes are occurring simultaneously to bring this about: one is the transition from manufacturing employment to service employment; the other is the movement of jobs from one geographical location to another. For the most part, market and conflict theorists do not disagree on the necessity of an overall shift in employment from manufacturing to services. Partly, this has been caused by a shift in final consumption from goods to services (Stanback, et al., 1981; Noyelle, 1986). More important has been a faster increase in productivity in manufacturing than in services (Fuchs, 1968; Stanback, et al., 1981).[11] Where market and conflict theorists strongly disagree, however, is on the reasons for the movement of jobs and investment from one geographical location to another.

The market explanation for the decline of manufacturing employment in central cities focuses on the lower factor costs in suburban, sunbelt, and overseas locations. Lower suburban land costs, for example, were a major factor in the decentralization of factory employment; lower wages contributed to the movement of factory jobs to the sunbelt. As in ecological theory, the market explanation of deindustrialization views it as the natural outcome of a competitive process that benefits society as a whole. If cities are losing industrial jobs it is because they can no longer compete efficiently with other cities as sites for industrial production. The President's Panel on *Urban America in the Eighties* expressed well the market attitude toward deindustrialization:

The nation can no longer assume that cities will perform the full range of their traditional functions for the larger society. They are no longer the most desirable settings for living, working, or producing. They should be allowed to transform into more specialized service and consumption centers within larger urban economic systems. The Panel believes that this nation should reconcile itself to these redistribution patterns (President's Commission, 1980: 4).

The mobility of capital insures that production takes place at the most efficient locations; everyone benefits from a more efficient economy. The social benefits of capital mobility are deduced, in market analysis, from the theory of comparative advantage, which extends back to the writings of David Ricardo (1772-1823).[12]   According to the theory of comparative advantage, geographical specialization according to different productive functions results in greater efficiency for the system as a whole.   The theory of comparative advantage is not static, however.   Changing consumer demand and new production technologies constantly alter the comparative advantages of regions and cities, necessitating what Joseph Schumpeter called a process of "Creative Destruction" (Schumpeter, 1950: 83).   (For a positive [market] treatment of Schumpeter's concept of Creative Destruction, see New York Stock Exchange, 1984; for a critical [conflict] treatment, see Bluestone and Harrison, 1982.)   While some workers and cities may be hurt by the movement of factory jobs overseas, overall, market theory views it as a healthy process because it increases the efficiency of the productive system as a whole and leads to lower prices for consumers (McKenzie, 1984: 25-26).

Capital mobility not only produces broad social benefits, market theorists argue, but it generates a self-correcting process that tends to even out the differences between regions and cities in the long run.   In the short run, market theorists acknowledge, disinvestment damages cities, decreasing income and increasing unemployment.   The market sets forces in motion, however, that automatically tend to correct geographical inequalities: workers migrate to high-growth regions in search of higher wages, thus reducing the unemployment rate in the disinvested area; companies, seeing the depressed wages in the disinvested area, eventually begin to reinvest in the region in pursuit of lower production costs (see Clark, 1983: 88).   As a case in point, *The President's National Urban Policy Report* presented evidence to show that regional per capita income in the U.S. between 1950 and 1980 tended to equalize (U.S. Department of HUD, 1982: 26-27).

Since capital mobility produces broad social benefits for society and, in any case, tends to automatically correct geographical inequalities over time, governmental interference into capital markets is viewed negatively by market theorists. Just as government, according to market theorists, should not attempt to slow down the gentrification process, it also should not interfere with the deindustrialization process. "Too often in the past, the Federal Government has responded to these temporary symptoms of national economic change with policies and programs intended to halt or slow rather than accommodate the process of adjustment" (U.S. Department of HUD, 1982: 23). Policies designed to help specific communities only end up rooting economic activity in inefficient locations. "Any policy which anchors poor people in a declining city -- whether it be by generous welfare payments, subsidized housing or subsidized employment -- is bound to be cruelly counterproductive" (Kristol, 1977; see also Kasarda, 1985: 38). Well-intentioned policies end up hurting the people they are designed to help. Plant-closing legislation, for example, is viewed as anti-labor because it depresses capital investment, and therefore job opportunities, in those communities that need jobs the most (McKenzie, 1984: 309).

While market theorists argue that governmental intervention into capital investment is counterproductive, they stress even more that efforts by the public sector to shape capital flows are futile. In explaining urban growth and decline, market analysts stress impersonal market exchange, not the power of public policies (U.S. Department of HUD, 1982: 23). "Urban growth in a free society is the result of decisions by many individuals, households, and firms, acting independently, to cluster together in particular places" (U.S. Department of HUD, 1982: 11).

Market conservatives favor a hands-off policy toward deindustriali-zation. To the extent that government should be involved in deindustrial-ization at all, its policies should be people-oriented, not place-oriented (Hicks, 1982: 585). People-oriented policies should be designed to facilitate adjustment to economic change, not to slow it down. Specific policies to further this goal correspond closely with policies to aid those who are dis-placed in gentrifying neighborhoods. Providing information to unemployed workers about job openings in new locations, for example, is analogous to a housing information service. Relocation allowances for displaced workers correspond to relocation allowances for displaced renters (see Figure 2 for a comparison of policies directed to job and housing displacement).

Market liberals agree that the market should decide the most efficient locations for jobs and investment. Market liberals differ from market conservatives in their willingness to let government play a more active role in promoting economic change. The idea is not to replace mar-ket priorities with government priorities but to complement market trends and even accelerate them (Reich, 1983: 234). Some market liberals advocate that government formulate a general "industrial policy" to enhance the mobility of capital and labor into high-productivity, "sunrise" industries (Thurow, 1980: 95).

Figure 2. Gentrification and Deindustrialization
Policy Comparisons

	Gentrification	Deindustrialization
Market-oriented policies	1. Housing information service 2. Relocation allowances 3. Housing vouchers (Sec. 8 certificates for displaced households) 4. Targeted subsidies to gentrifying neighborhoods	1. Job counseling 2. Transitional wage vouchers 3. Worker retraining programs 4. Targeted subsidies to sunrise industries
Conflict-oriented policies	1. "Right to stay put" 2. Advance notice: right of first purchase (limited equity coops) 3. Community development corporations 4. Targeted housing subsidies for existing residents (e.g. low-interest rehabilitation loans)	1. Job security 2. Advance notice: worker buyouts (employee stock ownership plans) 3. Workplace democracy 4. Targeted economic development subsidies to declining industries (e.g. low-interest loans)

Specific policies recommended by market liberals to help individuals hurt by deindustrialization resemble policies, discussed earlier, to help households displaced by gentrification. The common theme is that public policies should not stop or even slow down job displacement; instead, policies should help the individuals affected in such a way as to accelerate the process of economic adjustment. Job training programs are a good example (Thurow, 1980: 208-209; Reich, 1983: 204). The provision of transitional wage vouchers to better enable displaced workers to find new employment (Magaziner and Reich, 1982: 344-45) and the creation of public service jobs (Thurow, 1980: 203-206) are comparable to the provision of housing vouchers and the development of publicly-subsidized or owned low-income housing for households displaced by gentrification. Plant closing legislation which requires advance notice so that workers can begin a job search (Magaziner and Reich, 1982: 346-47) is similar to the policy requiring landlords to notify tenants of a planned condominium conversion.

The Conflict Approach to Deindustrialization

The conflict explanation of deindustrialization and its policy recommendations contrast in every way with the market approach. Conflict theorists do not view deindustrialization as the result of independent producers bidding for the most efficient locations for production. Rather, institutional power, exercised by governments and large corporations, has shaped the deindustrialization process (see Lustig, 1985; Bensman and Lynch, 1987). Central cities have not lost industrial jobs because they are less efficient locations for production in general, but because government policies have made them less profitable locations and because corporations are able to ignore the social costs of their investment decisions (Sclar, 1981; Adams, 1982; Bowles, Gordon, and Weisskopf, 1983: 233-34). Unlike market theory, conflict theory does not view capital mobility as broadly benefiting society as a whole; rather, the benefits are viewed as being bottled up in a narrow corporate sector.

Under market theory, capital mobility is determined by economic imperatives. If corporations do not move rapidly in search of lower factor costs, they will soon be forced out of business by the competition. Even in a competitive market, however, conflict theorists argue that many decisions made by corporations are not dictated by market imperatives. Charles Lindblom includes plant location among those decisions where executives cannot find one least-cost solution according to the market. Lindblom concludes, therefore, that executives must exercise "corporate discretion," which requires that political and social variables enter into decision-making (Lindblom, 1977: 152-55). Decisions in the market are not always Pareto Optimal, Lindblom contends; they are essentially political in nature and fraught with conflicts of values and interests.

In *The Deindustrialization of America*, Bluestone and Harrison maintain that large corporations are able to exert power over the market-place to their own narrow advantage. They describe how labor and capital agreed to an implicit social contract after World War II, which recognized unions and passed on productivity gains to workers, but gave control over production and technological innovation to management. When the economic problems of the 1970s squeezed profit margins, Bluestone and Harrison argue, the corporations broke the social contract and used capital mobility, enhanced by technological advances, to bust unions and undermine the social wage. In response to the profit crunch, many corporations pursued mergers instead of more efficient methods of production. Corporate conglomerates milked profitable plants, eventually shutting many of them down, with devastating effects on the communities involved. Geographical mobility, like an engineered recession, was used to discipline labor (see also Bowles, Gordon, and Weisskopf, 1983: 62-121). Instead of viewing mobility exclusively as a mechanism for improving growth and efficiency, conflict theory views it also as an instrument for influencing the distribution of wealth.[13]

Market analysts stress that government has played a minor role in economic change, and when it has been involved it has tended to retard capital mobility. Conflict theorists, on the other hand, stress that governmental policies have had an important effect on investment flows and that these policies have tended to promote mobility and change -- not retard it -- to the benefit of particular social interests. Of course, some federal grant programs have been targeted to deindustrializing areas, such as the CDBG and the Job Training Partnership Act (JTPA). Often, however, once given to the local governments, these grant monies have gone to subsidize gentrification and expansion of the corporate service sector.

More importantly, conflict analysts stress that analysis of spending programs ignores the equally powerful revenue side of the budget. Socially-oriented spending programs have been dwarfed by tax expenditures, which totalled $388.4 billion in 1984, and which *promoted* capital mobility and deindustrialization (Alperowitz and Faux, 1984: 21). Accelerated depreciation for new commercial and industrial property, for example, had the effect of rendering older buildings in central cities less attractive for investment, and accelerated the flight of industry out of central cities (Peterson, 1979; Adams, 1982: 14). By allowing corporations to credit foreign taxes against domestic tax liabilities, the U.S. tax code has subsidized the mobility of capital overseas, promoting the loss of thousands, if not millions, of American jobs (Bluestone and Harrison, 1982: 130). Michael P. Smith (1988) calls tax breaks for wealthy individuals and corporations "fiscal welfare" and argues that the revenue side of public budgets hides the essence of policy initiatives during the Reagan era.

Many federal spending programs, while purporting to be "place neutral," have also promoted deindustrialization at the expense of central cities. Military and space expenditures were keys to the rise of the sunbelt (Sale, 1974; Watkins, 1980: 233; Tabb, 1984: 7-8). "Military Keynesianism," as it is called, has played a major role in urban growth and decline (Smith, 1988). Ann Markusen has demonstrated how defense spending between 1951 and 1976 shifted from the industrial heartland to the "defense perimeter" where it "created relatively homogeneous, politically conservative, suburban communities favoring white male professional and technical workers" (Markusen, 1987: 106). The bias has continued into the 1980s. Other federal programs, such as the interstate highway program, FHA mortgage insurance and VA loan guarantees, as well as grants for new sewer and water systems, have also had the effect of subsidizing the disinvestment of older industrial areas (Vaughan, 1977; Glickman, 1980). Moreover, mobile capital has been able to play state and local governments against each other, forcing tax and spending concessions from them that have eroded the tax base and gutted social programs (Goodman, 1979).

The implication of the conflict explanation of deindustrialization is that mobility is greater than necessary for efficient economic adaptation and that it is often used as an instrument to benefit particular elite and regional interests. Moreover, conflict theorists view hypermobility in the American economy as tending to exacerbate class and regional inequalities. As noted earlier, market theory treats geographical inequalities as self-correcting: diminishing marginal returns in the winner regions eventually cause investors to shift back to the loser regions. Far from being self-correcting, conflict theorists view geographical inequalities as reinforcing (see Bluestone, 1972; Bluestone and Harrison, 1982: 202-205; Clark, 1983; and Markusen, 1987). Having fiscally stronger public sectors, for example, winner regions can more easily finance the infrastructure for profitable investment and growth, while loser regions find themselves in a vicious cycle of fiscal stress, infrastructural deterioration, and disinvestment.

For conflict theorists the question is not whether the U.S. should have an industrial policy or not. The U.S. already has an industrial policy, but it is an undemocratic one in which narrow elites confer market privileges on themselves by manipulating public policy. This ersatz industrial policy is hidden behind a veil of free market ideology (Smith and Judd, 1984). Since the U.S. cannot avoid having an industrial policy of some kind, conflict theorists recommend that we shift from our present one, which is elitist and regressive, to an industrial policy that is consciously democratic and egalitarian.

The policies recommended by conflict theorists to deal with deindustrialization resemble those recommended for gentrification (see Figure 2). Just as the goal in gentrification policy was "the right to stay put," the goal in deindustrialization is to bring jobs to the people, not force people to move to the jobs. "Community sustaining economics," Alperowitz and Faux call it (1984: Ch. 5). Since conflict theorists already view the government as heavily involved in deindustrialization, they are not shy about recommending government programs. Instead of the government response being haphazard and reactive, however, conflict theorists recommend a proactive planning approach that can prevent job displacement from occurring in the first place (Bensman and Lynch, 1987: Ch. 8; Blakely and Shapira, 1984: 104-109). In general, government policy should favor a "brownfield" approach, rebuilding existing industrial communities, instead of a "greenfield" approach, moving industry to rural areas and building up a whole new community to support it (Lynd, 1985). Older industrial cities, such as Detroit, are not obsolescent; they can be saved through a process of "rational reindustrialization" (Luria and Russell, 1981).

The specific policy instruments recommended by the conflict approach for deindustrialization are similar to those recommended for gentrification. First, conflict theorists recommend that democratic planning take place, as much as possible, at the local level (Alperowitz and Faux, 1984: Ch. 15; Whyte, 1985). Similar to the emphasis on community development corporations to give residents some control over gentrification, conflict theorists favor workplace democracy to give workers more control over industrial change. Similar to tenant approval of condominium conversions, conflict theorists advocate worker and community monitoring of, and influence over, disinvestment decisions (Bluestone and Harrison, 1982: 249; Bowles, Gordon, and Weisskopf, 1983: 323-37). Policies that require advance notice to workers of a plant closing are favored by conflict theorists, not primarily to enable workers to seek new jobs elsewhere, but to mobilize the community to retain the jobs through such mechanisms as worker buyouts. Government policy can support worker buyouts in many different ways, including tax incentives for employee stock ownership plans (ESOPs), low interest loans, and outright grants (see Rosen, 1985).

As in gentrification, behind the disagreements on the speed and desirability of industrial change lie contrasting theoretical frameworks: the market and conflict approaches. Policy recommendations flow, to a great extent, from the analysis of the phenomenon, which in turn is shaped by fundamental assumptions about the nature of economic change in American society. Whether dealing with rapid reinvestment (gentrification) or rapid disinvestment (deindustrialization), policy recommendations are consistent with the underlying policy perspectives.

Conclusion: Facts, Values and Public Policy

The purpose of this essay was to make explicit the implicit theoretical frameworks behind the policy debates on deindustrialization and gentrification. The preceding analysis has served that purpose, we believe. Figure 3 sums up the assumptions and implications of the two policy perspectives examined: conflict and market (which can, in turn, be divided

Figure 3. Job and Housing Displacement:
Public Policy Perspectives

	Market		Conflict
	Conservative	Liberal	
Cost of displacement	Low	Moderate	High
Main cause of displacement	Market exchange	Market exchange	Institutional power
Effect of state policy on gentrification	-Minimal effect -Where state policy does intervene, it decreases mobility and efficiency	-Moderate effect -State policy decreases the costs of mobility at minimum cost to efficiency	-Great effect -State policy tends to increase mobility at great cost to efficiency
Main influence over state policy	Liberal establishment	Plural interest groups	Corporate elite
Preferred role for state	Minimalist (umpire)	Ameliorative (handicapper)	Planning (player)
Main goal of public policy	Promote growth by encouraging mobility	Balanced growth (through mobility) and equality (through compensatory programs)	Promote stable communities by slowing displace- (through democrat-planning), at little or no cost to growth
Economic constraints on policy choice	Great (public policy has little effect on powerful market forces)	Great (public policy has little effect on powerful market forces, but it can compensate for the negative effects	Low (public policy can powerfully shape market outcomes)
Ideological vision	laissez-faire capitalism	welfare state capitalism	economic democracy

into conservative and liberal variants). The main paradigm split, we argue, is between the market and conflict approaches. While the liberal-conservative division dominates policy debates, we argue that it takes place within narrow confines because both basically accept the market as the allocator of resources. The market-Marxist/structuralist debate also receives a great deal of attention but we maintain that both approaches explain the phenomenon primarily in economic structural terms: the main difference is that one applauds the results, the other deplores them. In the American context, we argue, the division between market and conflict approaches is at the heart of the most vital policy debates.

Our analysis suggests that facts and values, normative and empirical judgments, cannot be easily separated; factual analysis is closely tied to values, and our values undoubtedly influence the way we look at facts. Whether a "problem" exists and whether it requires a public policy response (certainly value-laden questions) are determined, to a great extent, not by the facts but by how we interpret them. The same factual rate of economic change, for example, can be interpreted as too slow, appropriate, or too rapid, depending on the framework of analysis. Policy frameworks, then, are an integral part of what is called "agenda-setting" in the public policy literature (Cobb and Elder, 1983; Kingdon, 1984).

The central values of the debate between conservatives and liberals within the market approach are equality and efficiency. Market liberals and conservatives accept the idea of a steep trade-off between equality and efficiency that places limits on government intervention (Okun, 1975; Kristol, 1978: 239-43). The main difference is that liberals place more emphasis on equality and therefore are willing to support policies that target resources to distressed individuals and communities, even at some cost in efficiency or growth to the economy as a whole.

The problem is that the market liberal approach to public policy radically separates economic and social policy and subordinates the latter to the former. Like conservatives, the market liberal approach to public policy relies on the logic of the so-called Kaldor-Hicks principle. A policy is Kaldor-Hicks efficient if the resulting increase in aggregate wealth is sufficient to compensate the losers and still have something left over (Kaldor, 1939). (For a critical discussion of this approach to public policy, see Clark, 1983.) In other words, the idea is to first maximize the total size of the economic pie and only then to consider (and on this conservatives and liberals disagree) compensating the losers, whether individuals or geographical areas. In other words, economic policy (or growth) comes first, and should be treated separately from social policy (or redistribution). Since the market creates the resources that fund redistributive programs, social programs must fundamentally come after economic programs.

Applying this principle in the post-war period, market liberals have supported programs designed to aid mobility and growth, including accelerated depreciation, investment tax credits, the interstate highway program, and subsidies for homeownership, such as the deductibility of mortgage interest and property taxes. As we have seen, these policies have promoted deindustrialization and gentrification, helping to displace people from their jobs and homes. At the same time, liberals have supported programs that target resources to declining areas to cope with job and housing displacement, such as CDBG and JTPA. What liberal policy takes with its economic programs, it gives back with its social programs. (We are not the first to argue that liberal policies suffer from incoherence; see Lowi, 1979.)

The Achilles' heel of the market liberal approach is that it ties social policy to economic growth. The private economy generates the goods, so to speak, that government can redistribute, if it has the political will. In the high growth period of the 1950s and 1960s, liberals were able to support social programs for the poor on the grounds that even though they may have reduced economic growth somewhat, due to disincentive effects, there was still plenty of growth to go around. Indeed, Keynesian economics buttressed liberal policy by arguing that directing resources to the poor, who spend rather than save, would help smooth out demand-led recessions. Keynesian economics implied that the trade-off between equality and growth was less steep than conservatives maintained. Liberal social programs, in short, were founded on economic growth (Wolfe, 1981).

The economic stagnation of the 1970s and 1980s, however, has knocked this foundation out from under liberal social policy. The mounting trade and budget deficits have shifted the attention of policy makers from the demand side to the supply side, from inadequate demand to inadequate savings and investment. "Competitiveness" has replaced "compassion" as the policy buzzword. Market conservatives argue that we can no longer afford to trade off what little growth we have for greater equality. Accepting the trade-off (rooted in market thinking), liberals have found the policy ground for social programs shrinking.

Moreover, economic growth policies seem to have set in motion social forces that are overwhelming the coping abilities of social policies. Homelessness is a policy area where the separation of economic and social policy is reaching a crisis. Homelessness is caused by the rapid growth of high-level service-sector employment and major cities and the resulting gentrification of the housing stock and displacement of the poor (Adams, 1986). Meanwhile, government policies are exacerbating the problem by speeding up gentrification and making it difficult for the private market to respond to the demand for low-rent housing (Swanstrom, forthcoming). Phillip Clay estimates that by the year 2003, 18.7 million Americans will be in immediate risk of homelessness (Clay, 1987).   At the present rate of growth of homelessness, liberal shelter programs will be unable to keep pace with, let alone solve, the problem of homelessness.

Conflict theory presents an alternative framework that presents a way out of the market policy dilemma between growth and efficiency. Conflict theorists argue that the trade-off between equality and efficiency is not written in stone.   They maintain that it is possible to achieve greater job stability and geographical equality, without sacrificing efficiency and growth (Bluestone and Harrison, 1982: Ch. 2; Bowles, Gordon and Weiss-kopf, 1983: 262-73; Kuttner, 1984: 46-48; Alperowitz and Faux, 1984: 149; K. Dolbeare, 1986: 145).[14]

The means to achieving growth with equality, conflict theory implies, is to overcome the artificial separation between economic and social policy.   The animus of the conflict analysis of market-oriented growth policies is that the growth they promote has tremendous social implications. Growth-oriented economic policy is neither socially nor geographically neutral.   Economic policy is, by its very nature, social policy.   According to conflict theory, this connection has been hidden by market ideology, which says that economic growth is beneficial for society as a whole, while social policies benefit only narrow interest groups.   Conflict theorists challenge this notion by arguing that social policies can benefit society as a whole. As Mark Gottdiener writes: "[i]t is in everyone's interest, even the business community, to support public programs aimed at reducing crime, even if individuals are taxed for programs that do not benefit themselves directly" (Gottdiener, 1987: 88-89).   Social policies are not necessarily harmful to economic growth.

At the same time, economic growth policies have profound social implications, and policymakers should be more sensitive, conflict theorists argue, to these effects.   Equity considerations should be included before the fact in economic planning, not after the fact, as is usually the case with liberal social policy.   In the case of homelessness, for instance, instead of waiting for people to become homeless and then building shelters to house them, policymakers should try to attack homelessness before it occurs. Fundamentally, this means dismantling the policies that are fueling rapid gentrification and displacement in major American cities and increasing funding for programs to expand the supply of low-income housing.

It is interesting to note that the value position of the conflict school, which is normally viewed as being on the left, is more conservative, in the traditional sense, than either market liberals or conservatives.   As Garry Wills once remarked: "Our 'conservatives' are entrepreneurs of mobility and expansion -- their stake in society is the least conservative thing, capitalism" (Wills, 1977: 17).   While more willing to support government programs to deal with the costs of rapid change after they occur, market liberals, with their faith in the market, are just as committed to rapid social change as market conservatives. Conflict theory, on the other hand, defends the right of communities, rooted in space, to defend themselves against rapid economic and social change. As opposed to the market view of "place" as an abstract location for production and workers as mobile factors in production, conflict theory values place as a setting for the development of culture and valued social networks (Smith and Judd, 1984: 190). Conflict theory defends the use value of places, over and against their exchange values (Logan and Molotch, 1987). With its defense of territory, conflict theory is compatible with the often conservative grassroots citizen movements that have sprung up in recent years and which have been interpreted as a new American populism (Boyte and Riessman, 1986).[15]

If it is possible to achieve both economic growth and equity at the same time, why has it not been tried? Conflict theory suggests that it is not just a technical problem, such as inadequate information about the social impacts of economic growth policies. The fundamental reason why alternative policies have not been tried is because of the power of entrenched interest groups over policy. Accordingly, policy analysts cannot limit themselves to a technocratic role, analyzing the costs and benefits of alternative public policies. Following the advocacy or equity school of planning, policy analysts must become *advocates* for those who have been left out of the benefits of the American political economy (see Davidoff, 1965; Krumholz, 1975).

Notes

1.   Market analysts admit that, in practice, coercion does sometimes interfere with market efficiency. The most important market failures are externalities: costs (or benefits) that are forced on somebody who did not take part in an exchange. To the extent that externalities exist, even strict market conservatives admit that something should be done about them (Friedman, 1962: 30-32). Market failures, however, are viewed as the exception and not the rule in otherwise non-coercive market processes.

2.   Key works in the development of the conflict approach to urban and regional development include: Harvey, 1973; Molotch, 1976; Gordon, 1977; Bluestone and Harrison, 1982; Mollenkopf, 1983; Friedland, 1983; Clark, 1983; Feagin, 1983; Markusen, 1987; Logan and Molotch, 1987; Kantor, 1988; Gilderbloom and Appelbaum, 1988; and Smith, 1988. The conflict approach has also been applied in a number of case studies of specific cities: Stone, 1976; Whitt, 1982; Hartman, 1984; Swanstrom, 1985; Jones and Bachelor, 1986; Fainstein, et al., 1986; and Stone and Sanders, 1987.

3.   Besides the so-called "capital logic" school, exemplified in some of the work of David Harvey (1985: Ch. 6), reductionist tendencies are also evident in French structural Marxism (see Poulantzas, 1973; and Castells, 1979). Structural Marxism verges on economic functionalism, with outcomes explained as being functional for the accumulation of capital and the reproduction of the capitalist system. Both the capital logic and structural schools of Marxism are pitched at such a high level of abstraction that their policy implications in any particular area are usually unclear. In general, they imply that little progress can be made in any policy area until social ownership replaces private ownership of the means of production.

4.   Market theorists, such as Friedman, acknowledge that power often shapes markets. Such interference in markets, however, is viewed as undesirable, and they call for truly "free" markets. Conflict theorists, on the other hand, assume that power always shapes market outcomes; "free" markets never exist (see, for example, Smith, 1988: Chs. 5-6).

5.   As David Harvey has written: "The surface appearance of conflicts around the built environment -- the struggles against the landlord or against urban renewal -- conceals a hidden essence that is *nothing more* than the struggle between capital and labor" (our emphasis) (Harvey, 1976: 289, as quoted in Logan and Molotch, 1987: 11).

6.   The level of class consciousness may vary over time. Robert Kuttner, for example, suggests that in the past decade business interests have become more ideological- and class-united (1984: 257).

7.   More recently, Smith has attempted to integrate consumption- and production-side arguments in a Marxist explanation of gentrification (Smith, 1987).

8.   It is important to note that we are not claiming that all policy analysts fit neatly into our categories. Many who self-identify as liberals, for example, advocate policies to slow displacement or even plan jobs and housing. When they advocate such policies, however, they are implicitly assuming that markets are not fair and efficient allocators of resources. Hence, such policy prescriptions are more consistent with the conflict perspective that views markets as continually distorted by assertions of power. What our categories can accomplish, then, is to straighten out the relationship between empirical analysis and policy prescriptions and thereby help to clarify what is often a muddled policy debate.

9.   For the classic market liberal rationale for urban renewal, based on welfare economics, see Otis and Whinston, 1966.

10.   Michael Lang also recommends an approach that involves proactive planning. A "neighborhood indexing program" would delineate five areas of the city. In two of these areas experiencing gentrification pressures Lang recommends policies that would guarantee low-income residents either new or rehabilitated housing within the neighborhood with no increases in rent above the inflation rate (Lang, 1982: 94-95).

11.   Even here, however, there is disagreement on whether the movement out of manufacturing to services is occurring at an appropriate rate due to market forces or whether governmental policy and institutional power is forcing too rapid a transition to services.

Robert Reich, for example, argues that in the pursuit of "paper entrepreneurialism" American corporations have become top heavy with white collar service employees staff beyond rational requirements of the market (Reich, 1983: 142). In *Manufacturing Matters*, Stephen Cohen and John Zysman argue that the rapid shift from manufacturing to services, accelerated by governmental policies, is not a healthy market phenomenon but is undermining the long-term prosperity of the American economy (Cohen and Zysman, 1987).

12. In a famous example, Ricardo showed that if Portugal specialized in the production of wine and England specialized in the production of cloth, both countries would be better off trading with each other than if each tried to be self-sufficient in both commodities. This would be true even if England were more efficient in the production of both commodities.

13. Bluestone and Harrison's thesis resembles David Gordon's argument that manufacturers began to move out of cities at the turn of the century not for technical reasons but to flee radical trade unions and avoid paying city taxes that funded social services (Gordon, 1977).

14. Gordon Clark takes a different tack, maintaining that the trade-off between regional equality and efficiency is incoherent, involving, as he argues, essentially a trade-off between an end (equality) and a means (efficiency) (Clark, 1983: 40-44).

15. Conflict theory contrasts with the modernizing tendencies of Marxism. Harry Boyte, for example, criticizes Marx's "scientific socialism" for basing revolt on the freeing of workers from attachments to particular social values and places (Boyte, 1980: 21-22). Boyte instead commends grassroots citizen movements for their often conservative defense of place-oriented values against big business and big government.

References

Adams, C.T. (1982) The flight of jobs and capital: Prospects for grassroots action. In J.C. Raines, L.E. Berson, and D.M. Gracie (Eds.), *Community and Capital in Conflict*. Philadelphia: Temple Univ. Press.

Adams, C.T. (1986) Homelessness in the industrial city, *Urban Affairs Quarterly 21*: 527-549.

Alonso, W. (1964) *Location and Land Use: Toward a General Theory of Land Rent*. Cambridge, MA: Harvard University Press.

Alperowitz, G. and J. Faux (1984) *Rebuilding America: A Blueprint for the New Economy*. New York: Pantheon.

Anderson, C.W. (1978) The logic of public problems: Evaluation in comparative policy research. In D.E. Ashford (Ed.), *Comparing Public Policy*. Beverly Hills: Sage.

Anderson, M. (1964) *The Federal Bulldozer*. New York: McGraw-Hill.

Ashton, P.J. (1978) "The political economy of suburban development. In W.K. Tabb and L. Sawers (Eds.), *Marxism and the Metropolis*. New York: Oxford University Press.

Auger, D. (1979) The politics of revitalization in gentrifying neighborhoods, *Journal of the American Planning Association 45*: 515-522.

Avery, R.B. and T.M. Buynak (1981) Mortgage redlining: Some new evidence, *Federal Reserve Bank of Cleveland: Economic Review* (Summer): 18-32.

Beauregard, R.A. (1985) Politics, ideology and theories of gentrification, *Journal of Urban Affairs, 7*(4): 51-62.

Bensman, D. and R. Lynch (1987) *Rusted Dreams*. New York: McGraw-Hill.

Berry, B.J.L. (1985) Islands of renewal in seas of decay. In P.E. Peterson (Ed.), *The New Urban Reality*. Washington, DC: The Brookings Institution.

Black, H.A. and R.L. Schweitzer (1985) A canonical analysis of mortgage lending terms: Testing for lending discrimination at a commercial bank, *Urban Studies 22*: 13-19.

Black, J.T. (1980) The changing economic role of central cities and suburbs. In A.P. Solomon (Ed.), *The Prospective City*. Cambridge, MA: M.I.T. Press.

Blakely, Edward J. and P. Shapira (1984) Industrial restructuring: Public policies for investment in advanced industrial society, *The Annals, 475*: 96-109.

Bluestone, Barry (1972) Economic crisis and the law of uneven development, *Politics and Society* (Fall): 65-82.

Bluestone, Barry and Bennett Harrison (1982) *The Deindustrialization of*

America. New York: Basic Books.

Bluestone, Barry and Bennett Harrison (1986) *The Great American Job Machine*. Washington, DC: Joint Economic Committee.

Bowles, S., D.M. Gordon, and T.E. Weisskopf (1983) *Beyond the Wasteland*. Garden City, NY: Doubleday.

Boyte, H.C. (1980) *The Backyard Revolution: Understanding the New Citizen Movement*. Philadelphia: Temple University Press.

Boyte, H.C. and F. Riessman (Eds.) (1986) *The New Populism: The Politics of Empowerment*. Philadelphia: Temple University Press.

Business Week (1983) Industrial policy: Is it the answer? In V. Whitford (Ed.), *American Industry*. New York: H.W. Wilson.

Carnoy, M. and D. Shearer (1980) *Economic Democracy*. New York: M.E. Sharpe.

Castells, Manuel (1979) *The Urban Question*. Cambridge, MA: M.I.T. Press.

Center for Popular Economics (1986) *Economic Report of the People*. Boston, MA: South End Press.

Clark, G.L. (1983) *Interregional Migration, National Policy, and Social Justice*. Totowa, NJ: Rowman and Allanheld.

Clay, P.L. (1979) *Neighborhood Renewal*. Lexington, MA: Lexington Books.

Clay, P.L. (1987) *At Risk of Loss: The Endangered Future of Low Income Rental Housing Resources*. Washington, DC: Neighborhood Reinvestment Corporation.

Coalition for the Homeless and SRO Tenants Rights Coalition (1985) *Single Room Occupancy Hotels: Standing in the Way of the Gentry*. New York: Author.

Cobb, R.W. and C.D. Elder (1983) *Participation in American Politics: The Dynamics of Agenda-Building*, 2nd ed. Baltimore: Johns Hopkins University Press.

Cohen, S.S. and J. Zysman (1987) *Manufacturing Matters: The Myth of the Post-Industrial Economy*. New York: Basic Books.

Congressional Budget Office (1983) *The Industrial Policy Debate*. Washington, DC: Author.

Cummins, S. (1986) Urban policy research and the changing fiscal focus of the state: Sociology's ambiguous legacy and uncertain future. In M.S. Rosentraub (Ed.), *Urban Policy Problems*. New York: Praeger.

Cybriwsky, R.A., D. Ley, and J. Western (1986) The political and social construction of revitalized neighborhoods: Society Hill, Philadelphia, and False Creek, Vancouver. In N. Smith and P. Williams (Eds.), *Gentrification of the City*. Boston: Allen and Unwin.

Dahl, R. (1961) *Who Governs? Democracy and Power in an American*

City. New Haven: Yale University Press.

Daniels, P. (1982) *Service Industries: Growth and Location.* Cambridge, U.K.: Oxford University Press.

Danielson, M. (1976) *The Politics of Exclusion.* New York: Columbia University Press.

Davidoff, P. (1965) Advocacy and social concern in planning, *Journal of the American Institute of Planners, 31*: 331-337.

DeGiovanni, F. (1983) Patterns of change in housing market activity in revitalizing neighborhoods, *Journal of the American Planning Association, 49*: 22-39.

Dolbeare, C. (1986) How the income tax system subsidizes housing for the affluent. In R.G. Bratt, C. Hartman, and A. Meyerson (Eds.), *Critical Perspectives on Housing.* Philadelphia: Temple University Press.

Dolbeare, K. (1986) *Democracy at Risk: The Politics of Economic Renewal* (Rev. Ed.). Chatham, NJ: Chatham House.

Domhoff, G.W. (1978) *Who Really Rules? New Haven and Community Power Reexamined.* Santa Monica, CA: Goodyear.

Domurad, F. and R. Messinger (1983) *Citizen Program to Eliminate the Gap.* New York: The City Project.

Dunn, J.A. (1981) *Miles to Go: European and American Transportatin Policies.* Cambridge, MA: M.I.T. Press.

Edel, M. (1971) Urban renewal and land use conflicts, *The Review of Radical Political Economics, 3*(3) (Summer): 76-89.

Fainstein, Norman I. and Susan S. Fainstein (1978) Federal policy and spatial inequality. In G. Sternlieb and J.W. Hughes (Eds.), *Revitalizing the Northeast.* New Brunswick, NJ: Rutgers University, Center for Urban Policy Research.

Fainstein, Susan S., Norman I. Fainstein, Richard Child Hill, Dennis Judd and Michael Peter Smith (Eds.) (1986) *Restructuring the City*, 2nd ed. New York: Longman.

Feagin, Joe R. (1983) *The Urban Real Estate Game: Playing Monopoly with Real Money.* Englewood Cliffs, NJ: Prentice-Hall.

Foley, D.J. (1975) Institutional and contextual factors affecting the housing choice of minority residents. In S. Gale and E.G. Moore (Eds.), *The Manipulated City.* Chicago: Maaroufa Press.

Form, H.W. (1970) The place of social structure in the determination of land use. In R. Gutman and D. Popenoe (Eds.), *Neighborhood, City, and Metropolis.* New York: Random House.

Friedland, Roger O. (1983) *Power and Crisis in the City: Corporations, Unions and Urban Policy.* New York: Schocken.

Friedman, Milton (1962) *Capitalism and Freedom.* Chicago: University of

Chicago Press.

Fuchs, V.R. (1968) *The Service Economy.* New York: Columbia University Press.

Gale, D.E. (1979) Middle class resettlement in older urban neighborhoods, *Journal of the American Planning Association, 45*: 293-304.

Gale, D.E. (1984) *Neighborhood Revitalization and the Postindustrial City.* Lexington, MA: Lexington Books.

Gans, H.J. (1966) The failure of urban renewal. In J.Q. Wilson (Ed.), *Urban Renewal: The Record and the Controversy.* Cambridge, MA: M.I.T. Press.

Gilderbloom, J.I. and R.P. Appelbaum (1988) *Rethinking Rental Housing.* Philadelphia: Temple University Press.

Glickman, W. (Ed.) (1980) *The Urban Impacts of Federal Policies.* Baltimore: Johns Hopkins Unversity Press.

Goetze, R. (1979) *Understanding Neighborhood Change: The Role of Expectations in Urban Revitalization.* Cambridge, MA: Ballinger.

Goetze, R. (1981) The housing bubble, *Working Papers* (Jan.-Feb.): 44-52.

Goodman, R. (1979) *The Last Entrepreneurs: America's Regional Wars for Jobs and Dollars.* New York: Simon and Schuster.

Gordon, D. (1977) Capitalism and the Roots of urban crisis. In R.E. Alcaly and D. Mermelstein (Eds.), *The Fiscal Crisis of American Cities.* New York: Random House.

Gottdiener, M. (1977) *Planned Sprawl: Public and Private Interests in Suburbia.* Beverly Hills: Sage.

Gottdiener, M. (1985) *The Social Production of Urban Space.* Austin: University of Texas Press.

Gottdiener, M. (1987) *The Decline of Urban Politics: Political Theory and the Crisis of the Local State.* Newbury Park, CA: Sage.

Gottman, J. (1983) *The Coming of the Transactional City.* College Park, MD: University of Maryland, Institute for Urban Studies.

Harrison, Bennett (1974) *Urban Economic Development.* Washington, DC: The Urban Institute.

Harrison, Bennett, Charles Tilly, and Barry Bluestone (1986) Rising inequality. In D.R. Obey and P. Sarbanes (Eds.), *The Changing American Economy.* New York: Basil Blackwell.

Hartman, C. (1979) Comment on neighborhood revitalization and displacement: A review of the evidence, *Journal of the American Planning Association, 45*: 488-494.

Hartman, C. (1984) *The Transformation of San Francisco.* Totowa, NJ: Rowman and Allanheld.

Hartman, C. (1984a) The right to stay put. In C. Geisler and F. Popper (Eds.), *Land Reform, American Style.* Totowa, NJ: Rowman and

Allanheld.

Hartman, Chester, D. Keating, and Richard LeGates (1982) *Displacement: How To Fight It.* Berkeley, CA: National Housing Law Project.

Hartz, L. (1955) *The Liberal Tradition in America.* New York: Harcourt, Brace and World.

Harvey, D. (1985) *The Urbanization of Capital.* Oxford: Basil Blackwell.

Harvey, D. (1976) Labor, capital and class struggle around the built environment in advanced capitalist societies, *Politics and Society, 6*: 265-295.

Harvey, D. (1973) *Social Justice and the City.* Baltimore: Johns Hopkins University Press.

Hicks, D.A. (1982) Urban and economic adjustment to the post-industrial era, *Hearings Before the Joint Economic Committee, Congress of the United States, Ninety-Seventh Congress, Part 2.* Washington, DC: U.S. Government Printing Office.

Hinds, M. deC. (1987) 421a: A subsidy that cost $551 million, *New York Times* (March 29).

Hoch, C. and R. Slayton (forthcoming) *The New Homeless and Old.* Philadelphia: Temple University Press.

Housing and Development Reporter (1981), May 25: 1081-1082.

Houstoun, L. and F. O'Connor (1980) Neighborhood change, displacement, and city policy, in S.B. Laska and D. Spain (Eds.), *Back to the City.* New York: Pergamon Press.

Jackson, K.T. (1985) *Crabgrass Frontier: The Suburbanization of the United States.* New York: Oxford University Press.

James, F.J. (1980) The revitalization of older housing and neighborhoods. In A.P. Solomon (Ed.), *The Prospective City.* Cambridge, MA: M.I.T. Press.

Jessop, B. (1982) *The Capitalist State.* New York: New York Univ. Press.

Jones, B.D. and L.W. Bachelor (1986) *The Sustaining Hand: Community Leadership and Corporate Power.* Lawrence, KS: University Press of Kansas.

Kain, J.F. (1962) The journey-to-work as a determinant of residential location. *Papers and Proceedings of the Regional Science Association, 9*: 17-161.

Kaldor, N. (1939) Welfare propositions and interpersonal comparisons of utility, *Economic Journal, 49*: 549-552.

Kantor, P. with S. David (1988) *The Dependent City: The Changing Political Economy of Urban America.* New York: Little, Brown.

Kasarda, J.D. (1980) The implications of contemporary redistribution trends for national urban policy, *Social Science Quarterly, 61*: 373-400.

Kasarda, J.D. (1985) Urban change and minority opportunities. In P.E.

Peterson (Ed.), *The New Urban Reality*. Washington, DC: The
Brookings Institution.
Kingdon, J.W. (1984) *Agendas, Alternatives, and Public Policies*.   Boston:
Little, Brown.
Kleniewski, N. (1984) From industrial to corporate city: The role of urban
renewal.   In William K. Tabb and L. Sawers (Eds.), *Marxism and
the Metropolis*, 2nd ed.   New York: Oxford University Press.
Kristol, I. (1977) Sense and nonsense in urban policy, *Wall Street Journal*,
December 21.
Kristol, I. (1978) *Two Cheers for Capitalism*.   New York: Basic Books.
Krumholz, N. (1975) The cleveland policy planning report, *Journal of the
American Institute of Planners, 41*(5): 298-304.
Kuttner, R. (1984) *The Economic Illusion*.   Boston, MA: Houghton Mifflin.
Lang, M. (1982) *Gentrification Amid Urban Decline*.   Cambridge, MA:
Ballinger.
Lauber, D. (1984) Condominium conversions: A reform in need of reform.
In C. Geisler and F. Popper (Eds.), *Land Reform, American Style*.
Totowa, NJ: Rowman and Allanheld.
LeGates,   Richard   T.   and   Chester   Hartman   (1981)   Displacement,
Clearinghouse Review, 15: 207-249.
LeGates,   Richard   T.   and   Chester   Hartman   (1986)   The   anatomy   of
displacement in the United States.   In N. Smith and P. Williams
(Eds.), *Gentrification of the City*.   Boston: Allen and Unwin.
Lindblom, C.E. (1977) *Politics and Markets*.   New York: Basic Books.
Lipton, S.G. (1980) Evidence of central city revival.   In S.B. Laska and D.
Spain (Eds.), *Back to the City*.   New York: Pergamon Press.
Listokin, D. and S. Casey (1980) *Mortgage Lending and Race: Conceptual
and Analytical Perspectives of the Urban Financing Problem*.   New
Brunswick, NJ: Rutgers Univ., Center for Urban Policy Research.
Logan, J.R. and H. Molotch (1987) *Urban Fortunes: Making Place in the
City*.   Berkeley: University of California Press.
London, B. and J.J. Palen (1984) Introduction: Some theoretical and
practical issues regarding inner city revitalization.   In J.J. Palen and
B. London (Eds.), *Gentrification, Displacement and Neighborhood
Revitalization*.   Albany, NY: SUNY Press.
London, B., D.S. Bradley, and J.R. Hudson (1980) Approaches to inner city
revitalization, *Urban Affairs Quarterly, 15*: 373-380.
Low Income Housing Information Service (1987) *Special Memorandum*.
Washington, DC: April.
Lowi, T.J. (1979) *The End of Liberalism: Ideology, Policy, and the Crisis
of Public Authority*, 2nd ed.   New York: W.W. Norton.
Luria, D. and J. Russell (1981) *Rational Reindustrialization: An Economic*

Development Agenda for Detroit. Detroit: Widgetripper Press.

Lustig, Jeffrey (1985) The politics of shutdown: Community, property, corporatism, *Journal of Economic Issues, 19*(1), 123-52.

Lynd, S. (1985) Options for reindustrialization: Brownfield versus Greenfield approaches. In W. Woodworth, C. Meek, and W.F. Whyte (Eds.), *Industrial Democracy: Strategies for Community Revitalization*. Beverly Hills, CA: Sage.

Magaziner, I. and R. Reich (1982) *Minding America's Business*. New York: Vintage Books.

Manners, G. (1974) The office in metropolis: An opportunity for shaping urban America, *Economic Geography, 50*(2) (April): 93-110.

Marcuse, Peter (1986) Abandonment, gentrification, and displacement: The linkages in New York City. In N. Smith and P. Williams (Eds.), *Gentrification of the City*. Boston: Allen and Unwin.

Markusen, Ann R. (1978) Class and urban social expenditures: A Marxist theory of metropolitan government in William K. Tabb and L. Sawers (Eds.), *Marxism and the Metropolis* New York: Oxford University Press.

Markusen, Ann R. (1987) *Regions: The Economics and Politics of Territory*. Totowa, NJ: Rowman and Littlefield.

McKenzie, R.B. (1984) *Plant Closings: Public or Private Choices?* Washington, DC: Cato Institute.

Mills, D.E. (1983) Real estate speculation and antispeculation taxes, *Growth and Change* (July): 12-21.

Miron, J.R. (1982) Economic equilibrium in urban land use, in L.S. Bourne (Ed.), *Internal Structure of the City*, 2nd ed. New York: Oxford University Press.

Mollenkopf, John H. (1983) *The Contested City*. Princeton, NJ: Princeton University Press.

Molotch, Harvey (1976) The city as a growth machine: Toward a politicl economy of place, *American Journal of Sociology, 82*: 309-332.

Muth, R. (1969) *Cities and Housing*. Chicago: University of Chicago Press.

Nathan, R.P. and M.H. Schill (1983) *Revitalizing America's Cities*. Albany, NY: SUNY Press.

National Association of Neighborhoods (1980) *NAN Bulletin* No. 36 (February-March).

National Urban Coalition (1978) *City Neighborhoods in Transition*. Washington, DC: Author.

New York Stock Exchange (1984) *U.S. International Competitiveness: Perceptions and Reality*. New York: Author.

Novak, M. (1982) *The Spirit of Democratic Capitalism*. New York: Simon and Schuster.

Noyelle, T.J. (1986) Advanced services in the system of cities.   In E.M. Bergman (Ed.), *Local Economies in Transition.*   Durham, NC: Duke University Press.

Okun, A.M. (1975) *Equality and Efficiency: The Big Tradeoff.* Washington, DC: Brookings Institution.

Otis, A.D. and A.B. Whinston (1966) The economics of urban renewal.   In J.Q. Wilson (Ed.), *Urban Renewal: The Record and the Controversy.* Cambridge, MA: M.I.T. Press.

Park, R.E., E.W. Burgess, and R.D. McKenzie (1967) *The City.*   Chicago: University of Chicago Press.

Parker, R.A. (1983) Local tax subsidies as a stimulus for development: Are they cost-effective?   Are they equitable? *City Almanac, 17*(1): 8-15.

Pattison, T. (1983) The stages of gentrification: The case of Bay Village. In P. Clay and R. Hollister (Eds.), *Neighborhood Policy and Planning.* Lexington, MA: D.C. Heath.

Peterson, G.E. (1979) Federal tax policy and urban development.   In B. Chinitz (Ed.) *Central City Economic Development.*   Cambridge, MA: Abt Books.

Plotkin, Sidney and W.E. Scheuerman (1984) Industrial policy and theories of power.   Paper presented at the *Annual Meeting of the Northeastern Political Science Association,* Boston.

Poulantzas, N. (1973) *Political Power and Social Class.* Thetford, Norfolk, UK: New Left Books.

President's Commission for a National Agenda for the Eighties (1980) *Urban America in the Eighties.*   Washington, DC: U.S. Government Printing Office.

President's Commission on Housing (1982) *The Report of the President's Commission on Housing.*   Washington, DC: U.S. Government Printing Office.

President's National Urban Policy Report (1982).   Washington, DC: U.S. Government Printing Office.

Reich, R. (1983) *The Next American Frontier.* New York: Penguin.

Rosen, C. (1985) Financing employee ownership.   In W. Woodworth, C. Meek, and W.F. Whyte (Eds.), *Industrial Democracy: Strategies for Community Revitalization.* Beverly Hills, CA: Sage.

Sale, K. (1974) *Power Shift: Rise of the Southern Rim and Its Challenge to the Eastern Establishment.* New York: Random House.

Savitch, H.V. (1979) *Urban Policy and the Exterior City.*   New York: Pergamon Press.

Schafer, R. (1980) Discrimination in housing prices and mortgage lending. In S. Pynoos, R. Schafer, and C.W. Hartman (Eds.), *Housing*